LINCOLN
AND
NEW YORK

Brady,   New York.

LINCOLN AND NEW YORK

EDITED BY
HAROLD HOLZER

WITH CONTRIBUTIONS BY

JEAN H. BAKER
CATHERINE CLINTON
JAMES OLIVER HORTON
MICHAEL KAMMEN
BARNET SCHECTER
CRAIG L. SYMONDS
FRANK WILLIAMS

NEW-YORK HISTORICAL SOCIETY
PHILIP WILSON PUBLISHERS

This volume has been published in conjunction with the exhibition, Lincoln and New York,
organized by the New-York Historical Society, New York, New York,
and held at the Society from October 9, 2009 through March 25, 2010.

Lincoln and New York has been generously supported by JPMorgan Chase & Co.;
by the U.S. Department of Education Underground Railroad Educational and Cultural (URR)
Program; by the New York City Department of Cultural Affairs; and by the
National Endowment for the Humanities.

Co-Published by Philip Wilson Publishers Ltd.
109 Drysdale Street
The Timber Yard
London N1 6ND
www.philip-wilson.co.uk

ISBN (softcover edition) 978-0-91614-103-5
ISBN (hardcover edition) 978-0-85667-669-7

Distributed throughout the world (excluding North America) by:
I.B. Tauris & Co. Ltd. 6 Salem Road, London W2 4BU

Distributed in North America by:
Palgrave Macmillan, a division of St Martin's Press, 175 Fifth Avenue
New York NY 10010

For the New-York Historical Society
Volume Editor: Harold Holzer
Project Editor: Valerie Paley
Photographs are by Glenn Castellano unless otherwise noted

Designed in Centaur by Geoff Green Book Design, Cambridge
Printed in China on behalf of Latitude Press

Frontispiece: Mathew B. Brady (ca. 1823–96). *Abraham Lincoln*,
New York, February 27, 1860. Carte-de-visite. 4 x 2 ⅜ in (10.2 x 6.0 cm).
Gilder Lehrman Collection (GLC 05111.02.0001)

Cover, top, and back cover
Photographer unknown. [East side of Broadway, beginning with 534-6-8 Broadway, southeast corner at Spring Street,
New York City], ca. 1868. Print made from original negative. PR 020

Cover, bottom
Mathew B. Brady (ca. 1823–96). *Abraham Lincoln*, New York, February 27, 1860 (detail).
Carte-de-visite, 4 x 2 3/8 in. (10.2 x 6.0 cm). Gilder Lehrman Collection (GLC 05111.02.0001)

CONTENTS

PRESIDENT'S FOREWORD

LOUISE MIRRER

LTHOUGH AN EXHIBITION focused on Abraham Lincoln had been the New-York Historical Society's dream for easily a decade, *Lincoln and New York* began to take shape sometime in 2005, after a conversation with our board members about what we might do in 2009 to commemorate the bicentennial of Lincoln's birth. Lewis Lehrman offered, "How about 'Lincoln in New York'?" and, much to his surprise, our curatorial staff took him quite literally. Almost immediately we contacted our friend and Lincoln scholar Harold Holzer about acting as chief curator and historian. Happily for us, he agreed, and the idea for a show and accompanying book of essays was born.

Ironically, Lincoln was hardly ever in New York, yet the city figured in his career both before and during his presidency, and was the place where the enduring Lincoln image was created. This publication addresses New York's role in Lincoln's political life through several perspectives: New York Republicanism; the culture of opposition; the economy; Black New York; image making; civil liberties; New York women and Mrs. Lincoln; and his assassination and funeral. We are deeply grateful to the authors who have contributed to this effort: Jean H. Baker, Barnet Schecter, Craig L. Symonds, James Oliver Horton, Frank Williams, Catherine Clinton, and Michael Kammen. Their scholarship was gathered and edited under the direction of Harold Holzer, the volume editor, and Valerie Paley, the project editor. As always, the leadership of the Society's Board of Trustees has been invaluable. We are thankful to Chairman Roger Hertog, to Co-Chairs of the Trustees' Executive Committee Richard Gilder and Nancy Newcomb, and to the entire Board.

I also wish to acknowledge those who have participated in producing *Lincoln and New York*: our scholarly committee, consisting of James Oliver Horton, Peter Kunhardt, Richard Rabinowitz, Barnet Schecter, Craig L. Symonds, Craig Wilder, and Frank Williams; Richard Rabinowitz and Lynda Kaplan of the American History Workshop; image researchers Avi Mowshowitz and Lilly Tuttle; Marilyn Kushner and the N-YHS print room staff, Sue Kriete, Miranda Schwartz, and Kelly McAnnaney; N-YHS library personnel, including Edward O'Reilly, Eric Robinson, Joseph Ditta, and Mariam Touba; and Sarah Armstrong, who ably coordinated both in-house and outside image reproduction. I also must extend special thanks to the N-YHS Executive Vice President and Museum Director Linda Ferber, and her counterpart Jean Ashton, the institution's Executive Vice President and Library Director. They, along with Museum Director for Administration, Roy R. Eddey, skillfully and readily led the team that has labored on this book.

It is my pleasure to recognize vital lead partner support from JPMorgan Chase & Co. Focusing on the exhibition's dynamic school programs, these funds enable us to engage tens of thousands of teachers and students throughout New York City and beyond (many from under-resourced communities) via free teacher training, lesson plans and robust student materials, as well as interactive gallery experiences for school groups led by our enthusiastic Museum educators. This project is supported, in part, by public funds from the New York City Department of Cultural Affairs, which under the leadership of Commissioner Kate D. Levin so importantly advances the vitality of the New York City cultural community. Our ambitious vision for the *Lincoln and New York* exhibition and educational initiative was further made possible with grant funds from the U.S. Department of Education Underground Railroad Educational and Cultural (URR) Program, The Bodman Foundation, and the National Endowment for the Humanities. I express my deep gratitude for their partnership.

DR. LOUISE MIRRER
President and CEO
New-York Historical Society

LINCOLN
AND
NEW YORK

INTRODUCTION

HAROLD HOLZER

ALMOST NOTHING IS KNOWN about Abraham Lincoln's very first visit to—or rather *through*—New York. But brief as it was, it was surely filled with both irony and wonder, launching a unique and crucial relationship between one of the country's fastest-rising politicians and its fastest-growing city.

The year was 1848, and a presidential election loomed. Though only a freshman congressman from the West, not quite forty years old, Lincoln had been asked to campaign in the East for the Whig party's freshly anointed White House candidate, Zachary Taylor. Named just a few weeks earlier as an assistant elector, Lincoln was expected to stump convincingly for a military hero who had earned his greatest fame in the Mexican-American war that Lincoln had opposed. Yet he was fully prepared to do so. Lincoln had recently jettisoned his own lifelong political hero, Henry Clay, expediently switching his allegiance to Taylor for president for one simple reason: he thought the general could win. So Lincoln dutifully stayed behind in Washington after the House of Representatives adjourned for the summer in August, and agreed to undertake a speaking tour in Massachusetts.[1]

Together with his little family—his wife and two young boys—Lincoln left the capital on September 9, 1848, and headed to New England via New York City. It was by no means an easy journey. Just to reach Manhattan required frequent transfers on no fewer than five separate railroad lines. The Lincolns later proceeded by ferry to Norwich, Connecticut, and on to Worcester, Massachusetts, where he gave a ninety-minute free-soil, high-tariff speech, impressing one onlooker with his enormous height, "intellectual face," "searching mind," and "cool judgment."[2]

Preston Butler. *Abraham Lincoln,* Springfield, IL, August 13, 1860. Published in Meserve Historical Portraits. Ambrotype, 3 ¼ x 2 ⅛ in (8.26 x 5.40 cm). PR 231

LTH. & PUB. BY N. CURRIER.

VIEW OF THE PARK, FOUNTAIN & CITY HALL, N. Y. 1851.

Artist unknown. *View of the Park, Fountain & City Hall*, 1851. Lithograph, N. Currier, publisher, 10 ¼ x 14 in (26.04 x 35.56 cm). PR 020

But of Lincoln's reaction, if any, to the metropolis of nearly four hundred thousand people, neither he nor anyone he met here left a clue. Still, even if he merely passed through the city, he likely noticed its busy waterfront, the proliferation of crowded shops and bold street signs, the anarchic traffic along bustling Broadway, the thick skyline of church steeples, the majestic City Hall just a mile from the island's southern tip, and perhaps even the notorious nearby slum known as the Five Points, where "every nationality of the globe" lived in wretched, cheek-by-jowl misery.[3] But Lincoln was a man attracted to politics, not places, and his mission was to orate for Taylor, not to ogle the local sights. (If anyone in the family had the inclination or time to do any touring, it was probably Mary and her boys, five-year-old Robert and two-year-old Eddie.) Lincoln usually spent most of his time during such trips meeting like-minded politicians and writing and rewriting his speeches. He went on to speak in Taylor's behalf in New Bedford, Boston, Lowell, and other cities. The general won Massachusetts and the national election, and Lincoln, out of office after a single term in the House, lobbied for the reward of a federal patronage appointment he thought he deserved, but did not get. Ultimately he abandoned politics altogether and returned to the practice of law, his career in government apparently over for good. His trip north had done him little good.

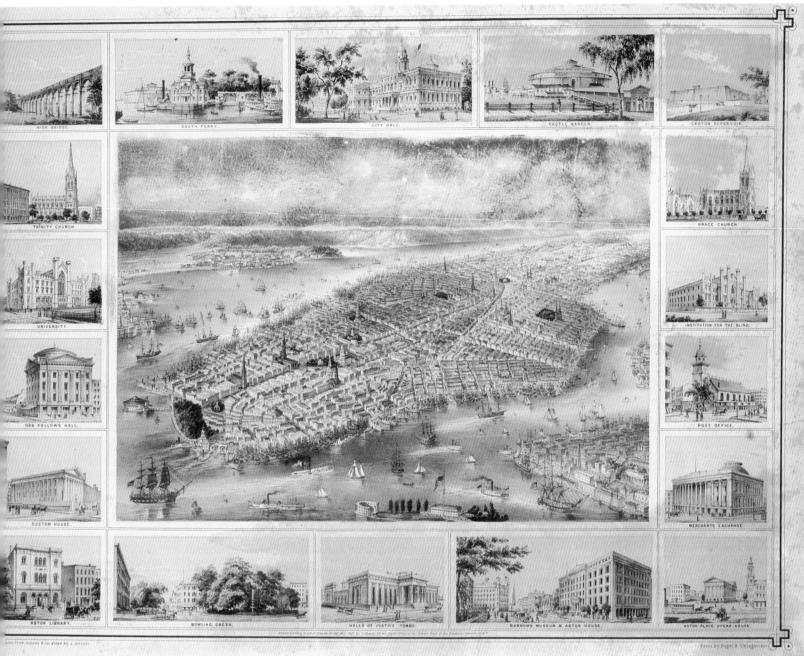

SOUVENIR OF NEW YORK.

By the time Abraham and Mary Lincoln returned to New York some nine years later, now purely for pleasure, the city had nearly doubled in population, and the former congressman had re-entered public life, inspired to action by opposition to the potential spread of slavery into the nation's new territories. "Mr. Lincoln has gone to New York," his junior law partner William H. Herndon confirmed on July 29, 1857, providing little detail save for reporting his colleague's absence—a tacit acknowledgment that Lincoln had made a spectacular political comeback and now needed to be seen and heard well beyond his home town of Springfield, Illinois.

J. Bornet. *Souvenir of New York,* 1851. Lithograph, J. Haasis, publisher, 19 ⅓ x 23 ¾ in (48.90 x 60.32 cm). PR 020

FORM 2.

ILLINOIS & MISSISSIPPI TELEGRAPH COMPANY

IN CONNECTION WITH ALL OTHER LINES IN THE UNITED STATES AND CANADAS.

Note.—This Company will assume no risk, or hold themselves liable for any damage, for errors, omissions or delays beyond the amount actually received by the Company for the transmission of any message, but will pledge themselves to use every exertion in their power to insure promptness and accuracy.

BY TELEGRAPH   Springfield Oct 12 1859

From New York Oct 12 185[...]

To Hon A Lincoln

will you speak in Mr Beechers Church Brooklyn on or about the twenty ninth (29) november on any subject you please pay two hundred (200) dollars

James A Briggs

James A. Briggs to Abraham Lincoln, October 12, 1859. Telegram; invitation. Library of Congress, Abraham Lincoln Papers

The Lincolns' idyllic summertime trip included a stop at romantic Niagara Falls, followed by a voyage to Manhattan—an interlude, Mary remembered, "spent most pleasantly." The couple stayed at the stylish Astor House on Broadway, noted for its opulent lobby and elegant shops. But much like her husband back in 1848, Mrs. Lincoln seemed to regard New York as a gateway more than a destination. Observing the maze of ships' masts thronging New York harbor, her thoughts wandered to foreign shores. "How I long to go to Europe," she wrote wistfully to her half-sister after seeing "the large steamers at the New York landing, ready for their European voyage." The thrill of visiting a posh hostelry in America's busiest city somehow increased her dread that "poverty was my portion" in life. So she teased Lincoln—more than once—"that I am determined my next Husband *shall be rich.*" It was perhaps just irritating enough to spoil the romantic vacation. In any event, her "current" husband's next—and most important—visit to New York would be undertaken alone.[4]

The opportunity arose two years later, in late 1859, on the eve of another crucial election for president. A group of political activists called the Young Men's Central Republican Union invited several western presidential aspirants to Brooklyn to audition for support by delivering lectures before elite audiences at Henry Ward Beecher's famous Plymouth Church in Brooklyn. As it happened, intrigued

THE COOPER UNION FOR THE ADVANCEMENT OF SCIENCE AND ART.

as he was by the summons, Lincoln delayed his acceptance just long enough to miss the Brooklyn lecture series entirely. This required his patient hosts to reschedule his speech in the handsome auditorium at a newly opened college in Manhattan: Cooper Union. The pressure on Lincoln was intense. Despite his earlier trips to town, one of his hosts was not incorrect in noting that he was still an "entire stranger" to the city.[5]

Not for long. Armed with a brilliantly conceived and crafted 7,700-word oration, fully understanding the potential impact of his maiden speech in the nation's media capital, Lincoln arrived in New York on February 25, 1860 and strolled up crowded Broadway to the Astor House, completely unrecognized. Only after registering did he first learn that his appearance had been moved from a religious to a secular setting, requiring significant rewriting at the last minute. Over the next two days, despite the distraction of meetings with well-wishers, obligatory visits to an antislavery newspaper office, the Beecher church, and the Broadway sights surrounding his hotel, Lincoln somehow found time not only to revise his prodigious manuscript, but to arrange for it to be typeset by the *New York Tribune*. This was perhaps accomplished in advance to facilitate its delivery—Lincoln preferred reading printed to handwritten scripts—but primarily to ensure that

Artist unknown. "The Cooper Union for the Advancement of Science and Art." Wood engraving, published in *Harper's Weekly*, March 30, 1861. E171.H29

Abraham Lincoln. *The Address of the Hon. Abraham Lincoln*, 1860. Pamphlet, George Nesbitt, publisher. CT.L7, Box L

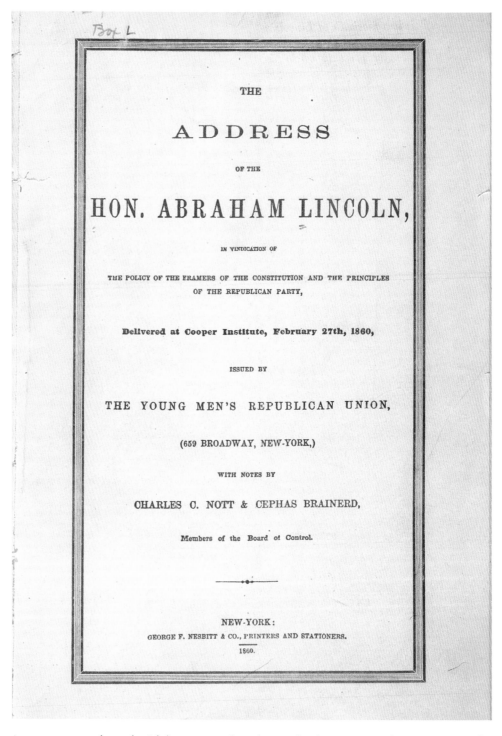

it was accurately and widely reprinted in this and other New York newspapers the day after.[6]

Lincoln triumphed at Cooper Union. Before a discriminating audience of some 1,200 people—"the pick and flower of New York"[7]—Lincoln succeeded in dramatically introducing himself to the East, allaying fears about his alleged rusticity, making a powerful case for the future of the Republican Party, and, most impressive of all, providing carefully researched historical arguments to show that the nation's founders had fully expected future generations of federal officials (perhaps

Abraham Lincoln. *The Address of the Hon. Abraham Lincoln*, 1860. Pamphlet, George Nesbitt, publisher. CT.L7, Box L

PREFACE.

This edition of Mr. Lincoln's address has been prepared and published by the Young Men's Republican Union of New-York, to exemplify its wisdom, truthfulness and learning. No one who has not actually attempted to verify its details can understand the patient research and historical labor which it embodies. The history of our earlier politics is scattered through numerous journals, statutes, pamphlets, and letters; and these are defective in completeness and accuracy of statement, and in indices and tables of contents. Neither can any one who has not travelled over this precise ground, appreciate the accuracy of every trivial detail, or the self-denying impartiality with which Mr. Lincoln has turned from the testimony of "the fathers," on the general question of Slavery, to present the single question which he discusses. From the first line to the last—from his premises to his conclusion, he travels with a swift, unerring directness which no logician ever excelled—an argument complete and full, without the affectation of learning, and without the stiffness which usually accompanies dates and details. A single, easy, simple sentence of plain Anglo-Saxon words contains a chapter of history, that, in some instances, has taken days of labor to verify, and which must have cost the author months of investigation to acquire. And, though the public should justly estimate the labor bestowed on the facts which are stated, they cannot estimate the greater labor involved on those which are omitted—how many pages have been read—how many works examined—what numerous statutes, resolutions, speeches, letters, and biographies have been looked through. Commencing with this address, as a political pamphlet, the reader will leave it as an historical work—brief, complete, profound, impartial, truthful—which will survive the time and the occasion that called it forth, and be esteemed hereafter, no less for its intrinsic worth than its unpretending modesty.

NEW-YORK, *September*, 1860.

himself) to control the spread of slavery. "Let us have faith," Lincoln memorably concluded his masterful address, "that right makes might, and in that faith, let us, to the end, dare to do our duty as we understand it."[8] The audience, skeptical at the outset, exploded with applause at the conclusion. Commented the influential *Tribune*: "No man ever before made such an impression on his first appeal to a New-York audience."[9] Lincoln had convincingly launched himself as a credible candidate for the presidency—even though New York Senator William H. Seward remained the overwhelming favorite—with just three months remaining before

Republicans were scheduled to choose their standard-bearer. At the convention, Seward faltered and Lincoln prevailed.

But his rise was not attributable to his Cooper Union appearance alone. As Lincoln learned on his milestone visit to New York, the city offered an ambitious politician far more than big crowds and capacious venues. Here, in the publishing center of the nation, what was *reproduced* in words and images could far exceed the impact of what was *produced* by an orator in a single speech. The *Tribune* obligingly published a pamphlet version of the Cooper Union speech, whose success inspired like-minded Republican journals around the country to do likewise. And Lincoln himself provided powerful visual accompaniment by consenting to pose at Mathew Brady's photography gallery on Broadway only hours before he took to the rostrum at the college. The striking portrait that resulted from that fortuitous sitting inspired engraved copies in the illustrated news weeklies, along with a multitude of lithographed sheets for display in the homes of supporters, and likenesses to adorn campaign buttons, broadsides, and banners.

Through these often-romanticized adaptations, the physically homely and virtually unknown Lincoln was successfully transformed and introduced to a broad voting public far beyond New York's borders. "While I was there I was taken to one of the places where they get up such things," Lincoln reported with folksy modesty a few weeks later in response to a request for his photograph, "and I suppose they got my shaddow [*sic*] and can multiply copies indefinitely."[10] That proved one of the most signal understatements of the entire campaign season.

After winning the nomination in May, Lincoln retreated back to Springfield and fell silent—true to a prevailing tradition that proscribed public appearances by White House candidates. Copies of his New York speech and New York image did the campaigning for him, and cast a "shaddow" nearly as large as Lincoln's own. In no other city but New York could a single appearance have stimulated such a powerful, widespread, and long-lasting impact. Although neither New York City's convention delegates in May nor its voters in November went on to support Lincoln for president (in fact he lost New York City on Election Day overwhelmingly), the city's artists and writers played as significant a role in his eventual victory as they did in subsequently making his troubled presidency a consistent challenge and frequent misery. As Lincoln later conceded, "Brady and the Cooper Union speech made me President."[11] It was not to be the last time New York exerted a major influence on Lincoln's—and the nation's—future.

This book—and the exhibition that inspired it—explore Abraham Lincoln's vastly under-appreciated impact on New York, and on New York's equally astonishing impact, in turn, on Abraham Lincoln. Although he visited the city only two more times, once during his voyage to Washington for his 1861 inauguration, and later en route, as commander-in-chief, to a clandestine wartime conference with retired general Winfield Scott at West Point, Lincoln and New York maintained their symbiotic and often crucial relationship. Despite ongoing political opposition, the state went on to provide more men and materiel to the Union war effort than any other, even as it incubated virulent, sometimes racist, occasionally violent resistance to Lincoln's presidency. The book will show how the city's politicians, preachers, and publishers—its citizens, white as well as black, rich as well as poor—continued variously to aid, thwart, support, undermine, promote, and sabotage Lincoln and his political party, and how Lincoln, in turn, came to influence the evolving history of New York.

Some of the nation's most prominent historians have contributed to this volume, richly exploring the nature and culture of the opposition, the vital influence of the press, the rapid growth of the Republican party, the local debate over executive powers and freedom of the press, the transformation of commerce, the role of African-Americans in nineteenth-century New York, its military and social upheavals, the city's contribution to shaping and proliferating the Lincoln image, Mary Lincoln's special ties to the city, and the widespread cultural impact of the president's death and the frenzied mass mourning it inspired. Utilizing the vast collections of the New-York Historical Society, these essays cast fresh light on one of the most dangerous periods in American history, with particular emphasis on how the country's greatest figure interacted with its greatest city to confront it.

That confrontation began just days before Lincoln took office as president. The public and press response to Lincoln's return visit to New York as president-elect in February 1861, nearly a year after his transformational Cooper Union appearance, naturally dwarfed that which greeted his 1860 trip. This time he did not merely stroll along Broadway in anonymity, carrying his own luggage; he rode down the thoroughfare in a vast official procession (his bags aboard a separate carriage), as tens of thousands of onlookers watched from the sidewalks. The cacophony of commercial signage that Lincoln had observed during his Cooper Union trip was now augmented by large banners welcoming him to the city: "Welcome, welcome, none too soon!" and, in echo of his 1860 address, "Right makes might."[12]

Even then, opposition to Lincoln continued to simmer. "All was comparative and ominous silence," Walt Whitman observed from a parked omnibus as Lincoln's caravan pulled up to the Astor House. "Cautious persons had fear'd that there would be some outbreak, some mark'd indignity or insult to the President elect on his passage through the city, for he possess'd no personal popularity in New York, and not much political. No such outbreak or insult, however, occur'd. Only the silence of the crowd was very significant to those who were accustom'd to the usual demonstrations of New York in wild, tumultuous hurrahs."[13]

Even in the absence of "hurrahs," Lincoln was treated royally on this visit—though opposition never lurked far from the surface. He was guest of honor at a reception at his hotel, though someone in the throng heckled him when he rose to speak. The mayor welcomed him to a public levee inside City Hall, but at the same time was audaciously plotting to have New York join Southern states in seceding from the Union. And while Lincoln attended a performance of Verdi's new opera, *Ballo in Maschera*, receiving a tumultuous ovation from the large audience at the Academy of Music, he exited shortly thereafter—before the climactic scene in which a public official is assassinated at a masked ball. "It is stated that Lincoln was to be assassinated at the same moment that the tenor falls by the hand of the baritone," the *Herald* breathlessly reported, "but some leaky vessel informed the police, and the president left the Academy precipitously."[14] In fact the president-elect's early departure likely owed more to exhaustion than fear, but the news item served as a reminder that deep and violent resistance to Lincoln's election still percolated in New York.

It is little wonder that when a committee of prominent Republicans invited Lincoln back to the city in 1863 for a tribute to Union armies fighting in the West, suggesting that his attendance would "afford the highest gratification to the people of this city," Lincoln declined, even though the summons offered an encore appearance at the scene of his great pre-presidential speech, Cooper Union.[15] Agreeing that "it would be exceedingly agreeable to me to join in a suitable acknowledgment to those of the Great West, with whom I was born, and have passed my life," Lincoln explained that "the now early meeting of congress, together with a temporary illness render my attendance impossible": he had come down with a mild case of smallpox after delivering the Gettysburg Address a few weeks earlier. But Lincoln probably would have avoided a return visit to the city even had Congress been in recess and his health restored. Deadly draft riots, punctuated by the hideous lynching of innocent African Americans, had only recently roiled the city, requiring the deployment of federal troops to stem the violence. So instead of visiting, Lincoln produced an eloquent public letter to be read aloud at Cooper Union. In it, he not only saluted soldiers in the West, as requested, but subtly alluded as well to the bravery of the soldiers who had restored order to New York: "Honor also to the citizen who cares for his brother in the field, and serves, as he best can, the same cause," he declared, adding: "honor to him, only less than to him, who braves, for the common good, the storms of heaven and the storms of battle."[16] In New York, those storms continued to rage unabated.

Of course, not everyone in the city opposed Lincoln. Back in 1860, a few days after causing a sensation at Cooper Union, Lincoln had returned to town for a visit to the Five Points slum, making an emotional speech to Irish orphan boys at the House of Industry. Told he had inspired the children, Lincoln replied: "No, they are the ones who have inspired me—given me courage. … I am glad we came—I shall never forget this as long as I live."[17] Neither did the boys. Three years later, the orphans—with names like Donague, McCarty, O'Neill, and Higgins—wrote to the President to remind him that they still recalled "with pleasure your visit to our School." Now, he had consecrated his message that "the way was open to every boy … if honest, industrious, and perserv[er]ing" by issuing the Emancipation Proclamation. "We take the liberty herein to congratulate you, sir," wrote the orphans. "We pray God … to further honor you as His instrument in liberating a race; and that so soon thereafter your own countrymen should have set their seal to your honesty and trustworthiness by conferring upon you the highest honors in the gift of a free people."[18]

One of Lincoln's final direct confrontations with the free—and unpredictable—people of New York came a full year later, when he was offered an honorary membership in a local group called the New York Workingmen's Democratic Republican Association. The Draft Riots were now receding into memory, but vociferous opposition to Lincoln's likely bid for a second term was building here quickly, punctuated by charges that if re-elected, the president would extend equal rights to blacks. Lincoln "gratefully accepted" the honorary membership, but casting his eye both to New York's past and its future, pointedly reminded the group that the rebellion was far more than a war to perpetuate "African Slavery," but "a war upon the rights of all working people." As he put it: "The most notable feature of a disturbance in your city last summer, was the hanging of some working people by other working people. It should never be so. The strongest bond of human sympathy, outside of the family relation, should be one uniting all working people, of all nations, and tongues, and kindreds."[19] Lincoln's pacific message went largely unheeded: the 1864 presidential campaign brought out in New York all the ugly internecine brawling against which he warned. Only in 1865 did violent opposition to Lincoln finally evaporate. And it required assassination and deification to remove him at last from the realm of political contentiousness here.

As the final chapter of this book will show, the man who made his first important visit to New York as a partisan, largely unknown orator, returned in death as an iconic national martyr, his remains attracting much the same silence the living man had elicited when he arrived here as president-elect. But this time the silence was reverential, not skeptical. "New York never before saw such a day," the *New York Herald* reported.[20] But neither had Lincoln—who, much as he had benefited from New York's commercial and political muscle, never completely conquered its prejudices or political hostility. He had won the enormous benefits of the support from its pro-Republican newspapers, the generosity of its wealthy financiers, the fruits of its manufacturing muscle, and the image-altering ingenuity and productivity of its robust picture publishing industry. But he never quite gained the hearts of its citizens, at least not while he lived.

The veneration he elicited at his New York funeral would likely have astounded Abraham Lincoln. Comparing his frosty welcome four years earlier—when Lincoln had been "scoffed and scowled" upon—to the "love and veneration" that greeted his return in death, the *Herald* argued, concluding, as if in apology for its years of criticism: "Yesterday witnessed the real triumphal march of Abraham Lincoln; for he had conquered the prejudices of all hordes and classes. . . . Better for his fame that it should come thus late than too soon."[21]

NOTES

1   *Illinois Daily State Journal* (Springfield), August 23, 1848. Donald W. Riddle, *Congressman Abraham Lincoln* (Urbana: University of Illinois Press, 1957), 132-33.

2   John W. Starr, Jr., *Lincoln and the Railroads: A Biographical Study* (New York: Dodd, Mead & Co., 1927), 49-50; Arthur P. Rugg, "Abraham Lincoln in Worcester," *Worcester Society of Antiquity Proceedings* 25 (1910): 228.

3   Tyler Anbinder, *Five Points: The 19th-Century New York City Neighborhood that Invented Tap Dance, Stole Elections, and Became the World's Most Notorious Slum* (New York: Free Press, 2001), 43.

4   Earl Schenck Miers, *Lincoln Day by Day: A Chronology, 1809-1865* (Washington, DC: Lincoln Sesquicentennial Commission, 1960), 2:198; Mary Lincoln to Emilie Todd Helm, September 20 1857, in Justin G. Turner and Linda Levitt Turner, *Mary Todd Lincoln: Her Life and Letters* (New York: Alfred A. Knopf, 1972), 50.

5   Quoted in Harold Holzer, *Lincoln at Cooper Union: The Speech that Made Abraham Lincoln President* (New York: Simon & Schuster, 2004), 27.

6   Lincoln had begun relying on pro-Republican newspapers to typeset his orations. He saw to the printing of his "House Divided" address in 1858, and in 1861 had his first inaugural address set in type by the local *Illinois Daily State Journal*. See Benjamin Perley Poore, Chapter 11 in *Reminiscences of Lincoln by Distinguished Men of His Time*, ed. Allen Thorndike Rice (New York: North American Publishing Co. 1886), 224.

7   Quoted in Holzer, *Lincoln at Cooper Union*, 105.

8   Roy P. Basler, ed., *The Collected Works of Abraham Lincoln* (New Brunswick, NJ: Rutgers University Press, 1953-55), 3:550.

9   *New York Tribune*, February 28, 1860. The paper reprinted the full text of the speech that day—as did the *New York Herald*, the *New York Times*, and the New York *Evening Post*.

10   Lincoln to Harvey Eastman, April 7, 1860, in Basler, *Collected Works of Abraham Lincoln*, 4:39.

11   George Alfred Townsend, "Still Taking Pictures," *New York World*, April 12, 1891, in *Mathew Brady and the Image of History*, by Mary Panzer (Washington, DC: Smithsonian Institution Press, 1997), 224.

12   For details of the welcome, see Harold Holzer, *Lincoln President-Elect: Abraham Lincoln and the Great Secession Winter 1860-1861* (New York: Simon & Schuster, 2008), 351-60.

13   Walt Whitman, *Specimen Days*, orig. pub. 1883, in *Memoranda During the War*, ed. Peter Coviello (New York: Oxford University Press, 2004), 39-40n.

14   *New York Herald*, February 27, 1861, reprinted in Edward K. Spann, *Gotham at War: New York City, 1860-1865* (Wilmington, DE: Scholarly Resources, 2002), 9.

15   George Opdyke, Joseph Sutherland, Benjamin F. Mannierre, Prosper M. Wetmore, and Spencer Kirby to Abraham Lincoln, November 28, 1860, Abraham Lincoln Papers, Library of Congress. Mannierre had been instrumental in inviting Lincoln to Cooper Union for

his 1860 speech.

16 Lincoln to George Opdyke et al., December 2, 1863, in Basler, *Collected Works of Abraham Lincoln*, 7:32.

17 Francis Fisher Browne, *The Every-day Life of Abraham Lincoln* (New York: N. D. Thompson, 1886), 323.

18 Patrick McCarty and others to Lincoln, October 16, 1863, Abraham Lincoln Papers, Library of Congress.

19 Lincoln to New York Workingmen's Democratic Republican Association, March 21, 1864, in Basler, *Collected Works of Abraham Lincoln*, 7:259.

20 *New York Herald*, April 28, 1861.

21 Ibid.

"WE ARE LINCOLN MEN": ABRAHAM LINCOLN AND NEW YORK REPUBLICANS

JEAN H. BAKER

OUT OF MANY, ONE

B Y 1855, the partisan choices of New Yorkers, like those of other Americans, had become confused and uncertain. For years, most voters had behaved as faithful members of a particular political party, supporting the same organization, election after election, year after year, and only rarely defecting to another party. There were, however, exceptions indicating the future of an unstable party system. In the 1850s partisans could still remember the presidential election in 1848 when nearly 27 percent—123,128 of 456,051 New York voters—had cast ballots for the upstart Free Soil Party and its candidate, former president Martin Van Buren. Choosing their local hero from Kinderhook rather than the Whig Zachary Taylor or the Democrat Lewis Cass, New Yorkers had given Van Buren a larger proportion of their vote than was the case in any other state. Van Buren—earlier dubbed the "fighting party man"—received only about one in every ten votes in the North and none in the South, in an era of growing sectional politics based on differences over slavery in the territories.

In the increasingly rancorous atmosphere dividing the North and the South, New York's Free Soilers were not only expressing their pride in a local politician, but were registering convictions that would soon reach fruition and permanency in the Republican Party. Free Soilers stood "for the rights of Free Labor against the aggressions of the Slave Power and to secure the Free Soil for a Free People…We plant ourselves upon the NATIONAL PLATFORM OF FREEDOM, in opposition to the Sectional Platform of slavery." But they proposed "no interference by Congress within the limits of any state," believing that the U.S. Constitution protected slavery in the states that had

Mathew B. Brady (ca. 1823–96). *Abraham Lincoln,* Washington DC, February 24, 1861. Jeffrey Kraus Collection

PROMINENT CANDIDATES FOR THE REPUBLICAN PRESIDENTIAL NOMINATION AT CHICAGO.—[From Photographs by Brady.]

Artist unknown, after photographs by Mathew B. Brady (ca. 1823–96). "Prominent Candidates for the Republican Presidential Nomination at Chicago." Wood engraving, published in *Harper's Weekly*, May 12, 1860. E171.H29

previously chosen it.[1] Their argument concerned the future, not the past, of the republic.

These Free Soilers, especially numerous in the northern and western counties of New York, represented precursors to the Republicans who were soon to become a durable political party and sweep across the United States after the passage of the Kansas-Nebraska Act in 1854. This controversial legislation, establishing the principle of popular sovereignty—that local self-determination must determine the status of slavery in the territories—outraged Northerners. Earlier, the compromises of the United States Constitution and the Missouri Compromise of 1820 seemingly guaranteed that slavery would be prohibited above the southern border of Missouri, with that state an exception to balance the admission of the new free state of Maine.

Now, as it appeared to New Yorkers like Senator William Henry Seward, aggressive Southern-supported measures threatened to nationalize slavery, an institution that many Northerners believed must be limited to the states where it already existed—there hopefully to wither away. Slavery was never to cross the boundary established at the latitude of 36/30, now compromised by the Kansas-

Artist unknown. "Anti-Republican Demonstration." Wood engraving, published in *New York Illustrated News*, November 3, 1860. *E171.D38

Nebraska Act. "What kind of popular sovereignty is it," asked the influential editor Horace Greeley in the *New York Tribune*, "that allows one class of people to vote slavery for another?" Without specifics, Greeley called for "a determined and overwhelming party for freedom."[2]

Amid this political uncertainty, several new organizations in the 1850s ran candidates in New York, as former Free Soilers, Whigs, and Democrats offered various alternatives. But New York's paper ballots during this period also included the names of candidates representing the Anti-Nebraska, Fusion, Free Soil, People's, Temperance, Republican, and American parties. The latter, promptly dubbed the Know Nothings, appeared almost overnight. They had begun as a tightly structured, highly disciplined organization whose members when asked for information replied, "I know nothing." Soon to spread throughout the United States, the Know Nothings were first organized as a secret society in New York City, where the foreign-born represented 47 percent of the population, and 40 percent of those in nearby Brooklyn.[3]

By 1856 the party had expanded well beyond New York and all thirty-one states had local chapters, which elected mayors and state officials. For a brief

(right, opposite, and following pages) William H. Seward to the Republican Central Committee [Charles C. Nott, William H. Ball, A. J. Williamson, C. S. Spencer, and F. W. Shepherd], May 21, 1860. Signed letter. Gilder Lehrman Collection (GLC04435). Seward expresses his disappointment at not receiving the Republican nomination for president but states that he is willing to support the Republican platform and Abraham Lincoln and Hannibal Hamlin. *I find in the resolutions of the Convention a platform as satisfactory to me as if it had been framed with my own hands, and in the candidates adopted by them, eminent and able Republicans with whom I have cordially cooperated in maintaining the principles embodied in that excellent creed. I cheerfully give them a sincere and earnest support.*

moment in the 1850s, the political future of the republic seemed to rest with a party that appealed to two groups of Americans: those nativists anxious to escape the perilous sectional politics of the 1850s and those who responded, during a time of high immigration, to anti-Catholic and anti-immigrant appeals. Specifically Know Nothings promised to lengthen the naturalization period for immigration, and to end office holding by Roman Catholics; on this platform in 1856, they ran their first and only national presidential candidate, Millard Fillmore of Buffalo. In New York as elsewhere, the party tried to avoid the slavery issue, and, split into Northern and Southern factions, it soon foundered, another casualty of sectional politics.[4]

The most commanding and enduring of New York's parties during this period of partisan realignment became the Republican Party, which from its

public a conventional form of manifestation. For this reason, if it were respectful and consistent with your own public purposes, I would have delayed my reply to you until I could have had an opportunity of making it verbally next week on my way to Washington, after completing the arrangements for the repairs upon my dwelling here, rendered necessary by a recent fire.

The same reason determines me also to decline your kind invitation to attend the meeting in which you propose some demonstration of respect to myself while so justly considering the nominations which have been made by the recent National Convention at Chicago. At the same time it is your right to have a frank and candid exposition of my own opinions and sentiments on that important subject.

My friends know very well that while they have always generously made my promotion to public trusts their own exclusive care, mine has only been to execute them faithfully, so as to be able at the close of their assigned terms to assign them into the hands of the people, without forfeiture of the public confidence.

Mathew B. Brady (ca. 1823–96).
William H. Seward (1801–72),
undated. Albumen print,
carte-de-visite, E. Anthony,
publisher, 3 ⅜ x 2 ⁵⁄₁₆ in
(8.57 x 5.88 cm). PR 011

very beginnings was a Northern organization. Its name emerged from a body of principles associated with freedom and a national culture that encouraged the ideals of liberty and civic participation. The label "republican" had been used during the American Revolution, and fifteen years later it appeared in Thomas Jefferson's Democratic Republicans, the latter name embracing both core principles of the new nation.

Later many communities claimed to be the site of the first Republican convention, but most historians now credit Ripon, Wisconsin with the first official meeting on July 6, 1854. New Yorkers were not far behind in a spontaneous eruption of partisanship that seemed to have spread, in the propaganda of the party's founders, like wildfire. What attracted voters was the Republican stand on prohibiting slavery in the territories. Still, to be more than just another

The presentation of my name to the Chicago Convention was thus their act, not mine. The disappointment therefore, is their disappointment, not mine. It may have found them unprepared. On the other hand, I have no sentiment either of disappointment or discontent, for who, in any possible case, could without presumption claim that a great national party ought to choose him for its candidate for the first office in the gift of the American People? I find in the resolutions of the Convention a platform as satisfactory to me as if it had been framed with my own hands, and in the candidates adopted by them, eminent and able Republicans with whom I have cordially cooperated in maintaining the principles embodied in that excellent creed. I cheerfully give them a sincere and earnest support. I trust, moreover, that those with whom I have labored so long that common service in a noble cause has created between them and myself relations of personal friendship unsurpassed in the experience of political men, will indulge me in a confident belief that no sense of disappointment will be allowed by them to hinder, or delay, or in

of the ephemeral movements of the 1850s, like the Free Soilers, required promotion, organization, and leadership. New York had an abundance of all three.

By the 1850s New York represented the most important political prize in the United States. The state's thirty-five electoral votes in the Union were more than in any other state, and its population of over 800,000 was 5 percent of the nation's total population. Just as significant in establishing the Republican Party was New York City's primacy in the publishing world. In a newspaper-reading society, the most influential papers in the United States were those published in New York, none more opinion-shaping than Horace Greeley's *Tribune* and Henry Raymond's *Times.* The city also was emerging as a commercial and financial center. Overall the state's significance, with the city as its beacon, was economic as well as intellectual, cultural, and political.

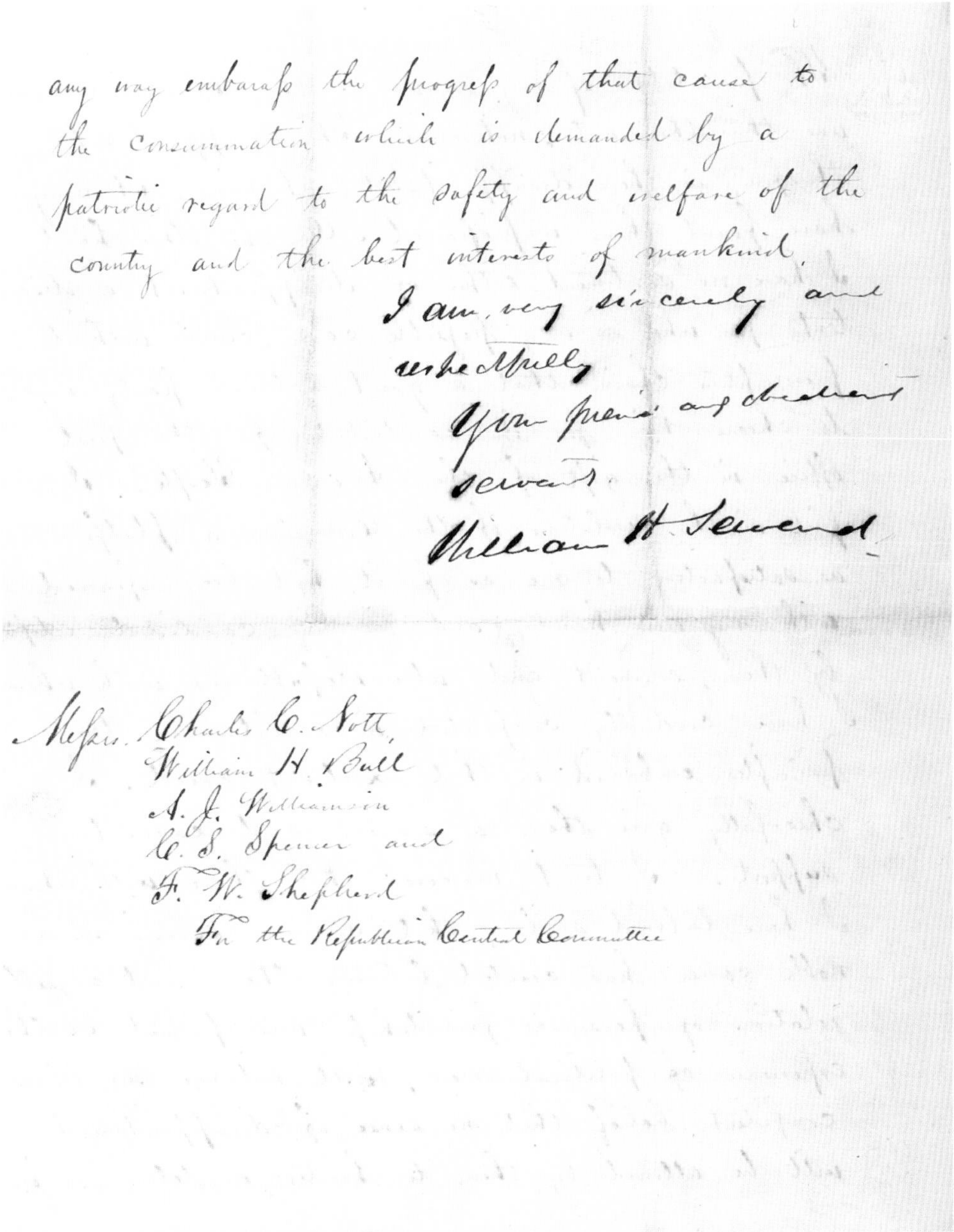

any way embarass the progress of that cause to the consummation which is demanded by a patriotic regard to the safety and welfare of the country and the best interests of mankind.

I am, very sincerely and respectfully

Your friend and obedient servant.

William H. Seward.

Messrs. Charles C. Nott,
William H. Bull
A. J. Williamson
C. S. Spencer and
F. W. Shepherd
For the Republican Central Committee

The first task of the neophyte Republican Party was to absorb voters who embraced other organizations. Chief among these were the Know Nothings. It needed as well to create a permanent structure, both nationally and in each state. Certainly the simultaneous meetings of Know Nothings and Republicans in Syracuse in the summer of 1855 had fulfilled the Republican prediction that Know Nothings might go into their meetings as members of a nativist organization, but partisans would emerge as one—and that one would be the Republican Party, a coalition of former Free Soil Democrats, former Whigs, as well as devotees of a party that appealed to new voters on the basis of morality and virtue. Included in the latter understanding was the central vision of party faith—free labor and its practical expression—no extension of slavery into new territories.

From the beginning of this prewar coalition-building, New York Senator

"Good, my lord; what is the cause of your distemper?" ×××××   1860
"Sir, I lack advancement .   Shakespere

Michael Angelo Woolf
(1837–99). "Good, my lord; what is
the cause of your distemper?" [James
Gordon Bennett], 1860. Lithograph,
9 7/16 x 13 5/16 in (24 x 8.41 cm).
PR 010

William Henry Seward, a former Whig but now an enthusiastic Republican, had predicted the possibilities for a party that shaped the slave issue as one of Southern aggression and Northern free labor. As he accurately predicted in 1854, "we will probably have a year of no popery extravaganza and then the contest between freedom and slavery will be resumed."[5]

And so it was. In 1856, barely two years old, New York Republicans carried the state in the three-way presidential election. Not even the presence of a local candidate—Millard Fillmore of Buffalo who ran as a Know Nothing—staunched the movement of New York Whigs, Free Soil Democrats and new voters into the Republican Party represented by John C. Fremont. The Democrat James Buchanan easily won the national electoral vote, but for Republicans, the presidential election of 1856 stood as a "victorious defeat."[6] And during Buchanan's feckless administration from 1857–61, Republicans benefited from the bloody events in Kansas first orchestrated by Southerners, a Southern congressman's vicious attack on Republican Senator Charles Sumner in the United States Senate, and the Dred

THE POLITICAL GYMNASIUM.

Scott decision. All seemed to demonstrate a central tenet of the Republican Party: with their aggressive behavior, Southerners were trying to nationalize slavery, even to the point of empowering slaveowners to take their human "property" anywhere in the United States.

Such events encouraged Abraham Lincoln, an aspiring but wary politician in Illinois who had been slow to leave the Whigs and join the Republicans, to believe that at first "we were without party history, party pride or party idols. We were a collection of individuals but recently in political hostility one to another."[7] Now Republicans were a powerful organization that had every reason to believe they could elect the next president. And Lincoln understood the inspiring core principle of Republicans: "in the organization of the Republican Party this question of Slavery was more important than any other …."[8]

MR. LINCOLN COMES TO TOWN

In the beginning of 1860, Abraham Lincoln, on the basis of his growing reputation among Republican partisans, was invited to lecture in New York's famed Cooper Union Hall. At the time the frontrunner for the Republican nomination

Artist unknown. *The Political Gymnasium*, 1860. Lithograph, Currier & Ives, NY, publisher, 10 ⅝ x 16 ½ in (27 x 42 cm). PR 010

STORMING THE CASTLE
"OLD ABE" ON GUARD.

Artist unknown. *Storming the Castle "Old Abe" on Guard*, 1860. Lithograph, Currier & Ives, NY, publisher, 10 ¹¹/₁₆ x 15 in (27.15 x 38.10 cm). Gift of Daniel Parish Jr., PR 010

(opposite page) Report of Lincoln's nomination in *New-York Daily Tribune*, May 19, 1860. Gilder Lehrman Collection (GLC0872609)

was Senator William Henry Seward. Aware of the political importance of New York, the sometimes untidily dressed Lincoln even bought a new suit for the occasion. But it was his words, according to the *Tribune*, that mesmerized one of the largest and most enthusiastic audiences in New York history.[9] This speech, according to contemporary historian Harold Holzer, won him the nomination.[10]

Lincoln spoke compellingly to the Republican conviction that Southerners intended to install their odious vision of a reopened slave trade on the United States along with their plan to extend slavery into the territories. Lincoln painstakingly attacked the Northern Democracy's support of popular sovereignty, arguing the negative proposition that the founders never supported any policy that prevented the U.S. Congress from prohibiting slavery in the territories. He denied that his was a sectional party, and assailed the Southern purpose as that of either ruling or ruining the nation. And in the moral ethic that sustained the Republican faith, he emphasized "the wrong of slavery" and ended with the thrilling peroration: LET US HAVE FAITH THAT RIGHT MAKES MIGHT, AND IN THAT FAITH LET US TO THE END DARE TO DO OUR DUTY AS WE UNDERSTAND IT."[11]

BY TELEGRAPH TO THE NEW-YORK TRIBUNE.

From Washington.

Special Dispatch to The N. Y. Tribune.

WASHINGTON, Friday, May 18, 1860.

THE CHICAGO NOMINATION.

The nomination at Chicago was the absorbing subject of interest to-day in both branches of Congress. Mr. Mason was hardly able to preserve a quorum during his speech in the Senate. Various dispatches were received early; and one from Mr. Haskin to Mr. Wendell, indicating that Mr. Seward would be chosen, seemed to express most positive knowledge of the purpose there.

About 2 o'clock Mr. Haskin telegraphed Mr. Douglas that Mr. Lincoln was nominated, but the fact was discredited in consequence of several bogus dispatches having been circulated, even though one of the operators testified to its genuineness. An hour and a half elapsed before any confirmation was obtained, and then telegrams announcing the result multiplied rapidly.

During the period of suspense, groups were collected in different parts of the hall, discussing the probabilities, and Senators and Members passed between the two Houses, comparing notes and exchanging such imperfect information as had been procured. Finally, when all doubts were removed, an evident sense of relief was visible on all sides, and then began a comparison of opinions as to the policy of Mr. Lincoln's nomination. He is well known here, and left, on retiring from Congress, the reputation of an able, genial, and worthy man, of unquestioned integrity and great popularity. A Whig of the olden time, he was devoted to the principles and policy of Mr. Clay, and was always regarded among his most earnest supporters.

Aside from the disappointment occasioned to Mr. Seward's friends, who were confident of success to the last moment, Mr. Lincoln's name has been received with general expressions of favor and rejoicings, and is regarded as furnishing every assurance of victory.

Mr. Douglas spoke of him in presence of Republicans and Democrats as an upright, gifted, and popular candidate, who had great strength in the North-West, and would carry Illinois against any other candidate but himself, by 20,000.

The conviction has already spread that the whole North-West and East are certain beyond doubt. Pennsylvania and New-Jersey take the

THE TREASURY.

The following is the weekly statement of the Treasury:

Receipts............$884,895 54 | Drafts issued.........$536,536 66
Drafts paid............ 666,401 17 | Net balance.........5,083,372 88

Special dispatch to The N. Y. Tribune.

WASHINGTON, Friday, May 18, 1860.

MR. LINCOLN'S NOMINATION

The nomination of Mr. Lincoln has been received with remarkably unanimous and hearty expressions of satisfaction by the Republican members of Congress.

The Democratic members are equally unanimous in asserting that Mr. Seward should have been taken. The conviction is everywhere expressed that Mr. Lincoln will make a clean sweep in the North-West, carrying every State in that section.

The opinion that no man has been named among all the candidates who possesses greater running qualities than Mr. Lincoln, finds prompt assent in all quarters. There was a strong desire and expectation that a candidate for the Vice-Presidency would be taken from Pennsylvania, it being believed that such a course would strengthen the ticket in that State; but confidence is felt that the Convention has acted wisely, it having the means of deciding upon the propriety of that course. Mr. Hamlin is considered a wholly unexceptionable candidate, and one possessing unquestionable elements of popularity, with no drawbacks.

All things considered, the action of the Convention is regarded as eminently satisfactory. The enthusiasm of the North-Western men knows no bounds.

SANDERS TO BUCHANAN.

The following is an exact copy of the famous dispatch of George Sanders to the President, which created such an excitement in the White House:

"CHARLESTON, 27th April, 1860.

"Slidell and Bright are here trying to break up the government. The occasion may arrive to-day for you to act. Northern delegates, with exception of a few from Pennsylvania, New-Jersey, Massachusetts, Oregon, and California, in concert with half the delegates from Alabama, two Florida, five Tennessee, half Kentucky, half North Carolina, half Maryland, half Missouri, a few from Georgia and Arkansas, agreed to the following addition to the Cincinnati Platform, which will be offered this morning as an amendment to the Slave-code programme of the majority. [Here was inserted the minority platform.] The amendment will receive one hundred and seventy-five to ninety votes. Alabama, Mississippi, and Louisiana will probably withdraw from the Convention. Douglas will then receive decided majority on first ballot, and on second or third will approximate to two-thirds. It is believed that the Collectors of Boston, Philadelphia, and New-Orleans will make factious opposition, but the Douglas majority will not be intimidated by anything that the

Artist unknown. "Wide Awakes,"
1860. Watercolor, 11 ⅞ x 22 ³/₁₆ in
(29.9 x 56.8 cm). PR 020

Three months later, on the third ballot at the party's nominating convention in Chicago, Abraham Lincoln became the Republican nominee for president. It was a blow to Seward, who had suffered from the strident opposition of his former political ally Horace Greeley. Ever since Seward had failed to support Greeley for a host of offices including the New York governorship, these two powerful Republicans had attacked each other in a bitter factional fight. In fact Greeley, an unlikely politician but brilliant editor, had roamed the corridors of the Republican convention, saying to anyone who would listen, "anyone but Seward."[12] Ultimately, however, Seward played a critical wartime role as Lincoln's Secretary of State, guiding Lincoln's patronage choices for New York as well as his foreign policy.

During the campaign that followed, Republicans led by Thurlow Weed, the party's clever strategist, organized effective party rituals and ceremonies. Republican loyalists underscored their devotion and enhanced their solidarity by dressing in parade uniforms and calling themselves the "Wide Awakes." In public ceremonies they marched in New York City and other communities carrying torchlights and chanting, "We are Lincoln men." In October, Greeley's *Tribune* described an event in Manhattan as a "Monster Torchlight Parade —20,000 Lincolnites in Line— Seventy acres of Republicans—Over a half million spectators."[13] New Yorker George Templeton Strong, the diarist, noted after one parade that the "Republican turnout is the town talk. Everyone speaks of the good order and the earnest aspect of the 'Wide Awakes' … Certainly, all the vigor and enthusiasm of this campaign are thus far confined to the Republicans."[14]

On Election Day November 6, 1860, Lincoln carried New York, running

E. A. Daggett (fl. 1860). *The Wide-Awake Vocalist; or Rail Splitters' Song Book. Words and Music for the Republican Campaign of 1860*, 1860. Gilder Lehrman Collection (GLC03430)

George Edward Perine (1837–85). *Henry J. Raymond (1820–69)*, undated. Engraving, 6 ⅝ x 4 ¹¹/₁₆ in (16.83 x 11.91 cm). PR 052

strongly in the state's rural central, western, and northern counties where voters were attracted to not just the party's antislavery position, but its commitment to free land and a Homestead Act. But in that enduring polarization of state politics, Lincoln failed to carry New York City by 30,000 votes despite the support of Greeley, Seward, Raymond, and Edmund Morgan, the New Yorker who had been the head of the Republican National Committee and was soon to be governor of the state. Thus, while the president-elect carried New York State by 53 percent of the vote, in the city his electoral percentage was a dismal 34 percent. A year later, on his way to Washington to take the oath of office, Lincoln returned to New York. This time he offered his commitment to maintain the Union as well as to fulfill his private promise to young Grace Bedell of Westfield, New York, to grow whiskers if she persuaded her brothers to vote for him.

LINCOLN AND WARTIME NEW YORK, 1861–1863:
UNION NOW AND FOREVER

During the months after South Carolina seceded in December of 1860 and secession spread to six other states by February, nowhere in the North were allegiances as complicated as those in New York. With their commercial connections to the cotton planters of the Confederacy and their dependence on trade as the financial center of the United States, many New Yorkers opposed war. "The South have not offended us," said U.S. Senator Daniel Dickinson.[15] "Let them go in peace" became the early, though soon reversed, mantra of Greeley's *Tribune*.[16] New York's quixotic Democratic mayor Fernando Wood argued for the secession of the city from the Union so that it might operate as a free port.

Yet after the firing on Fort Sumter and Lincoln's calling up of the militia in the spring of 1861, New York chose the Union. The legislature immediately authorized and funded the enlistment of 30,000 volunteers. Ten days later, 100,000 New Yorkers assembled in Union Square to rally for the nation and to denounce the South's destruction of the republic. To be sure, there were permanent pockets of Southern sympathizers composed mostly of what came to be known as the Peace Democrats or Copperheads, but the overwhelming majority of the citizens of New York and their state officials vigorously supported Lincoln's call for troops. By the spring of 1861, supported mostly by private donations, New York's Seventh Regiment, soon to be incorporated into the Army of the Potomac, reached Washington in the perilous days when a Confederate attack on the nation's capital seemed imminent. Overall the state mobilized 123,000 volunteers by the summer of 1861, with a disproportionate number coming from upstate. Eventually the War Department credited New York with 448,500 enlistments, more than any other state in the Union.

Lincoln depended on New York for more than troops. In the crisis-filled days of the war's first spring, the president conferred extraordinary powers on several New York Republicans, who were empowered to act as if they were Treasury Department officials. Serving as agents of the federal government, but giving no security, John Dix and others used federal money to pay contracts for uniforms. They signed vouchers and hired steam ships though they had no public standing.

The Republicans, the clear beneficiaries of this early war-borne patriotism, immediately attempted to merge their party into a new nonpartisan nationalism. "No Party Now, but All for Our Country" emerged as the strategy of New York Republicans. Later the sentiment was codified into a widely distributed pamphlet written by New Yorker Francis Lieber, a Columbia College professor.[17] Echoing the earlier opposition of the Founding Fathers to political parties because they were dangerous factions, Republicans successfully framed their newly christened Union Party as a necessary wartime alternative to earlier rivalries. But such tactics were only briefly successful.

In 1862, after a year and a half of a war that many expected to end in three months, New York Democrats scored victories in the off-year elections. Most surprising and troubling to Republicans was the victory of Democrat Horatio Seymour in the governorship contest against James Wadsworth. During this campaign which took place after Lincoln's issuance of the Preliminary Emancipation Proclamation, Democrats labeled Republicans as revolutionary abolitionists whose wartime policies violated individual liberties. They pointed to the military suspension of city newspapers such as the *Journal of Commerce*. Seymour attacked the Lincoln administration as inept and called for "the Constitution as it is, the Union as it was, and the Negroes where they are."[18] The latter sentiment expressed the racist fears that Southern blacks freed by Lincoln would flood New York and take jobs from Irish workers.

A few months later, the city's 12,000 blacks, along with thousands of Republicans, had cause for celebration after Lincoln signed the final Emancipation Proclamation on January 1, 1863. At a meeting at Cooper Union, Henry Highland Garnet, the African American pastor of the Shiloh Presbyterian Church, and Lewis Tappan, the ancient advocate of New York's prewar anti-slavery movement, joined Republicans like Horace Greeley to endorse a policy that for some had been too long in the making. Indeed, six months before, Greeley and other New York Republicans had sent Lincoln their famous "Prayer of Twenty Millions," a letter demanding that the president emancipate slaves under the authority of the recent confiscation act. Now the president acted under his powers as commander-in-chief. In the words of the final Emancipation Proclamation: "All persons held as slaves within said designated

J[ohn]. C[hester]. Buttre (1821–93), after a photograph by Mathew B. Brady (ca. 1823–96). *Maj. Gen. John A. Dix*, undated. Steel engraving, John Chester Buttre, publisher, 5 x 4 ½ in (12.70 x 11.43 cm). PR 052

Thomas Nast (1840–1902). *Study for "Departure of the Seventh Regiment for the War, April 19, 1861,"* ca. 1865–69. Oil over graphite on brown paper, varnished, laid on heavy board, nailed and mounted on a wood panel, 22 ½ x 32 ¾ in (57.15 x 83.19 cm). Gift of George A. Zabriskie, 1946.174

Artist unknown. "Departure of the 7th Regt. N.Y.S.M Friday April 19th 1861. View of Broadway, Cor. Courtland St." in D.T. Valentine's Manual, 1862. Lithograph, Sarony, Major & Knapp, lithographer, 5 ¾ x 8 ¹⁄₁₆ in (14.60 x 20.48 cm). PR 020

(opposite page) Artist unknown. *A Great Rush 36th Regiment New York Volunteers,* ca. 1861–63. Woodcut and letterpress, Baker & Godwin, printer, 37 ¾ x 24 ¹³⁄₁₆ in (95.88 x 63.02 cm). PR 055

States or parts of states are, and henceforward shall be free." Furthermore, former slaves could now join the army.

Two months later, in a city full of complaints about Lincoln and his proclamation, Republicans rallied the city's influential supporters of the president. Intended to be an organization of young city leaders committed to Lincoln and his administration, the Union League Club located on Union Square quickly became a powerful propaganda voice for the Republican Party. Its pamphlets sponsored by its publication arm influenced Northerners across the country, as men like Frederick Law Olmsted and Henry Bellows used their prominence to encourage younger men to support Lincoln and the raising of black troops. When Governor

A GREAT RUSH

Cost what it may,

The Nation must be Saved!

TO JOIN THE

36TH REGIMENT

NEW YORK VOLUNTEERS,

Commanded by COLONEL W. H. BROWN.

This fine Regiment, one of the best in the Army of the Potomac, has been an active participant in the engagements on the Peninsula, and particularly distinguished itself during the "SEVEN DAYS' FIGHTING," having captured the Colors of the 14th North Carolina Regiment at the Battle of Malvern Hill. The term of enlistment of this Regiment will be out in

NINE MONTHS.

DON'T WAIT TO BE DRAFTED!

☞ THE USUAL BOUNTY GIVEN. ☜

Recruiting Office, No. 17 CENTRE STREET,

BETWEEN CHAMBERS AND READE STREETS.

Lieut. G. H. MOORE, Recruiting Officer.

BAKER & GODWIN, Printers, Printing-House Square, Opposite City Hall, New York.

Seymour resisted efforts to recruit a black regiment from the city, club members raised private money. By 1864, the Twentieth United States Colored Regiment marched down Broadway on its way to action in Louisiana.

Emancipation and the recruitment of black soldiers continued to alienate some conservative Republicans, who like Henry Raymond, had at first believed that the war was solely to restore the Union and who had not incorporated emancipation into their war goals. But overall, most party members supported, however tepidly, a policy undertaken not so much on moral grounds but as a wartime necessity. It was the Democrats who overwhelmingly opposed emancipation as well as the new policy of conscription, requiring military service of men aged twenty to forty-five unless they found a substitute or paid a commutation fee of $300. Such arrangements favored the rich and inflamed young Irishmen who believed they were the victims of an unfair, class-based policy.

Amid these simmering tensions, New York City erupted in the summer of 1863 in a bloody riot lasting from July 13 through 16. A mob of mostly Irish workers and firemen had first vented their anger on draft offices on Forty-sixth Street where the so-called "wheels of misfortune" were determining who would be sent to war. Later the violence expanded. Blacks were lynched and tortured in a brutal orgy that included the burning of the Colored Orphans' Asylum at Fifth Avenue and Forty-third Street. Prominent Republicans found themselves targets of rioters armed with sticks and stones as well as guns, swords and torches. When the riot finally ended, and over 100 mostly African-American New Yorkers lay dead, explanations took on a political tone. Governor Seymour informed Lincoln that the unconstitutional draft with its unfair quotas for New York had been the cause of the conflict. Lincoln forcefully responded that the Union could not wait for a constitutional test at a time when the Confederacy was forcing every able-bodied man into its army. Eventually Seymour yielded, and the draft proceeded with public money sometimes used for bounties and substitutes.[19]

Meanwhile, Republicans excoriated Governor Seymour for his role in triggering the riot. A few days before the riot, he had made the intemperate suggestion in a speech that "the bloody and treasonable and revolutionary doctrine of public necessity can be proclaimed by a mob as well as the government." Peace Democrats, charged the Republicans, had organized the conspiracy in order to sabotage the war effort.[20]

(opposite page) Artist unknown. *Phoenix Regiment! Corcoran Zoaves! 4th Regiment Spinola's Empire Brigade!,* undated. Hand-colored woodcut and letterpress, Baker & Godwin, publisher, 23 7/16 x 37 ¾ in (59.53 x 95.89 cm). PR 055

AND ON TO SUCCESS

The year 1864 heralded another electoral challenge to New York Republicans as the war continued, even after the victories at Gettysburg and Vicksburg in July

PHŒNIX REGIMENT!
CORCORAN ZOUAVES!

4th REGIMENT SPINOLA'S EMPIRE BRIGADE!

JAMES C. BURKE, Colonel.   **M. D. SMITH, Lieutenant Colonel.**

"OH, COME AND WEAR A GREEN COCKADE
AND LEARN THE SOLDIER'S GLORIOUS TRADE;
'TIS OF SUCH STUFF A HERO'S MADE--
THEN COME AND JOIN THE BOLD BRIGADE."

This splendid Regiment of Irish Volunteers is the best for all young Irishmen to join, as they will be amongst as fine a lot of fellows as ever followed the Green Flag to Battle.

RECRUITS WANTED

For **COMPANY H**, to fill up to the maximum standard.

QUARTERS, RATIONS, and a NEW AND DASHING UNIFORM furnished immediately.

PAY FROM $13 TO $23 PER MONTH,
TO COMMENCE FROM DATE OF ENROLLMENT.

$25 Bounty and One Month's Pay in ADVANCE! RELIEF TICKETS, signed by the Colonel, will be furnished to Soldiers' families immediately.

RECRUITS WILL BE RECEIVED DAILY, FROM 9 A. M. TO 6 P. M., AT

62 SPRING STREET, NEAR MARION ST

RICHARD OULAHAN, 1st Lieut.   **DANIEL O'SULLIVAN (Agreem), Capt.**
JAMES A. O'SULLIVAN, 2d Lieut., Recruiting Officer.

BAKER & GODWIN, Printers, Printing-House Square, cor. Nassau and Spruce Streets, New York.

SENATORIAL REGIMENT

COLONEL ANTHONY CONK.

RESPOND — TO YOUR COUNTRY'S CALL!

RECRUITS WANTED

FOR COMPANY A,

To serve for three years or during the War, under experienced Officers.

$75 BOUNTY!

From the Government and State will be paid to each Recruit before leaving the State;
also, ONE MONTH'S PAY IN ADVANCE, as soon as the Company is
mustered into the service of the United States.

ALSO, $ BOUNTY FROM THE COUNTY OF KINGS.

PAY COMMENCES IMMEDIATELY!

CLOTHING AND SUBSISTENCE FURNISHED FROM DATE OF ENLISTMENT.

Apply to CAPT. GILBERT BOGART,
or LIEUT. THEODORE MILLER, Recruiting Officers,

No. 12 COURT STREET, BROOKLYN.

BAKER & GODWIN, Printers, Printing-House Square, opposite City Hall, N. Y.

Abraham Lincoln,

President of the United States of America.

To all whom these presents may concern, Greeting:

Whereas, an insurrection continues to exist in the United States, and whereas there are in the military Department of the East, now under the command of Major General John A. Dix, combinations of evil disposed persons armed to oppose the civil and military authorities, which combinations are dangerous in their character, have already seriously disturbed the public peace, occasioned the murder of innocent citizens and the destruction of valuable property; and whereas those combinations are believed to require the employment of military force for their suppression and the restoration of the public tranquillity;—

Now, therefore, be it known, that I, Abraham Lincoln, President of the United States of America and Commander in Chief of the Army and Navy thereof, do, hereby, authorize Major General John A. Dix, Com-

mander in the Department aforesaid, to suspend the Habeas Corpus and to declare and exercise martial law within that Department, whenever and to such extent as in his judgment may be necessary for the suppression of the combinations above referred to.

In testimony whereof, I have hereunto signed my name and caused the Seal of the United States to be affixed. Done at the City of Washington this Seventeenth day of July, A.D. 1863, and of the Independence of the United States the Eighty eighth.

Abraham Lincoln

By the President:

William H. Seward.
Secretary of State.

1863. War weariness led a few New York Republicans to support negotiations with the Confederacy. The erratic Greeley orchestrated a plan to bring a Southern delegation to Washington; Thurlow Weed supported a conditional surrender. But Lincoln shrewdly required unresolvable preconditions before he would agree to any meeting. Then, in a year filled with difficulties for the president, former Secretary of the Treasury Salmon Chase and John Fremont, the Republican candidate in 1856, presented themselves as alternatives to Lincoln. But both movements fizzled into cranky expressions of distaste for the president who continued to command the allegiance of most mainstream Republicans—in New York and elsewhere.

In May, at the party's nominating convention in Baltimore, the opportunities for Republicans to demonstrate their commitment to black liberation and military victory manifested themselves. It was New York's Edwin Morgan, the former governor and retiring head of the National Union Executive Committee, who as presiding officer urged the convention to support a constitutional amendment to prohibit slavery. Lincoln had encouraged him to do so, knowing that this further commitment—which became the Thirteenth Amendment after its ratification in

Abraham Lincoln Authorizes Suspension of Habeas Corpus and Imposition of Martial Law during the New York City Draft Riots, July 17, 1863. Manuscript document signed by Abraham Lincoln, countersigned by William H. Seward. Two sides of a folded sheet affixed with embossed seal of the United States. Private collection

(opposite page) Artist unknown. *Senatorial Regiment Colonel Anthony Conk.* ca. 1862. Hand-colored woodcut and letterpress, Baker & Godwin, publisher, 23 11/16 x 38 1/8 in (60.17 x 96.84 cm). PR 055

MAY THE BEST MAN WIN!---UNCLE SAM REVIEWING THE ARMY OF CANDIDATES FOR THE PRESIDENTIAL CHAIR.

Artist unknown. *May the Best Man Win! – Uncle Sam Reviewing the Army of Candidates for the Presidential Chair*, 1864. Wood engraving, 12 ¹¹⁄₁₆ x 19 ⅛ in (32.28 x 48.58 cm). PR 010

1865—would make emancipation irreversible. The sixty-six New York delegates, including Henry Raymond who had written the pro-Lincoln platform, cheered their approval. In a hopeful expression that the war would end soon, the delegates looked ahead, supporting peacetime initiatives such as a railroad to the Pacific Coast. Earlier the party, in efforts to move beyond its founding principles opposing the extension of slavery, had resolved to promote land grants to institutions of higher learning and a homestead policy of 160 acres of land to those who farmed it for five years. During the war, Congress passed and Lincoln signed both measures, designed to appeal to farmers.

By late summer, however, Lincoln's reelection was by no means certain. The news from the battlefront was dreary; the draft rankled, and there was a distaste for presidential second terms. Some observers predicted that New York would go for the War Democrat General George B. McClellan, a New York resident. Then on September 1 a triumphant General Sherman occupied Atlanta, and turned his vast army toward the coastal city of Savannah, Georgia. Meanwhile in several engagements, General Sheridan defeated the Confederate Jubal Early in the Shenandoah Valley.

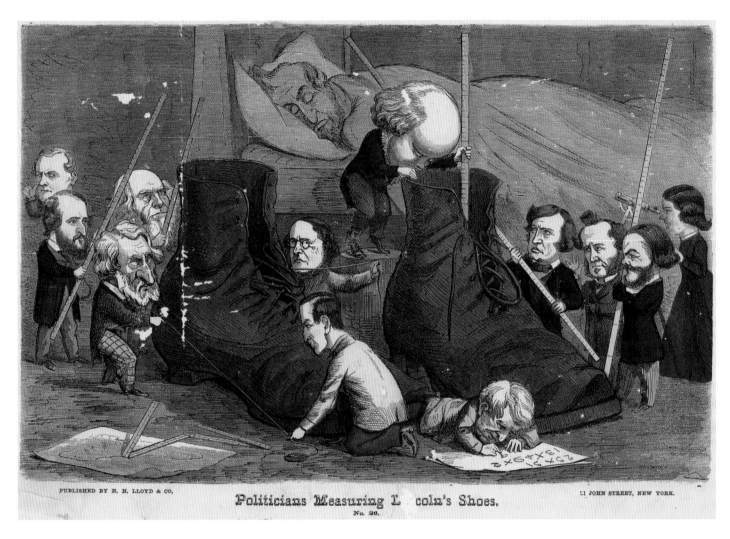

PUBLISHED BY H. H. LLOYD & CO,

Politicians Measuring L coln's Shoes,
No. 26.

51 JOHN STREET, NEW YORK.

As the war news turned positive, New York Republicans became more sanguine about the outcome of the election. From his headquarters in the Astor House, Thurlow Weed, the party's masterful political operative, campaigned for the Lincoln ticket, circulating pamphlets, organizing rallies, seeking the support of local ward captains upstate, and always, always, calculating to keep the expected Democratic majority in the city to a minimum. The poet and hospital nurse Walt Whitman observed one of these spectacles in October: " I go ... as to shows, fireworks, cannon, clusters of gaslights, countless torches, banners and mottos, 15, 20, 50,000 people—."[21]

In November 1864 Abraham Lincoln was reelected president of the United States in an election he later saluted as demonstrating "that a people's government can sustain a national election, in the midst of a great civil war."[22] He carried New York and its thirty-five electoral votes, along with those of every other Union state except New Jersey, Delaware and Louisiana, now under the control of the army. But the popular vote was close and in New York, amid rumors of a Confederate conspiracy to shut down the polls, the president won by the hairbreadth's margin of only 6,749 of 730,723 votes cast. The city and Brooklyn returned impressive

Artist unknown. *Politicians Measuring Lincoln's Shoes*, 1864. Hand-colored woodcut, H. H. Lloyd & Co., publisher, 8 ⅞ x 13 ⅞ in (22.54 x 35.24 cm). PR 010

FOR PRESIDENT,

ABRAHAM LINCOLN.

FOR VICE PRESIDENT,

ANDREW JOHNSON.

THE UNION AND THE CONSTIT

Campaign banner, 1864.
Lithograph on cotton,
16 ½ x 25 ½ in (41.91 x 64.77 cm).
Samuel T. Shaw Memorial
Collection, 1946.243

majorities for McClellan, which cut into Lincoln's upstate support. The soldier vote went overwhelmingly for the president, as did the vote from counties such as Allegany, Broome, Cayuga, Genesee, Jefferson, Madison, Ontario, St. Lawrence, Schuyler, Steuben, and Washington. In these areas farmers, artisans and especially young men, some first-time voters, voted Republican in disproportionate numbers. Such a victory, however narrow, was cause for celebration.

There had been local successes as well. The party sent two Republican stalwarts—William Dodge and Henry Raymond—to Congress; Horatio Seymour, an impediment to Republican hopes for a Union Party and a thorn in Lincoln's side, was no longer governor. Now it was certain that the war would continue until the Confederacy surrendered. "The crisis has been past," exulted George Templeton Strong. "The most momentous popular election ever held since ballots were invented has decided against treason and disunion."[23]

Peace brought hope for the future, but then sudden special grief for New York's pared for his final visit to the state. Throughout his presidency he had depended on many New Yorkers, including his loyal Secretary of State William Seward and the party's leader Edwin Morgan. He had maneuvered his way through the thickets of the Seward-Greeley factions, keeping the respect of both. He had exchanged significant policy statements with New Yorkers who had pressed him

(opposite page) *Union Nomination for President, Abraham Lincoln of Illinois, for Vice President, Andrew Johnson of Tennessee*, 1864. Election poster. 99 ⅞ x 43 ¾ in (253.68 x 111.25 cm). PR 055

UNION NOMINATION

FOR PRESIDENT,
Abraham Lincoln
OF ILLINOIS.

FOR VICE PRESIDENT,
Andrew Johnson
OF TENNESSEE.

JOB PRINTERS, AND ENGRAVERS ... LLIAM STREET, N... K   NEW DESIGNS FOR ALL POLITICAL P...

(above) Lantern with portrait of
Lincoln and Union Flag, 1864.
Tin, glass, and paper,
8 ½ x 5 ⅜ x 5 ⅜ in (21.59 x
13.65 x 13.65 cm). Purchased
from Elie Nadelman, 1937.585

(right) Emanuel Gottlieb Leutze
(1816–68), designer. Banner,
1864. Produced by Tiffany & Co.,
presented to General Dix at the
NY Sanitary Fair, April 23, 1864.
38 x 43 in (96.52 x 109.22 cm).
Private collection

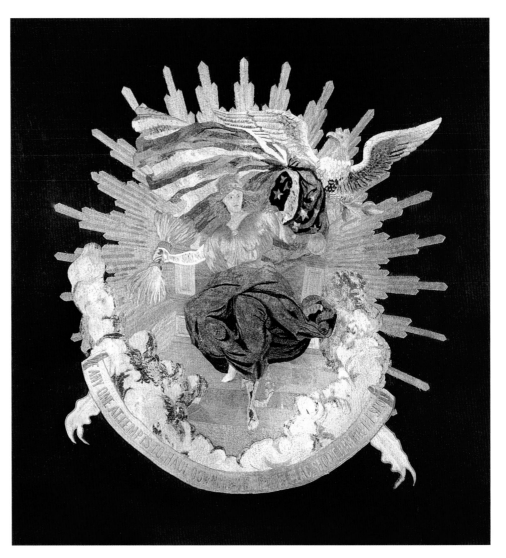

on his decisions about patronage, civil liberties, and slave emancipation. He had
earned his way to the White House with a New York speech, and he had been
elected two times by Republican voters in the state.

On April 25, 1865, the president came to New York for the last time. The city
had shut down; all was draped in black. Lincoln's funeral cortege moved slowly up
Broadway to City Hall where it was placed on a catafalque. Only through the
intercession of the Union League Club had blacks been allowed to march in the
procession, and then only at the back.[24] The next day the funeral car moved on
through the state as silent observers along the tracks bowed their heads and wept.

By the end of 1865, New York Republicans faced different challenges during
the period of Reconstruction. New issues emerged involving tariffs, commercial
policies, and especially during the 1870s, currency matters. But the legacy to the
post-war party remained an optimistic one of growth—from 276,007 voters in
1856 in eight years to 368,736 in 1864. Perhaps as notably, the party had held
true to its original organizing principles by supporting Lincoln's progressive, but
controversial, policies of emancipation, the draft, and finally the Thirteenth

1.

It has long been a grave question whether any government, not <u>too</u> strong for the liberties of its people, can be strong <u>enough</u> to maintain its own existence, in great emergencies.

On this point the present rebellion brought our republic to a severe test; and a presidential election occurring in regular course during the rebellion added not a little to the strain.

If the loyal people, <u>united</u>, were put to the utmost of their strength by the rebellion, must they not fail when <u>divided</u>, and partially paralized, by a political war among themselves?

But the election was a necessity—.

We can not have free government without elections; and if the rebellion could force us to forego, or postpone a national election, it might fairly claim to have already conquered and ruined us. The strife of the election

(above) Mathew B. Brady's (ca. 1823–96) National Portrait Gallery. *George B. McClellan (1826–85)*, 1862. Albumen print, carte-de-visite, E. & H. T. Anthony, publisher, 3 ⅝ x 2 ⅛ in (9.21 x 5.40 cm). PR 011

(left) Abraham Lincoln (1809–65). The First Page of Abraham Lincoln's November 10, 1864 victory speech, November 10, 1864. Courtesy of Christie's. *"It has long been a grave question whether any government, not <u>too</u> strong for the liberties of its people, can be strong <u>enough</u> to maintain its own existence in great emergencies. On this point the present rebellion brought our republic to a severe test; and a presidential election occurring in regular course during the rebellion added not a little to the strain...."*

Alexander Hay Ritchie
(1822–95). E[dwin]. D[enison].
Morgan (1811–83), undated.
Engraving, 6 %16 x 3 %16 in
(16.67 x 9.05 cm). PR 052

Photographer unknown. *Salmon
Portland Chase (1808–73)*, undated.
Albumen print, carte-de-visite,
C. D. Fredericks and Co.,
publisher, 3 %16 x 2 ⅛ in
(9.05 x 5.40 cm). PR 011

(opposite page) Artist unknown.
*To His Excellency the President of the
United States. For God & Liberty*,
1864. Lithograph, sheet music
cover, H. Millard, composer.
13 ⅜ x 10 ¼ in (33.97 x 26.04 cm).
PR 031

Amendment. Party members had done this in a state that was competitive, where there was a temptation to compromise. In step with their president, these articulate and energetic Republicans had demonstrated that democracy could survive during the most trying times.

NOTES

1   Kirk Porter and Donald Bruce Johnson, *National Party Platforms* (Urbana: University Press, 1966), 13.

2   *New York Tribune*, January 5, 1854.

3   Edward Spann, *Gotham at War* (Wilmington: Scholarly Resources, 2002), 107.

4   Jean H. Baker, *Ambivalent Americans: The Know Nothing Party in Maryland* (Baltimore: Johns Hopkins Press, 1982).

5   William Henry Seward, *William Henry Seward at Washington 1846–1861* (New York: Derby and Miller, 1891), 239. For the Republicans in the 1850s see Hendrik Booram, *The Formation of the Republican Party in New York* (New York: New York University Press, 1983), 64.

6   William Gienapp, *The Origins of the Republican Party 1852–1856* (New York: Oxford University Press, 1987), 442.

7   Roy P. Basler, ed., *The Collected Works of Abraham Lincoln* (New Brunswick: Rutgers University Press, 1953–55), 2:390–1.

8   Abraham Lincoln, *Speeches and Writings, 1859–1865*, ed. Don E. Fehrenbacher (New York: The Library of America, 1989), 132.

9   *New York Tribune*, February 28, 1860.

10 Harold Holzer, *Lincoln at Cooper Union: The Speech That Made Lincoln President* (New York: Simon Schuster, 2004).

11 *Abraham Lincoln: Speeches and Writings* (New York; Library Association of America, 1984) 111–130.

12 Robert Williams, *Horace Greeley: Champion of Freedom* (New York: New York University Press, 2006), 216.

13 *New York Tribune*, October 4 and 5, 1860, cited in Edward Spann, *Gotham At War* (Wilmington: Scholarly Resources, 1860), 4.

14 George Templeton Strong, *Diary of George Templeton Strong*, ed. Allan Nevins and Milton Halsey (New York: Macmillan, 1952), 3:41.

15 Quoted in DeAlva Alexander, *A Political History of the State of New York* (Fort Washington: Ira Friedman, 1909), 4.

16 Williams, *Horace Greeley*, 216.

17 Francis Lieber, *No Party Now But All For the Union* (Philadelphia: Crissy and Markley, 1863).

18 Joel Silbey, *A Respectable Minority: Northern Democrats in the Civil War, 1860–1865* (New York: W.W. Norton, 1977), 51.

19 Basler, *Collected Works of Abraham Lincoln*, 6:369–70, 391.

20 Spann, *Gotham at War*, 95–102.

21 Walt Whitman, *The Correspondence*, ed. Edwin Miller (New York: New York University Press, 1961), 1:243.

22 Basler, *Collected Works of Abraham Lincoln*, 8:101.

23 Strong, *Diary*, 3:511.

24 Edwin Burrows and Mike Wallace, *Gotham: A History of New York City to 1898* (New York: Oxford University Press, 1999), 904–5.

THE CULTURE OF OPPOSITION IN NEW YORK

BARNET SCHECTER

WHILE LINCOLN'S COOPER UNION appearance in February 1860 helped galvanize his Republican supporters, the speech and his subsequent nomination as the party's presidential candidate were the target of ridicule by Democratic, proslavery forces in New York City. In May, James Gordon Bennett's *New York Herald* called the choice "a remarkable indication of small intellect, growing smaller." Passing over able statesmen, "they take up a fourth-rate lecturer, who cannot speak good grammar." The *Herald* called the Cooper Union speech "hackneyed, illiterate ... the most unmitigated trash, interlarded with coarse and clumsy jokes," while denouncing Lincoln's $200 speaking fee as "dollars coined out of Republican fanaticism."[1]

Among Lincoln's opponents, "Republican fanaticism" was shorthand for the radical wing of the party and its demand for the immediate abolition of slavery. Distrusting Lincoln's carefully worded statements opposing only the expansion of slavery, New York's Democrats and proslavery independents like Bennett took every opportunity to paint him as a radical.

A LEGACY OF SLAVERY AND JACKSONIAN WHITE SUPREMACY

In New York, opposition to the Republican Party and to Lincoln's candidacy in 1860 was rooted in a long history of slavery, dating back to the founding of the city more than two centuries earlier by the Dutch, who used African slaves on their farms and to build the settlement in lower Manhattan. During the British period, beginning in 1664, laws for controlling slaves became harsher, and two

Mathew B. Brady (ca. 1823–96). *Abraham Lincoln*, Washington, DC, probably 1862. Published in Meserve Historical Portraits. Albumen silver print from collodian plate. 3 ¼ x 2 ⅛ in (8.26 x 5.40 cm). PR 231

Studio of Mathew B. Brady
(ca. 1823–96). *James Gordon Bennett*
(1795–1872), ca. 1851–52.
Half plate daguerreotype, gold
toned. Library of Congress,
Daguerreotype collection,
LC-USZC4-4150

slave uprisings, in 1712 and 1741, were brutally repressed. After the American Revolution, slavery persisted throughout the state while New York's Federalists, including John Jay and Alexander Hamilton, pressed for abolition. It was not until 1827 that the gradual emancipation laws of 1799 and 1817 ended slavery in New York State.[2]

The withering of slavery precipitated white opposition to black equality and civil rights. After the Revolution, free blacks had only to meet a minimal property requirement to vote in New York, but when the Democrats came to power in the state in 1801 with the election of Thomas Jefferson to the White House, they began to challenge the voting qualifications for blacks. In 1821 the Democrats ushered in a new state constitution that eliminated the property requirement for all white men while raising it prohibitively—to $250—for blacks.[3] This incendiary linkage of racial and class conflict—the pitting of poor whites' aspirations against those of free blacks—would become a staple of Democratic politics, sparking violent resistance to abolition for decades, through the Civil War, and beyond.

By the late 1820s and early 1830s, Thomas Jefferson's political heirs in the Democratic party of President Andrew Jackson had proclaimed themselves defenders of the common man against the northeast's increasingly powerful commercial and industrial urban elite.[4] While the Democrats condemned inequality between the rich and poor, they believed blacks were inherently inferior to whites, and Jackson himself owned slaves. The party embraced all whites, no matter how poor, as equals—as voting citizens of the republic and members of the master race.[5]

New York's social and racial divide was widened by ethnic and religious hatred. As New York's newly freed blacks looked for menial jobs in the late 1820s and early 1830s, the easing of immigration restrictions by the British flooded American port cities with tens of thousands of Irish Catholics, also looking for unskilled work. The growth of New York's archdiocese and Archbishop John Hughes's aggressive leadership against the Protestant establishment's anti-Catholic bigotry provoked public hysteria about a papal conspiracy to topple American democracy. The Second Great Awakening, a surge in Protestant revivalism radiating from New England during the first few decades of the nineteenth century, brought numerous Protestant evangelists to New York. Their wildly popular revival meetings helped intensify religious divisions, while their denunciation of slavery as a grave sin alarmed proslavery advocates.[6]

When the Republican Party formed in 1854, the North's largely immigrant working class was alienated from this coalition of its Protestant enemies—abolitionists, prohibitionists, Know-Nothing nativists, and former Whigs. Since industrialization threatened to turn workers into "wage slaves," most urban laborers were infuriated by evangelicals and abolitionists who lectured them about hard work and self-help, while bestowing sympathy on blacks in the distant southern states.

Working as much as nineteen hours a day in garrets and factories, men, women, and children barely scraped by in New York's filthy slums. In a single year, between 1853 and 1854, inflation drove the cost of living up by almost a third, while wages failed to keep pace.[7]

Fernando Wood, a Democrat, was elected to the first of three terms as mayor in 1854. He garnered votes from the working class, particularly Irish longshoremen, by denouncing the rich as idle "non-producers." For the aristocratic merchants and landowners who had traditionally dominated New York politics, Wood's rise represented a dangerous new phenomenon made possible by the Jacksonian era of universal white male suffrage: the emergence of demagogic, professional politicians, completely lacking in social pedigree, who pandered to the newly enfranchised masses. Wood also pitted whites against blacks: He opposed abolition, saying freed blacks would take jobs from white workers in the North and drive down wages.[8]

By 1860, New York's merchants and financiers had extended loans amounting to hundreds of millions of dollars to Southern planters, whose cotton was insured and shipped to European textile factories by companies in New York, and who bought agricultural tools and machinery from the city's manufacturers. Amid this dense web of commercial ties to the South, some New York investors and ships even continued, illegally, to participate in the slave trade. As the prospect of abolition and disunion loomed over Lincoln's candidacy in 1860, New York's businessmen were convinced his election would spell financial ruin, and grass would grow in the once-bustling streets of the great city.[9]

THE DEMOCRATIC OPPOSITION IN 1860

In the presidential election of 1860, Democrats stirred up fears of racial equality, interracial sex, and black labor competition, especially in New York, where a Republican-sponsored amendment to the state constitution appeared on the ballot, proposing to do away with the $250 property requirement for black voters. Democratic editorials and campaign speeches accused Republicans of believing "a nigger is better than an Irishman." A parade in New York City included a float bearing effigies of abolitionist *Tribune* editor Horace Greeley and a "good looking nigger wench, whom he caressed with all the affection of a true Republican." Nearby, a banner warned that "free love and free niggers will certainly elect Old Abe." Even though Lincoln had not denounced the fugitive slave law or called for immediate abolition in the South, the New York *Daily News*, owned by Fernando Wood and edited by his brother Ben, predicted "negroes among us thicker than blackberries swarming everywhere" if he were elected, while Bennett's *Herald* envisioned labor competition from "four million emancipated negroes."[10]

In the country as a whole, Lincoln was elected with only forty percent of the

THE GREAT EXHIBITION OF 1860.

Artist unknown. *The Great Exhibition of 1860*, 1860. Lithograph, Currier & Ives, publisher, 8 ½ x 15 ⅞ in (21.60 x 40.32 cm). Gift of Henry O. Havemeyer, PR 010

popular vote. "Has not the election of Lincoln ruined and broken up the country?" The proslavery *New York Day-Book* asked. "What Republican editor will dare answer that question?" Lincoln won New York State but lost in the Democratic stronghold of New York City, where conservative merchants—dreading a disruption of trade and hoping secession would be temporary—urged that the South be allowed to go peacefully if compromise failed. [11]

At the state level, Republican control during the previous four years had exacerbated Democratic opposition in New York City. While the newly formed Republican Party had lost the 1856 presidential election, it had won several important Northern states; in New York, Republicans had won the governor's office and control of the state legislature. In 1857, the state legislature had replaced New York City's "Municipal" police force with the "Metropolitans," run by a state-appointed commission dominated by Republicans. The arrival of the Metropolitans had sparked deadly rioting, and tensions had continued to simmer.

The commission had free rein not only over the police, but enforcement of election laws, health codes, and Sabbath closings. Coupled with the Liquor Excise

Law, which created stringent regulations and costly liquor licenses, the Sunday closings attacked the foundations of Democratic power in the city's wards: the saloons and grocery-grogshops were the local nerve centers of the political machine and sources of revenue from liquor industry lobbyists. The new laws, passed by a coalition of Republicans, nativists, and temperance advocates, also infuriated German and Irish Catholic laborers by policing their leisure time.[12]

After Lincoln's election in 1860, thousands of workers were laid off as trade with the South diminished and many Southern planters repudiated their debts to New York's merchants. However, the South's predictions of New York's demise, and those of the city's own merchants, proved inaccurate. Through Union war contracts, trade with the Midwest, and infusions of gold from California, the city soon rebounded commercially and financially. During the Civil War its industrial output would rival that of the entire Confederacy.[13]

South Carolina became the first state to secede, on December 20, 1860. With his annual address in January 1861 Mayor Wood fanned the flames of disunion by suggesting that New York should secede as well and become a "free city"—free from federal control and from the state government in Albany that deprived New York City of home rule. The city could then tap its good commercial relationships with all parts of the U.S., including the South. Despite Wood's claims, the city did not have the resources to sustain independence, and Lincoln calmly observed that it would be a long time "before the front door sets up house-keeping on its own account." By the end of the month, encouraged by South Carolina's example and the sympathetic pronouncements of New York Democrats, six more states had seceded.[14]

When Lincoln visited New York City on his way to Washington in February 1861, 250,000 people filled the streets to see the president-elect as he rode to his hotel. However, the *Day-Book* refused to fly the American flag over its offices, and the red, white, and blue banners, pennants, and flags waving throughout the city were absent from the East River docks that hosted Southern ships, and where one captain hanged Lincoln in effigy from a mast.[15] At a formal City Hall reception, Mayor Wood shocked his guests by openly confronting Lincoln. The South's departure "sorely afflicted" New York and threatened its "commercial greatness," Wood declared, and he insisted on "a restoration of fraternal relations between the states—only to be accomplished by peaceful and conciliatory means—aided by the wisdom of God." Unfazed, Lincoln thanked Wood for his hospitality and professed to share his feelings, saying he would work for the good of the city and the country. However, Lincoln added, "There is nothing that can ever bring me willingly to consent to the destruction of this Union, under which not only the commercial city of New York, but the whole country has acquired its greatness."[16]

Artist unknown. *Inauguration of the President and Vice-President of the Southern Confederacy,* 1861. Wood engraving, published in the *New-York Illustrated News,* March 9, 1861. *E171.D38

INAUGURATION OF THE PRESIDENT AND VICE-PRESIDENT OF THE SOUTHERN CONFEDERACY, AT MONTGOMERY, ALA., ON THE MORNING OF FEB. 18. FROM A PHOTOGRAPH TAKEN EXPRESSLY FOR THIS PAPER BY A PHOTOGRAPHER IN MONTGOMERY. See page 284.

Morse. [Abraham Lincoln boxing with Jefferson Davis], 1861. Woodcut, 19 ¹³/₁₆ x 21 ⅝ in (50.32 x 54.93 cm). PR 010

THE ANTIWAR MOVEMENT

On April 13, 1861, the day after the Confederacy fired on Fort Sumter, the *New York Day-Book* appeared with heavy black borders on every column, declaring itself in mourning "for the fate of our once happy and glorious country, now plunging into the abyss of war, under the black and piratical lead of Abolitionism." The Fort Sumter headline screamed: "The Abolition Crusade!! Civil War Begun!"[17]

For the next eighteen months Lincoln strove to deny this linkage of the war and abolition, arguing that secession was treason, and the war's purpose was none other than to restore the Union. Putting aside his personal antislavery views, Lincoln focused on a conservative purpose that would bind together his pro-war coalition of slave-holding border states, Republicans, and War Democrats. In New York City, these pro-war Democrats included Tammany Hall, the dominant Democratic Party organization in the city, and the Catholic Church.

Lincoln could not hope to influence the likes of James McMasters, editor of New York City's leading Irish Catholic newspaper, the *Freeman's Journal*, an organ

T. S. Peirce. *Champion Prize Envelope: Lincoln & Davis in 5 Rounds*, 1861. Lithograph. Five envelopes, J. H. Tingley, publisher. Each: 3 15/16 x 5 7/8 in (8.41 x 14.92 cm). PR 117

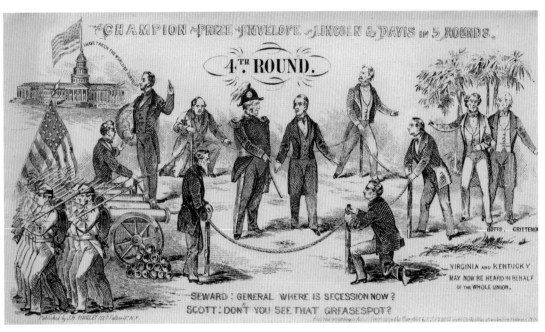

of extreme opposition to the war. Archbishop John Hughes, however, was a different matter. He had founded the paper and influenced its content for some time after it changed ownership, but it no longer reflected his views. Grateful to America for absorbing so many Irish Catholic refugees, Hughes was strongly pro-Union: Every steeple in the archdiocese flew the Stars and Stripes. Like Hughes, the New York Irish community's most influential secular paper, the *Irish-American*, backed the Union but denounced the Republican Party and abolition.[18]

When Fort Sumter fell, Lincoln called on the states to provide 75,000 national guardsmen for ninety days of federal service—the longest enlistment the president

Studio of Mathew B. Brady (ca. 1823–96). [August Belmont (1813–90), half-length portrait], ca. 1844–60. Half plate daguerreotype, gold toned. Library of Congress, Daguerreotype collection, LC-USZ62-109850

could legally require of the militia. The excitement of the war's opening days led most Northerners to believe three months would be ample time to crush the rebellion. In a burst of patriotism, New York's merchants abandoned their calls for conciliation and rallied behind the war effort. They hoped a massive show of force would end the war quickly, reunite the country, and restart the flow of trade.[19]

The disastrous Union defeat at Bull Run (Manassas) on July 21, 1861 crushed Northern hopes for a quick victory over the Confederacy and also gave Peace Democrats across the North a fresh impetus for attacks on Lincoln. The "effusion of blood" must be stopped through a negotiated settlement and recognition of the Confederacy, Democratic newspapers insisted. To demonstrate the popular groundswell for a truce, the *New York Daily News* published a list of 154 anti-war newspapers in the North on August 12, 1861 and condemned "the present unholy war." The *Journal of Commerce* and the *Day-Book* reprinted the list over the next two days.

However, Bull Run also inspired supporters of the war to redouble their efforts, and the idea of all-out war on the Confederacy gained ground. To circumvent constitutional protections for slavery, Republicans began to defend emancipation as a "military necessity." Slaves, they argued, made up more than fifty percent of the South's workforce, laboring in fields, mines, and factories as well as numerous non-combat roles in the Confederate army. Conservatives, including many Irish Americans who were eager to defend the nation that had offered them asylum, had volunteered enthusiastically, but now the assumption that they were fighting in a war to preserve the Union—not for abolition—came into question.[20]

DEMOCRATS UNITED AGAINST EMANCIPATION

In Congress, Republican calls for a "radical revolution" to destroy slavery reinforced Lincoln's fear that his increasingly fragile coalition of moderate Republicans, War Democrats, and Southern Unionists from the border states would shatter if emancipation became the Union's avowed goal. The Republicans would then have to fight the war alone, Lincoln said, "and the job on our hands is too large for us."[21]

The Democrats were also beset by factions and, having lost their entire Southern wing—now absent from Congress, where the all-Northern Republican Party held sway—they could not afford further divisions. Peace Democrats, especially the Wood brothers and Ohio's Clement Vallandigham, were particularly aggravating to the mainstream party leadership in New York, which included the "swallow-tail" Democrats, named for their fancy coats, who bankrolled the party: wealthy corporate lawyer Samuel Barlow; Democratic National Committee chairman August Belmont; and Samuel Tilden, a powerful corporate lawyer

Albert Berghaus (fl. 1869–80). *"24 Weeks on the Potomac": Illustration for* Frank Leslie's Illustrated Newspaper, 1862. Black ink over graphite on ivory paper, 6 ¼ x 9 ⅛ in (15.88 x 23.18 cm). James B. Wilbur Fund, 1945.580.82

and master political organizer. William Tweed and Tammany Hall, and former governor Horatio Seymour of the upstate organization dubbed the "Albany Regency", like the swallowtails, were pro-war but anti-emancipation. The anti-war rhetoric of the Peace Democrats—also called Copperheads—drove patriotic War Democrats out of the party and into the Republican camp. Moreover, the Copperheads' insistence on negotiations with the Confederacy enabled the Republicans to label the entire Democracy as disloyal. The peace faction kept growing, dividing the Democrats and enabling Republicans to campaign on their party's unblemished record of support for the war. In November 1861, Republicans triumphed in elections across New York State, including the three-way mayor's race in New York City, where Republican businessman George Opdyke prevailed and Fernando Wood lost.

Attempting to unify the party in early 1862, the War Democrats and Peace Democrats submerged their disagreements and rallied around their shared opposition to emancipation. Racism, they predicted, would bring the party's factions together and might pull some conservative, anti-abolition Republicans into the Democracy. In addition to emancipation, the question of civil rights for freed blacks provided a wedge to drive between radical and conservative Republicans. Barlow, Belmont, and Tilden remained alert, watching for a chance to exploit public fears about the growth of abolitionist sentiment in the North. For the moment, however, Lincoln's refusal to embrace emancipation deprived the Democrats of a galvanizing issue.[22]

By the spring of 1862, General George B. McClellan, commanding the Union's Army of the Potomac, had moved his forces down to the Yorktown peninsula in

Ferd. Mayer & Co. Lith. 96 Fulton St. N.Y.

Published by A. Marpé.

THE MAN OF THE PEOPLE !
GOVERNOR HORATIO SEYMOUR.
Elected by ten thousand majority, November 1862.
SURROUNDED BY HIS FRIENDS.

1. Martin Kalbfleisch.   5. M. Speyer.
2. Isaac G. Boyce.   6. I. A. Phillips.
3. M. Cassidy.   7. James Reed.
4. A.H. Dutsneier.   8. B.W. Osborn.
9. August Belmont.

10. C. Godfrey Gunther.   14. W. Tryon.
11. John R. Giles.   15. F. J. A. Boole.
12. J.R. Steers.   16. G. C. Howard.
13. M.F. Branian.   17. E.O. Bernet.
18. August Marpé.

Virginia and was slowly closing in on Richmond. Across the country, Union forces had captured 50,000 square miles of territory and pressure was mounting to free the tens of thousands of fugitive slaves who had fled to their protection. On May 9, 1862, Union general David Hunter freed the slaves in his military district, consisting of South Carolina, Georgia, and Florida.

Lincoln immediately countermanded the order, while asserting that emancipation might soon "become a necessity indispensable to the maintenance of the government." In the meantime, Lincoln continued to urge the Border States to embrace gradual, compensated emancipation in order to make the transition as smooth as possible. However, representatives of these states and Northern Democrats still hoped the war could be ended by McClellan's capture of Richmond, a decisive military victory that would reunite the country with slavery preserved.[23]

Hunter's proclamation was exactly the opportunity Barlow, Belmont, and Tilden had hoped for, and they made anti-emancipation the rallying cry to unite the War and Peace factions of the Democratic Party. To denounce Hunter's proclamation, the Albany Regency, the swallowtails, and Tammany orchestrated a series of mass meetings across New York State that set the stage for a huge demonstration in New York City. A Fourth of July celebration sponsored by Tammany welcomed the Peace Democrats back to the fold. Tammany sachem Elijah Purdy made a great show of marching arm in arm with Fernando Wood.[24]

However, Democratic hopes for the capture of Richmond, a limited war, and the "Union as it was" receded once again after Union forces under McClellan were defeated in the Seven Days' Battles of June 25-July 1, 1862. Lincoln vowed to fight on "until successful, or till I die, or am conquered … or Congress or the country forsakes me." A manifesto from border state congressmen on July 13th again rejecting gradual emancipation finally moved Lincoln away from courting the middle to favoring radical action on slavery. "As commander in chief of the army and navy, in time of war," he said, "I suppose I have a right to take any measure which may best subdue the enemy." By July, the failure to take Richmond, disillusionment in the ranks of the army, and dwindling enlistment all impressed on Lincoln the need for drastic action. To Secretary of State William Seward and navy secretary Gideon Welles, Lincoln revealed that he "had about come to the conclusion that we must free the slaves or be ourselves subdued."[25]

Republicans pressured Lincoln to dismiss McClellan after his defeat in the Seven Days' Battles. Not only was McClellan an outspoken Democrat and opponent of emancipation, he blamed the Administration for his defeat in Virginia, claiming he had not received adequate reinforcements. In fact, he vastly outnumbered the rebels, but Democrats spread McClellan's complaints among their constituents, and party leaders, including Fernando Wood, had visited the general at his battlefield headquarters asking him to run for president. Many Union

(opposite page) Ferd. Mayer & Co. *The Man of the People! Governor Horatio Seymour. Elected by ten thousand majority, November 1862*, ca. 1863. Lithograph on wove paper, August Marpé, publisher, 22 x 16 in (55.88 x 40.64 cm). Library of Congress, LC-DIG-pga-02137, 2004665359

soldiers idolized McClellan for whipping the army into shape and shared his opposition to an "abolition war." Hoping to forestall a mutiny in the Army of the Potomac and a surge of Democratic unity in the North, Lincoln hesitated to replace McClellan.[26]

Lincoln also postponed a proclamation to free the slaves in the Confederacy. In part, he wanted to protect Republicans from a political backlash in the upcoming fall elections. He was also following Seward's advice to wait until Union forces were winning, so that the declaration did not appear completely rhetorical and unenforceable.[27] During the summer, Democrats on the campaign trail continued to stir up fears of emancipation and labor competition from free blacks. Riots against blacks erupted across the North. In Brooklyn, an Irish mob set fire to a tobacco factory, targeting the black women and children working inside, who had to be rescued by police.[28]

With the Union victory at Antietam on September 17, 1862 Lincoln felt he had the military success and momentum to issue his Preliminary Emancipation Proclamation. On September 22, 1862 Lincoln proclaimed that in any state of the Confederacy that remained in rebellion on January 1, 1863, the slaves would be "thenceforth and forever free." With the stroke of a pen, the war became a struggle to end slavery. While it did not free slaves in the Border States for fear of driving them out of the Union, the proclamation nonetheless put the war on a moral footing, which abolitionists welcomed wholeheartedly. "GOD BLESS ABRAHAM LINCOLN ... It is the beginning of the end of the rebellion ... it is the beginning of the new life of the nation," Greeley's *Tribune* declared.[29]

THE PRELIMINARY EMANCIPATION PROCLAMATION AND THE ELECTIONS OF 1862

For Democratic Party strategists, headquartered in New York, the Preliminary Emancipation Proclamation provided the great issue around which to continue the process of Democratic unification and resurgence that had peaked in July 1862 with the state-wide anti-emancipation meetings and the rally in Manhattan. The Proclamation also exploited divisions within the Republican Party, spurring some conservatives to defect to the Democrats.

Among them was Manton Marble, editor of the struggling *New York World*, who revived the paper with financing from Samuel Barlow. Marble sold large stakes in the *World* to Barlow and three other Democrats—including Fernando Wood and George Barnard, a Tammany judge. Party leaders, including former governor Horatio Seymour, attended strategy sessions at the *World's* offices. Their immediate goal was to unify the party by attacking the Preliminary Emancipation Proclamation. Democratic newspapers threw off all restraint, declaring that Lincoln was influenced by "insane radicals," who had once promised they only wanted to stop the spread of slavery. Marble wrote that the president was "fully adrift on the current of radical fanaticism." If anyone was a danger to the government, he asserted, it was not the Copperheads, but rather the radical Republicans, who were hounding Lincoln to end slavery and overturn white supremacy in America. Glossing over the divisions among Democrats, Marble portrayed the party as the loyal opposition, vital to the two-party system.[30]

In the fall of 1862 Democrats nominated Horatio Seymour for governor and the party rallied around him. A decade earlier, his stand against prohibition in large part had cost him a second term, but now, his opposition to temperance became an asset, as did his racism and denunciations of Lincoln's policies. By contrast, the Republicans nominated an abolitionist, General James Wadsworth, a choice that divided the party. Predicting defeat, Greeley lamented to abolitionist Gerrit Smith that "the Rum-sellers, the Irish and the Slavery idolaters make a big crowd and they are fiendish in their vote against the president's proclamation of freedom."[31] Fernando Wood, after three terms as mayor of New York, was running for a seat in Congress. In campaign speeches that fall, pandering to Irish and German immigrants, Wood crystallized his message of class warfare and racial hatred. Emancipation, he asserted, was another attempt to exploit poor whites by deluging the North with cheap black laborers.[32]

J. Gurney & Son. *Manton Marble (1834–1917)*, undated. Albumen print, carte-de-visite, 3 9/16 x 2 1/8 in (9.05 x 5.40 cm). PR 011

Democrats charged that the Metropolitans, the Republican-controlled police force in New York City, had become the instrument of Lincoln's civil rights abuses, arbitrarily arresting political opponents and detaining them without charges in the city's prisons and the dungeons of Fort Lafayette in the harbor. Superintendent John Kennedy was allegedly intimidating Democratic voters with the threat of arrest, not—as he asserted—because they were aliens who claimed to be exempt form military service, but rather for the Republicans' political advantage.[33]

Northerners' despair over Union losses on the battlefield during the previous eighteen months, opposition to emancipation, and fear of British intervention in the war all helped the Democrats, who nearly doubled their seats in Congress. In New York, Democrats submerged their differences over the issue of war and peace, sending both Ben and Fernando Wood to Congress and Seymour to the governor's mansion by a significant margin. Greeley was furious and declared that the state had abandoned the Union cause.[34] However, the Republicans still had a majority in the House and an even firmer grip on the Senate. Voters had signaled their disapproval of emancipation and of the administration's handling of the war, but indicated they were willing to give Lincoln and his party another chance. Nonetheless, the Democrats had successfully exploited public fear of abolition to unite the party, and they celebrated their victories across the North. A popular Democratic song declared that abolition "has died before it was weaned, weaned, weaned; it

Draft Wheel, ca. 1863. Wood and metal cylindrical drum with a rectangular, lockable hatch and an iron and wood handle, set on trestle frame with bracket feet and a turned stretcher; with 100+ cards with names of draft-eligible men; brass plaque on side, engraved:

DRAFT WHEEL/USED JULY 13, 1863/ WITH NAMES OF RESIDENTS IN THE/ 7TH CONGRESSIONAL DISTRICT N.Y. CITY/COMPRISING THE 11TH AND 17TH WARDS/PRESENTED BY FREDERIC C. WAGNER/CAPTAIN AND PROVOST MARSHALL/JUNE 20TH 1865.

23 x 25 ½ x 21 ¾ in (58.42 x 64.77 x 55.25 cm). Gift of Frederic C. Wagner, 1865.6

has died before it was weaned."[35]

Bennett's *Herald* declared that Republicans had been "rebuked and repudiated," by voters demanding a war to preserve the Union, not for "the bloody extermination of slavery."

Writing to Carl Schurz, Lincoln listed three reasons for the electoral upheaval. "1. The democrats were left in a majority by our friends going to the war. 2. The democrats observed this & determined to reinstate themselves in power, and 3. Our newspapers, by vilifying and disparaging the administration, furnished them all the weapons to do it with. Certainly, the ill-success of the war had much to do with this."

Lincoln summed up his paradoxical relationship to the Empire State and New York City with his trademark folksy humor. When asked how he felt about the losses in New York, he reportedly said: "Somewhat like that boy in Kentucky, who stubbed his toe while running to see his sweetheart. The boy said he was too big to cry, and far too badly hurt to laugh."[36]

EMANCIPATION, THE DRAFT LAW, AND THE RIOTS OF JULY 1863

On January 1, 1863 Lincoln's Emancipation Proclamation declared the slaves in the Confederacy "forever free," and effectively marked the beginning of Reconstruction—not the physical rebuilding of a nation ravaged by war, but rather the

THE DRAFT RIOTS IN NEW YORK.—THE BATTLE IN SECOND AVENUE.

process of thoroughly revolutionizing American race relations and society. The Declaration of Independence and Lincoln's Proclamation had both endorsed the ideal of human equality; to make it a reality, the Civil War generation would first have to demolish the slaveholding culture in the South, and along with it the caste system and racial bigotry in the North, where the "peculiar institution" had still existed, only decades earlier.[37]

African Americans and white abolitionists rejoiced, while most Democrats, many of them Irish Americans, were filled with anger and dread. Having sacrificed for the Union, many Irishmen saw that they would now be fighting to liberate blacks, who would compete not only for jobs, but—once enrolled as soldiers and citizens—for glory on the battlefield and acceptance in American society. The elevation of blacks to equality with whites lowered the status of the Irish worker, New York's *Weekly Day-Book* declared; he was "degraded to a level with negroes."[38] The Irish Brigade's terrible losses, particularly at Fredericksburg in December, deepened Irish suspicion that their men were being used as cannon fodder by the Lincoln administration. The Emancipation Proclamation made the brutal war even more painful. Denouncing abolitionists as "Nigger propagandists," the *Irish-American* declared: "We have no words to express the loathing and contempt we feel for the besotted fanatics."[39]

Governor Seymour was a long-time political ally of the Irish, a friendship sealed by the building of the Erie Canal by Irish laborers in the early 1820s when

Artist unknown. "The Draft Riots in New York: The Battle in Second Avenue", Wood engraving, published in *Frank Leslie's Illustrated Newspaper*, August 1, 1863. PR620

THE RIOTS IN NEW YORK: CONFLICT BETWEEN THE MILITARY AND THE RIOTERS IN FIRST-AVENUE.—SEE NEXT PAGE.

Artist unknown. "The Riots in New York: Conflict Between the Military and the Rioters in First-Avenue." Wood engraving, published in the *Illustrated London News*, August 15, 1863. 7 ⅜ x 9 ¹¹⁄₁₆ in (18.73 x 24.61 cm). PR 100

Seymour was a boy and his father was a state canal commissioner. The father's political connections made for the son's smooth entry into state politics, where his expertise in canal issues kept him at the center of power, leading to his first term as governor.[40] Seymour reaffirmed his opposition to emancipation and the enlistment of black troops in February 1863 when top Democratic leaders met at Delmonico's Restaurant in New York.

In this elegant setting, the party chieftains and intellectuals formed a propaganda arm called the Society for the Diffusion of Political Knowledge. Hoping to force a retraction of Lincoln's proclamation, the Society published pamphlets and scholarly articles defending slavery and predicting dire economic consequences for both sides if it were abolished. Manton Marble attended the summit at Delmonico's and the *World* continued to be a major part of the anti-emancipation campaign. General George McClellan, dismissed from command a few months earlier, was also on hand. He had moved to New York and was being groomed by

THE RIOTS IN NEW YORK : DESTRUCTION OF THE COLOURED ORPHAN ASYLUM.

August Belmont to unseat Lincoln the following year.[41]

Democrats soon had another powerful issue to unite them. The nation's first federal draft, approved by Congress on March 2, 1863 and signed by the president the following day, included a clause exempting any man who could present a substitute or pay $300, nearly the annual salary of an average worker. Instead of depending on quotas of men from the states, for the first time the War Department was empowered to draft men directly for service in the national army. On the same day it passed the new draft law, Congress authorized the suspension of habeas corpus throughout the United States, enabling the administration to detain political prisoners indefinitely without charges or any other due process of law.[42] The draft law also empowered the secretary of war to create a police arm, the office of the provost marshal general, whose assistants scoured the country arresting deserters, spies, and others deemed disloyal to the Northern war effort.

Artist unknown. "The Riots in New York: Destruction of the Colored Orphan Asylum." Wood engraving, published in the *Illustrated London News*, August 15, 1863. 7 ⅜ x 9 ¹¹/₁₆ in (1873 x 24.61 cm). PR100

In New York, and across the North, the Democratic press charged that like Lincoln's decrees and civil rights abuses, and the myriad wartime laws passed by a Republican-controlled Congress, the draft was part of a dangerous, unprecedented centralization of power in the federal government.[43] New York's *Freeman's Journal* called the federal draft an "outrage" and challenged the citizenry to prove they were not an "enervated, emasculated and slavish people," by resisting the new law.[44] When the provost marshal general's office completed registration for the draft lottery across the North by sending agents from door to door in May and June, more than one hundred were attacked and two were killed.

On July 4, 1863, as news trickled into New York City from Gettysburg, and it remained unclear whether or not the Union had won a decisive victory, Governor Seymour addressed a gathering of the party faithful at the Academy of Music. His words were aimed at Congress and the Lincoln administration:

> Is it not revolution which you are thus creating when you say that our persons may be rightfully seized, our property confiscated, our homes entered? Are you not exposing yourselves, your own interests to as great a peril as that which you threaten us? Remember this, that the bloody and treasonable and revolutionary doctrine of public necessity can be proclaimed by a mob as well as by a government.[45]

For the rest of his career, Seymour would face Republican accusations that his speech was an incitement to riot.[46]

In New York City, the draft lottery began on a Saturday, July 11th. As it resumed on Monday the 13th, the *Daily News* denounced "The Inquisition Conscription," charging that the "miscreants at the head of the Government" were using the draft "to kill off" Democratic voters, enfranchise blacks, and remain in power for another four years.[47] Thousands of protesters stormed the draft office on Third Avenue and Forty-seventh Street that morning and burned it to the ground, along with the entire block.

Scattering policemen, militia, and federal troops from its path, the mob moved downtown in search of guns, while the city's poor, at the fringes of the crowd, embarked on a spree of indiscriminate looting. After targeting the homes of the wealthy and of Republican officials, the rioters focused their attacks on African Americans, torching their homes, lynching the men from lampposts, and driving them off the docks into the rivers. An orphanage for black children on Fifth Avenue and Forty-fourth Street was looted and burned. On July 16th, troops returning from Gettysburg quelled the last of the rioting. More than one hundred people were confirmed dead, and five thousand blacks became refugees. The draft riots still rank as the largest civil insurrection in American history.[48]

(opposite page) Photographer unknown. Colored Orphan Asylum, 1861. Stereograph (detail), 3 x 6 ⅛ in (7.62 x 15.56 cm). Purchase, PR 065

1

At a Meeting of the Managers of the Colored Orphan Asylum held at the house of A. S. Murrays 7th Mo. 25th 1863 — in company with J. B. Collins Wm. F. Mott Jr of the Advisers

Present of the Managers R. Phelps E Bown A S Jotwell Caroline Hull, Sarah Lankford, Harriet Onderdonk, S. F. Underhill, S. S. Murray.

Information having been received that on the 13th Inst at 4 P.M. an infuriated Mob, which had commenced its ravages in the Neighbourhood, surrounded the premises of the Asylum — and some 500 of them entered the house — without previous notice After despoiling it of Furniture, Bedding Clothing &c &c — they deliberately set fire to it, in different parts — Simply because it was the home of unoffending Colored Orphan Children

The Superintendent, Matron and others were quietly collecting the Children, who were permitted to pass out of the North wing on 44th St unmolested to the 35th St Station House. — Here they were compactly stowed together, three days and three nights — when arrangements had been made for their

The COMMANDER-IN-CHIEF conciliating the SOLDIER'S VOTES on the Battle Field.

"Now, Marshal, sing us 'Picayune Butler,' or something else that's funny."

Through a compromise with Tammany boss William Tweed, Lincoln was able to resume the draft peacefully in August. Tweed arranged a $3 million bond issue that paid the $300 exemption fee for the city's poor draftees. Lincoln reasserted federal authority, and New York's Democrats reaped the political bounty of protecting their constituents from the draft. Tweed's largesse with public money blunted the draft, but Lincoln continued to fill the ranks of the Union army, because the threat of the draft prompted men to volunteer and collect a bounty.[49]

More than simply a protest against the draft, the so-called draft riots were the first battle of the Reconstruction era, an outcry against emancipation and the powerful currents of social change unleashed by Lincoln's proclamation.[50] There is no direct evidence that New York's Copperheads conspired to spark the draft riots, or intended them as a fire-in-the-rear during Robert E. Lee's invasion of Pennsylvania.[51] Nonetheless, having failed to prevent emancipation, the city's Democrats skillfully managed the political fallout of riots and, during the next decade and a half, embarked on a successful campaign to thwart black equality, helping to perpetuate a racial caste system in America far into the twentieth century.[52]

C.A.L. *The Commander-in-Chief Conciliating the Soldier's Votes on the Battle Field,* 1864. Etching, 11 x 16 ½ in (27.95 x 41.91 cm). PR 010

(opposite page) *Colored Orphan Asylum Board Minutes, July 25, 1863.* Records of the Association for the Benefit of Colored Orphans. *"Information having been received that on the 13th Inst. at 4 P.M. an infuriated mob, which had commenced its ravages in the neighbourhood, surrounded the premises of the Asylum and some 500 of them entered the house without previous notice. After despoiling it of Furniture, Bedding, Clothing &c. &c. —they deliberately set fire to it, in different parts, —simply because it was the home of unoffending Colored Orphan Children."*

Artist unknown. "The National Joker. Salary 25,000 Dollars Per Annum." Published in *The Funniest of Phun,* April 1, 1864. Gary Bunker Collection

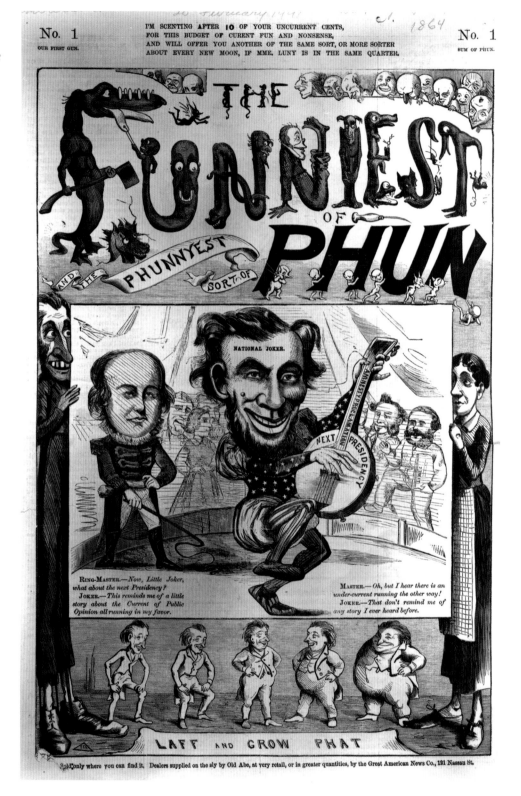

NOTES

1   *Herald* editorial reprinted in the *New York Tribune*, May 21, 1860, quoted in Robert S. Harper, *Lincoln and the Press* (New York: McGraw Hill, 1951), 56.

2   The law left some blacks in bondage until 1848. Leslie Harris, *In the Shadow of Slavery* (Chicago: University of Chicago Press, 2003), 11–12, 32–38, 42–47, 61, 94.

3   Edwin Burrows and Mike Wallace, *Gotham: A History of New York City to 1898* (New York: Oxford University Press, 1999), 554; Paul Gilje, *The Road to Mobocracy* (Chapel Hill: University of North Carolina Press, 1987), 159–60; Harris, *In the Shadow of Slavery*, 5, 97, 118–19. In 1826, sixteen blacks in New York County could vote; that number increased only to about 300 by 1861.

4   James McPherson, *Battle Cry of Freedom* (New York: Oxford University Press, 1988), 23–27; Arthur Schlesinger, Jr., *The Age of Jackson* (Boston: Little, Brown, 1944), 8–10, 30–33 and 90–92; Burrows and Wallace, 571–73.
    Jefferson's Democratic-Republicans renamed themselves Democrats upon Jackson's re-election in 1832. When Jackson vetoed a new charter for the Bank of the United States in 1832, pro-Bank forces called him a tyrant and themselves the Whigs, after the opponents of King George III in the Revolutionary era. The Whigs carried on the traditions of the recently disbanded Federalists in the American two-party system.

5   James McPherson, *Ordeal by Fire* (New York: Knopf, 1982), 32–33, 498; McPherson, *Battle Cry*, 31 and 88; Noel Ignatiev, *How the Irish Became White* (New York/London: Routledge, 1995), 100.

6   McPherson, *Battle Cry*, 8; Burrows and Wallace, *Gotham*, 543–44.

7   Burrows and Wallace, *Gotham*, 553, 772, 785–90; Horace Greeley, *Recollections of a Busy Life* (New York: J.B. Ford, 1868), 145.

8   Jerome Mushkat, *Fernando Wood* (Kent, Ohio: Kent State University Press, 1990), 8, 16, 18 and 68–69 (including footnote); Eric Homberger, *Scenes from the Life of a City* (New Haven, Yale University Press, 1994), 151.
    Wood was elected mayor in 1854, 1856, and 1859. Republicans moved the mayoral race to odd years in 1857 and cut his second term short.

9   Edward K. Spann, *Gotham at War* (Wilmington, DE: Scholarly Resources, 2002), 4, 5, 7 and 10; David Quigley, "Slavery in a Free City," in *Slavery in New York*, ed. Ira Berlin and Leslie M. Harris (New York: New Press, 2005), 269; Burrows and Wallace, *Gotham*, 867–68.

10 McPherson, *Battle Cry*, 224; Burrows and Wallace, *Gotham*, 865; Spann, *Gotham at War*, 4.

11 Harper, *Lincoln and the Press*, 120–22; Spann, *Gotham at War*, 5.

12 Mushkat, *Fernando Wood*, 68–71; Burrows and Wallace, *Gotham*, 838, 840; Tyler Anbinder, *Five Points: The 19th-Century New York City Neighborhood that Invented Tap Dance, Stole Elections, and Became the World's Most Notorious Slum* (New York: Penguin, 2002), 278–79.

13 Burrows and Wallace, *Gotham*, 872–76; Edmund Ruffin, *Diary* (Baton Rouge: Louisiana State University Press, 1989) 1:504; Spann, *Gotham at War*, 7–10.

14 Mushkat, *Fernando Wood*, 111–13; Spann, *Gotham at War*, 6; Burrows and Wallace, *Gotham*, 867–68; Basil Leo Lee, *Discontent in New York City* (Washington, DC: Catholic University of America Press, 1943), 2; McPherson, *Battle Cry*, 234–35.

15 Harper, *Lincoln and the Press*, 120–122; Spann, *Gotham at War*, 8.

16 Mushkat, *Fernando Wood*, 114; Spann, *Gotham at War*, 8.

17 Harper, *Lincoln and the Press*, 120–22.

18 Edward K. Spann, "Union Green," in *The New York Irish*, ed. Ronald Bayor and Timothy Meagher (Baltimore: Johns Hopkins University Press, 1996), 194; Brian Cogan, "The Irish-American Press," *New York Irish History* 14 (2000): 37–38; D.P. Conyngham, *The Irish Brigade and Its Campaigns*, ed., with intro. Lawrence Frederick Kohl (New York: Fordham University Press, 1994), xv. Tammany Hall, a patriotic society dating back to the American Revolution, was named for Chief Tamanend, a mythic warrior of the Delaware Indians.

The club's hierarchy consisted of "sachems," "warriors," and "braves" and the headquarters was dubbed the "wigwam."

19   McPherson, *Ordeal*, 149; Richard Lowitt, *A Merchant Prince of the Nineteenth Century: William E. Dodge* (New York: Columbia University Press, 1954), 212; Spann, *Gotham at War*, 14–15.

20   McPherson, *Battle Cry*, 333, 347, and 354; Harper, *Lincoln and the Press*, 113–15; James Geary, *We Need Men* (Dekalb: Northern Illinois University Press, 1991), 6; Conyngham, *Irish Brigade*, xvi; Florence Gibson, *The Attitudes of the New York Irish* (New York: Columbia University Press, 1951), 144.

21   McPherson, *Battle Cry*, 356–58.

22   Jerome Mushkat, *The Reconstruction of the New York Democracy* (Rutherford, NJ: Fairleigh Dickinson University Press, 1981), 27–33; Frank L. Klement, *The Copperheads in the Middle West* (Gloucester, MA: Peter Smith, 1972), 2.
     The Regency's Albany *Argus*, edited by Dean Richmond, and Tammany Hall's New York *Leader*, edited by John Clancy, were the War Democrats' main newspapers for voicing the party line.
     Republicans denounced Confederate sympathizers as Copperheads: traitors, poisonous snakes-in-the-grass within the "loyal" states. Copperheads adopted the label and wore copper badges made from Liberty-head pennies to decry Northern oppression.

23   McPherson, *Battle Cry*, 437 and 496–99; Mushkat, *Reconstruction of the New York Democracy*, 32–34; David Herbert Donald, *Lincoln* (New York: Simon and Schuster, 1995), 355 and 363.

24   Mushkat, *Reconstruction of the New York Democracy*, 32–34, and Mushkat, *Fernando Wood*, 128.

25   McPherson, *Battle Cry*, 490–91 and 499–500; Donald, *Lincoln*, 187–95, 236, 362–64.

26   McPherson, *Battle Cry*, 504–6.

27   Donald, *Lincoln*, 364–66; McPherson, *Battle Cry*, 504–6.

28   McPherson, *Battle Cry*, 506–9; *New York Commercial Advertiser*, August 5, 1862.

29   McPherson, *Battle Cry*, 532–45; McPherson, *Ordeal*, 285. William Harlan Hale, *Horace Greeley* (New York: Harper and Brothers, 1950), 262–63 and 265.

30   Mushkat, *Reconstruction of the New York Democracy*, 34–35; George T. McJimsey, *Genteel Partisan: Manton Marble* (Ames: Iowa State University Press, 1971), 39–42.

31   Mushkat, *Reconstruction of the New York Democracy*, 35–37; Alexander J. Wall, *Sketch of the Life of Horatio Seymour* (New York: 1929. Privately printed, copy 68 of 300), 20–21.

32   Mushkat, *Fernando Wood*, 130; Spann, *Gotham at War*, 90.

33   Stewart Mitchell, *Horatio Seymour* (Cambridge, MA: Harvard University Press, 1938), 284–85.
     In New York, federal prisoners were held at Fort Lafayette, which stood near the Brooklyn shore in the Narrows, where the eastern pier of the Verrazano Bridge now stands.

34   Mitchell, *Horatio Seymour*, 254; George Templeton Strong, *Diary of George Templeton Strong*, ed. Allan Nevins and Milton Halsey (New York: Macmillan, 1952), 3:264; Mushkat, *Reconstruction of the New York Democracy*, 36–37; Carl Sandburg, *Abraham Lincoln: The War Years* (New York: Harcourt Brace, 1939), 1:610.

35   Maria Daly, *Diary of a Union Lady* (New York: Funk and Wagnalls, 1962), 194–95; Strong, *Diary*, 271.

36   Sandburg, *Abraham Lincoln*, 1:610–12.

37   Eric Foner, *Reconstruction* (New York: Perennial, 1989), xxv and 585.

38   Conyngham, *Irish Brigade*, xvi; Spann, "Union Green," 203; Gibson, *Attitudes*, 142.

39   Conyngham, *Irish Brigade*, xvi; Spann, "Union Green," 203, 207; Gibson, *Attitudes*, 144; *Irish-American*, January 17, 1863.

40   Wall, *Sketch*, 5–20; Mitchell, *Horatio Seymour*, 12, 16–17, 19–20, 22–23, 33–35, 44–45, 57–58, 63–64, 95, 111, 131.

41   Burrows and Wallace, *Gotham*, 886; Iver Bernstein, *The New York City Draft Riots* (New York: Oxford University Press, 1990), 146–47; McJimsey, *Genteel Partisan*, 46.

42 Geary, *We Need Men*, 50–51, 57–64; Joseph E. Stevens, *1863: The Rebirth of a Nation* (New York: Bantam Books, 1999), 108.

43 Bernstein, *Draft Riots*, 7–8; Stevens, *Rebirth of a Nation*, 108.

44 Quoted in Spann, "Union Green," 204.

45 *Daily News*, July 6, 1863.

46 See for example, "Seymour, Vallandigham, and The Riots of 1863" (London, 1867) in "U.S. Civil War & Reconstruction: A Collection of Pamphlets in the New York Public Library." Microform. (Republican campaign literature from 1867, attacking Horatio Seymour.) Quoted at length in Barnet Schecter, *The Devil's Own Work* (New York: Walker, 2005), 322–24.

47 *Daily News*, July 13, 1863. The Academy of Music, on Fourteenth Street and Irving Place, opened in 1854 and was then the largest opera house in the world.

48 Official death toll: Adrian Cook, *The Armies of the Streets* (Lexington: University Press of Kentucky, 1974), 193–95, 213–18; *Report of the Committee of Merchants for the Relief of Colored People, Suffering from the Late Riots in the City of New York* (New York: George A. Whitehorn, steam printer, 1863), 7. For a discussion of higher estimates, see Schecter, *Devil's Own Work*, 251–52. Largest civil insurrection: Foner, *Reconstruction*, 32.

49 Kenneth Ackerman, *Boss Tweed* (New York: Carroll and Graff, 2005), 28; George Opdyke, *Official Documents, Addresses, etc.* (New York: Hurd and Houghton, 1866), 277, 290; Cook, *Armies of the Streets*, 174; Spann, *Gotham at War*, 103–5; Burrows and Wallace, *Gotham*, 896; Bernstein, *Draft Riots*, 201–2; Eugene Murdock, *One Million Men* (Madison: State Historical Society of Wisconsin, 1971), 335, 334.

50 Foner, *Reconstruction*, xxv and 585; McPherson, *Battle Cry*, 559–60; McPherson, *Ordeal*, 497; Mushkat, *Reconstruction of the New York Democracy*, 27–28.

51 For a discussion/rejection of the conspiracy theory, see Schecter, *Devil's Own Work*, 3–4 254.

52 For a discussion/narrative of the draft riots' aftermath as a prelude to the demise of Reconstruction, see Schecter, *Devil's Own Work*, 6, 8, 253–370.

THE ECONOMICS OF CIVIL WAR: MONEY, MANUFACTURING, AND COMMERCE

CRAIG L. SYMONDS

NEW YORK CITY's commercial and financial community, like the rest of the city, had favored Stephen Douglas over Lincoln in the presidential election, and its leaders had predicted that if the rail-splitter gained the White House, it would result in economic and social disaster for the city. Now with Lincoln elected and South Carolina seceded, it appeared that their warnings were about to come true. For decades, New York City and the cotton South had sustained a symbiotic financial relationship. New York provided the capital investment, manufactured goods, and shipping; the South supplied the cotton. Southerners sometimes complained that New York factors and brokers took too big a share of the profit simply for handling the cotton and carrying it away to foreign markets. This proto-Populist view of many Southern cotton planters had an ugly anti-Semitic edge as Southerners often portrayed New York as the Temple of the Moneychangers whose denizens cared more about their bottom line than about honor or fairness, a stereotype that many Southerners applied to all Yankees. For their part, some New Yorkers ascribed an equally stereotypic image of slave-beating to aristocratic Southern planters. For both, however, the fabulous profits to be made during the heyday of "King Cotton" in the 1850s overrode these uncharitable caricatures. Now, however, many New Yorkers feared that James Dunmore De Bow, the influential editor of the New Orleans-based *De Bow's Review*, might be right when he predicted that with New York cut off from the South's cotton trade, "The ships would rot at their docks; grass would grow in Wall Street and Broadway, and the Glory of New York, like that of Babylon and Rome, would be numbered with the things of the past."[1]

As other states followed South Carolina out of the Union, the great fear of

Alexander Gardner (1821–82). *Abraham Lincoln*, Washington, DC, August 9, 1863. Albumen print on carte-de-visite mount. Library of Congress

THE MISSISSIPPI IN TIME OF PEACE.

NEW YORK, PUBLISHED BY CURRIER & IVES, 152 NASSAU STREET

Frances Flora Bond Palmer (1812–76). *The Mississippi in Time of Peace*, 1865. Hand-colored lithograph, Currier & Ives, publisher, 18 x 27 ¾ in (45.72 x 70.49 cm). PR 230

the New York business community was that the city would lose both the Southern market and the profitable carrying trade. Indeed there was a kind of mini panic in the days immediately following Lincoln's election during which goods intended for sale in the South piled up on shelves and in warehouses unbought and unshipped, and some merchants advertised drastic sales for fear that their products would not be sold at all. Even more unsettling was the fear that Southern creditors would default on their debts. Eager to curry favor with Southern planters, New York merchants had extended them generous credit terms, in some cases postponing payment for as much as a year. Now with secession, the merchants feared that these debts, which totaled some $150 million, might never be paid. It did not help when, a month after Fort Sumter, Georgia's governor, Joseph Brown, declared that because he suspected (incorrectly) that New Yorkers were appropriating

Southern property, Georgians would not be allowed to pay any outstanding debts to New York City creditors. All this undermined the hope of many that, war or no war, business could continue as usual.[2]

New Yorkers were divided about how to respond to these unprecedented circumstances. Before the first shot was fired at Fort Sumter, there was talk about New York becoming a "free city." More than a few bankers and merchants feared that with the loss of Southern markets, and deterred by the high rates of the Morrill Tariff, trade would go elsewhere and New York would lose its leadership position in business matters. One New York City banker, who preferred to remain anonymous, argued in print in December 1860 that New York should become a free city. "Not a free city with respect to the liberty of the negro," he hastened to add, "but a free city in commerce and trade." He noted that other great commercial cities, such as Hamburg, Bremen, and Frankfort [sic], had survived, even thrived, as free cites. He was convinced that "there is no other way in which New York

After Frances Flora Bond Palmer (1812–76). *The Mississippi in Time of War*, 1865. Lithograph, Currier & Ives, publisher. 18 x 27 ¾ in (45.72 x 70.49 cm). © Museum of the City of New York/ The Bridgeman Art Library

Artist unknown. "U.S. Vessels of War at Anchor Off the Battery." Wood engraving, published in *New-York Illustrated News*, March 30, 1861. *E171.D38.

City can preserve her position." Not surprisingly, Southerners encouraged such thinking. George Fitzhugh, the Southern gadfly who had published *Cannibals All* in 1857 to wide acclaim (and condemnation), urged New York to seize the moment and declare herself free of "the dominion of the corrupt, venial, wire-workers at Albany." Otherwise she would lose her status as a great world port. "In fine," Fitzhugh declared, "she must set up for herself or be ruined."[3]

Lincoln did not take such claims seriously. When asked about it while en route to Washington for his inauguration, Lincoln is said to have replied, "I reckon that it will be some time before the front door sets up house-keeping on its own account." And he was right. Though the city's mercurial mayor Fernando Wood jumped onto this bandwagon during the secession winter of 1860–61, the first shots at Fort Sumter in April swept away this pie-in-the-sky notion and undercut Wood's political posturing. August Belmont spoke for most of New York's financial community when he declared that the honored title of "American citizen" was more valuable than "the gilded prospects of New York merchant princes." Southerners were both surprised and angered by this reaction. Southern papers redoubled their invective against what one paper called "Execrable New York" which they described as "the metropolis of shoulder-hitters, prize-fighters, blackguards, and mercantile gamblers."[4]

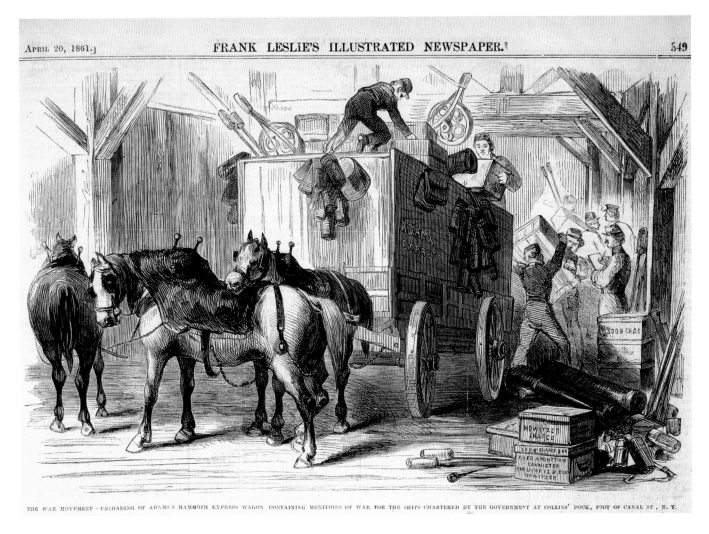

THE WAR MOVEMENT—UNLOADING OF ADAMS'S MAMMOTH EXPRESS WAGON CONTAINING MUNITIONS OF WAR FOR THE SHIPS CHARTERED BY THE GOVERNMENT AT COLLINS' DOCK, FOOT OF CANAL ST., N. Y.

Once the war began, New York City and Brooklyn, which were the first and third largest cities in the country, contributed significantly to the Union war effort, and to eventual Union victory, in a number of important ways. They supplied men, money, and manufactured goods, and throughout the war New York Harbor remained a center of shipbuilding and international commerce. In terms of manpower, by war's end some 150,000 men from New York City had served in Union blue. That represented 18 percent of the city's population, and 6 percent of all Union soldiers. It is noteworthy that New York City sent more men to the war than did the states of Connecticut, Massachusetts, Michigan, or Wisconsin. Indeed, only four *states*—Illinois, Indiana, Ohio and Pennsylvania—sent more soldiers to the war than the *city* of New York.[5]

Important as that was, it was the economic, financial, and manufacturing strength of the city that constituted New York's most significant contribution to victory. Wars are expensive, and the national government's antebellum revenue system was completely inadequate to the financial needs of modern war. The total budget of the U.S. government in 1860 had been $67 million, 90 percent of which came from customs fees. That amount in 1863 would have paid for

Artist unknown. "The War Movement—Exciting Scenes on Collins' Dock, New York … " Wood engraving, published in *Frank Leslie's Illustrated Newspaper,* April 20, 1861. *E171.L63

Photographer unknown. *Wall Street, South Side, from Broad Street to Hanover Street*, 1864. Gelatin silver copy print, 4 ⅛ x 5 ⅜ in (10.48 x 13.65 cm). PR 020

only about two or three weeks of war. By 1864, the federal budget had grown to twenty-two times its pre-war levels. To fund the war, the United States had to raise unprecedented sums of money, and to do that, Lincoln's Treasury Secretary Salmon P. Chase issued government bonds to the public in 1861. The most popular form of these bonds were called "five twenties," because the government could pay them off at its discretion as soon as in five years but no later than twenty years. In the meantime they would pay the bearer 7.3 percent, which was a point and a quarter more than good railroad stocks at the time. New York bankers overcame their annoyance that Chase relied on Philadelphia's Jay Cooke as his primary agent for this offering, and New York City banks subscribed $35 million of the first $50 million. Moreover, they sustained a leadership role throughout subsequent bond issues.[6]

The first government bond offering of $150 million proved to be insufficient, and as early as December 1861, Lincoln's government faced a financial crisis with cash

reserves of only $29 million and obligations of over $600 million. Chase traveled to New York City that month to discuss the crisis with several New York bankers, and the result of their meeting was a decision to suspend specie payment and issue paper money. The Legal Tender Act, creating the famous "greenbacks," passed Congress the following February. Putatively, this paper currency was redeemable in gold, but only if the government could make good on its debts, and that, of course, depended on eventual Union victory. Thus it was that the value of greenbacks against gold on any given day was a measure of public confidence in the war's outcome. With every Union military defeat, the price of gold rose, and with every hopeful victory, confidence in the greenbacks rallied and the price of gold fell. Naturally this led to speculation, which some observers found distasteful

Photographer unknown. *N.Y. Stock Exchange*, 1865. Gelatin silver copy print, 7 ⅜ x 8 in (18.73 x 20.32 cm). Gift of Mrs. Elihu Spicer, PR 020

CHRISTY, CONSTANT & CO.
PAPER-HANGINGS MANUFACTORY.
NO. 510 TO 544 WEST 23ᴿᴰ ST. NEW YORK.

Artist unknown. *Christy, Constant & Co. Paper-Hangings Manufactory*, ca. 1865. Hand-colored lithograph, Endicott & Co., lithographers. 16 ⅜ x 29 in (41.59 x 73.66 cm). PR 020

since by betting on the price of gold, investors were also betting on Union military success—or defeat. The New York Stock Exchange forbade gold speculation, but the market, as usual, found a way around this, and soon a separate gold exchange was operating on William Street.[7]

Moreover, the issuing of paper money was naturally inflationary, which led to higher prices (though not necessarily higher wages). Retail prices in the city rose 43 percent from 1860 to 1863, with food prices leading the way. Lamb that had cost ten cents a pound in 1860, cost twenty-three cents a pound by 1863; beef went from eight cents a pound to fifteen cents; and coffee from ten cents to fifty cents a pound. Wages, which rose by only 12 percent in this same period, failed to keep up with these new prices in spite of the fact that the city's labor pool was reduced by the absence of the tens of thousands of men who had marched off to war, as well as immigration rates that actually fell in 1861 and 1862. Two dollars a day was considered a good wage in 1862, though men working in the various war industries such as in the shipyards could make as much as five or six dollars a day. Some workers, however, found themselves unable to pay the new higher prices. Particularly hard hit were the large number of women who went to work in manufacturing and retail jobs to replace the men who had gone to war. Women in the

INTERIOR ESPLANADE FRONTING THE NAVY YARD, BROOKLYN, N. Y., WITH THE SHIP NORTH CAROLINA ALONGSIDE.

Artist unknown. *Interior Esplanade Fronting the Navy Yard Brooklyn, N.Y., with the Ship North Carolina Alongside,* 1851. Wood engraving, 7 ½ x 9 ¾ in (19.05 x 24.77 cm). PR 020

U. S. NAVY YARD, BROOKLYN, N. Y.

Artist unknown. *U.S. Navy Yard, Brooklyn, N.Y.,* 1857. Wood engraving, 5 ⅞ x 6 ⅜ in (14.92 x 16.19 cm). PR 020

UNITED STATES NAVY YARD. BROOKLYN. NEW-YORK

Artist unknown. *United States Navy Yard. Brooklyn. New-York*, undated. Lithograph, 3 $^{11}/_{16}$ x 7 $^{11}/_{16}$ in (9.37 x 19.53 cm). PR 020

garment industry—many of them girls—were paid as little as seventeen cents for a twelve-hour day to sew shirts and underwear, and they had to supply their own thread. Then, too, in the early days of battle, the Department of War was remarkably inefficient in paying its soldiers, which complicated the lives of their families at home. As a result of all this, a struggling underclass fell further and further behind even as a new wealthy class emerged at the top. One modern authority has calculated that by 1863 the top 1 percent of New Yorkers was earning 61 percent of all income in the city.[8]

Of course the new circumstances also created opportunities. The historian Ernst McKay has noted that during the Civil War, "aggressive money-makers, some honest, some dishonest, some loyal, some disloyal, found business opportunities as never before." Due to regular employment, itself a product of wartime contracts, "thousands of men who had never been rich before now suddenly acquired wealth," including many who had little experience in handling money. The editors of *Harper's* complained that New Yorkers were "spending money with a profusion never before witnessed in our country," and William Cullen Bryant bemoaned the "extravagant luxury" and the "vain show" of New Yorkers during a time of war.[9]

In addition to spending, New Yorkers also saved. Deposits in New York City banks jumped from $80 million to $224 million during the war. In 1864 alone, some 13,000 new depositors opened savings accounts in New York banks. Significantly, 600 of those new accounts were opened by seamstresses, and 300 by washerwomen. Indeed, a full 77 percent of the 52,000 savings accounts in all New York banks by

NOVELTY IRON WORKS, FOOT OF 12th ST. E.R. **NEW YORK.**
STILLMAN, ALLEN & C°
Iron Founders Steam Engine and General Machinery Manufacturers.

the end of the war were for amounts of $100 or less, suggesting a democratization of banking and saving that had not existed before the war.[10]

Another measure of how the war economy affected New Yorkers was the dramatic explosion of the insurance business. The number of insurance companies in New York jumped from seventeen to thirty during the war, and the number of policies from 49,000 to 305,000 (out of a population of 805,000). Mutual Life of New York doubled the number of its policy holders from 12,000 to 24,000 during the war, and New York companies wrote a total of a quarter of a million dollars in polices. Whether in finance, banking or insurance, New York City not only retained its lead over other metropolitan centers during the war, but actually increased it.[11]

*

Artist unknown. *Novelty Iron Works, Foot of 12th St. E[ast]. R[iver]. New York,* ca.1855–70. Lithograph, 5 7/16 x 8 13/16 in (13.81 x 22.38 cm). PR 020

CONTINENTAL WORKS, GREEN POINT, BROOKLYN.
T. F. ROWLAND, PROPRIETOR.
IRON SHIPS, IRON BRIDGES, BOILERS, TANKS AND GENERAL IRON WORK. VESSELS OF EVERY DESCRIPTION FURNISHED READY FOR SEA.
BUILDER OF U. S. IRON CLAD BATTERIES.

Artist unknown. *Continental Works, Green Point, Brooklyn*, 1865. Hand-colored lithograph, Endicott & Co., publisher, 22 ⁵⁄₁₆ x 35 in (56.67 x 88.90 cm). PR 020

New York's role as a manufacturing, shipping, and shipbuilding center was equally important to eventual Union success. To be sure, some manufacturing concerns were badly hurt by the loss of Southern markets—hoop skirt manufacturing disappeared almost overnight, as did companies that shipped ice to the South. But other industries took their place as the wartime economy kicked into full gallop. In addition, the closure of the Mississippi River meant that Midwestern goods now had to be shipped eastward by railroad for export rather than southward by river barge to New Orleans. This not only increased the overland shipment of goods through New York, it boosted railroad stocks such as the New York Central.[12]

Lincoln's announcement of a blockade of the seceded states on April 19, 1861, galvanized the shipbuilding industry. In Manhattan alone there were thirty-three shipyards on the East River with a dozen more in Brooklyn, including the government-owned Brooklyn Navy Yard, which covered some 290 acres and which at its peak employed over 6,000 men. Another 1,500 worked

at the Continental Works at Greenpoint in Brooklyn, and 1,200 more at the Novelty Iron Works between Twelfth and Fourteenth streets on the East River in Manhattan. Even before Congress met in July to pass new spending bills, Lincoln's Secretary of the Navy Gideon Welles, on his own authority, contracted for the construction of two dozen new gunboats—the largest single addition to the Navy since 1816. The first of these so-called ninety-day gunboats, the *Unadilla*, was built at the shipyard of John Englis & Son at the foot of Tenth Street in Manhattan, and was launched in only fifty-eight days, twelve days ahead of schedule.[13]

In addition to new construction, New York shipyards also took the lead in converting merchant steamers to wartime use. It was both quicker and cheaper to convert an existing hull into a war vessel than to build a new one from the keel up. Often all that was necessary to accomplish this transformation was to strengthen the deck to hold the weight of the naval guns. A significant number of these conversions took place at the Brooklyn Navy Yard where workers spent twelve-hour shifts reinforcing the decks and bulwarks, expanding the crew space, and constructing magazines below the water line. The Brooklyn Navy Yard took the lead in this activity, refitting as many as 190 ships during the war. In one exceptional case, the *Monticello* was completely converted from merchantman to warship in less than twenty-four hours.[14]

Lincoln himself played what was very likely a crucial role in obtaining approval for the construction in New York of the vessel that subsequently became USS *Monitor*, designed by Brooklyn resident John Ericsson. When Cornelius Bushnell showed the president a model of Ericsson's revolutionary ironclad, Lincoln was immediately interested, and he agreed to accompany Bushnell to the meeting of the Ironclad Board the next day. Lincoln's comment there that "it strikes me there's something in it," helped sway skeptical Board members and earn Ericsson a contract. The hull for this iconic vessel was constructed at the Continental Iron Works in Brooklyn, while the revolutionary revolving turret was fabricated at the aptly-named Novelty Iron Works across the East River in Manhattan. The *Monitor*'s subsequent success in Hampton Roads in March 1862 sparked a kind of "monitor fever" in the Navy Department, and led to many more contracts for several new classes of monitors, many of which were constructed in New York shipyards.[15]

John Ericsson (1803–89), designer. Maker unknown. *Builder's Half-Model of the U.S.S. Monitor*, 1862. Wood, metal. 14 ½ x 98 x 12 in (36.83 x 248.92 x 30.48 cm). Gift of Thomas Fitch Rowland, 1862.9

George Edward Perine (1837–85). *J[ohn]. Ericsson* (1803–89), undated. Steel engraving, 7 ⅝ x 7 ⁵⁄₁₆ in (19.37 x 18.57 cm). PR 052

THE "MONITOR" AS SHE IS—INTERIOR AND EXTERIOR.—SKETCHED BY OUR SPECIAL ARTIST.—[SEE PAGE 237.]

Artist unknown. "The Monitor as She Is." Wood engraving, published in Harper's Weekly, *April 12, 1862. G71.H29*

Other New York businesses also thrived as the nation shifted into a wartime economy. Phelps, Dodge & Company on Clift Street made iron forgings and marine engines for the ships that were being built at the shipyards; Conrad Pappenhusen, who had bought the rights to Charles Goodyear's vulcanization process and opened the Enterprise Rubber Works in Queens in 1854, produced hard rubber flasks (canteens) for the soldiers as well as thousands of uniform buttons. There were a few stumbles. Brooks Brothers at the corner of Catherine and Cherry Streets got an order for 12,000 army uniforms in April only days after the first shot at Fort Sumter. Though the company's motto was "to make and deal only in merchandise of the finest body," Brooks Brothers did not have sufficient woven cloth in stock to fill so large an order. It met the challenge by developing an artificial cloth made by combining lint-like piles of shredded rags

Frances Flora Bond Palmer
(1812–76). *The Terrific Engagement
Between the 'Monitor' and 'Merrimac':
Study for a Lithograph*, ca. 1862.
Watercolor, black ink, gouache,
and graphite on gray paper,
18 ½ x 26 ¼ in (46.99 x 66.68 cm).
Gift of Daniel Parish, Jr., 1900.10

Artist unknown. *Interior View of the
Turrets of the Monitor Fleet*, 1862.
Lithograph, Endicott & Co.,
publisher. Courtesy of the
Mariners' Museum, Newport
News, Virginia.

INTERIOR VIEW OF THE TURRETS OF
THE MONITOR FLEET.

C[harles]. Parsons (1821–1910).
The First Naval Conflict Between Iron Clad Vessels, 1862. Lithograph, Endicott & Co, lithographers.
13 11/16 x 21 in (34.77 x 53.34 cm).
PR 100

with glue and rolling it flat. The result was an ersatz cloth called "shoddy." Brooks Brothers was able to meet the terms of the contract, though the uniforms had a tendency to come apart in the rain, and "shoddy" soon came to refer to poor quality items of all kinds. Brooks Brothers was hardly the worst culprit in this regard, however. Two New York police officers found that the firm of Neutrick & Brothers at 4 Dey Street was actually engaged in manufacturing uniforms for the Confederacy.[16]

Crucial to New York's commercial establishment was the fact that despite the gloomy pre-war predictions, trade boomed. Thanks in part to the closing of the Mississippi River, shipping in and out of New York Harbor actually increased in 1861 and 1862. To accommodate the rail cars filled with western wheat destined for Europe, Brooklyn's Atlantic Dock was the first in the nation to construct floating grain elevators. This surge in trade also helped fill the coffers of the Federal government as the revenue from customs collected at New York increased from an

THE U.S. SLOOP OF WAR "KEARSARGE" 7 GUNS, SINKING THE PIRATE "ALABAMA" 8 GUNS.
Off Cherbourg, France, Sunday, June 19th 1864.
The "Alabama" was built in a British Ship-yard, by British workmen, with British Oak, armed with British Guns, manned with British Sailors, trained in the British Navy, and was sunk in the British channel, in 80 minutes, by the Yankee Sloop of War "Kearsarge" Capt. John A. Winslow.

average of $1.85 million per month in the last half of 1861 to an average of over $4 million a month in the first half of 1862. That fall, the revenue from customs reached $250,000 per day.[17]

✳

The war news that fall was that George B. McClellan had finally won a victory of sorts over the rebel army on the banks of Antietam Creek in Maryland, an event followed swiftly by Lincoln's announcement of an Emancipation Proclamation. Within the business community, however, there was almost as much interest in the rampage of Confederate commerce raiders on the high seas, and particularly the notorious CSS *Alabama* commanded by Raphael Semmes. By 1863, Confederate raiders, including the *Alabama*, had destroyed 150 Union merchant vessels, and before the war was over these rebel commerce raiders would capture or destroy a total of 284 Union ships with a value of over $25 million. New York newspapers routinely referred to Semmes as a "pirate," and the *Alabama* as "a pirate ship." After all, the ship had been built in the Birkenhead Shipyard at Liverpool in England under the subterfuge that she was intended for another government, and

Artist unknown. *The U.S. Sloop of War "Kearsarge" 7 Guns, Sinking the Pirate "Alabama" 8 Guns,* ca. 1864. Lithograph, Currier and Ives, publisher, 6 15/16 x 9 5/16 in (17.62 x 23.65 cm).

Captain Semmes.

Frank Thomas Beard
(1842–1905). *Captain [Raphael]
Semmes.*, 1864. Wood engraving,
9 x 8 15/16 in (22.86 x 22.70 cm).
PR 010

though her officers were from the southern states, her crew was an international one dominated by Englishmen. Semmes had already earned a reputation as an effective commerce raider in the CSS *Sumter*, but his exploits in the *Alabama* made him a celebrity in the South and a nemesis in the North. The New York Chamber of Commerce pressed the Lincoln administration to organize convoys from New York to the British Isles, Brazil, and the Cape of Good Hope. Welles opposed the idea because it would have depleted the blockade of the southern coast. Though Lincoln was sensitive to the problem, he declined to interfere with the dispositions made by his Navy Secretary. His decision cost him some political capital in New York since the U.S. Navy seemed helpless against this Confederate will-o-the-wisp.[18]

The fear that Semmes inspired was almost as effective a weapon of war as were his actions. By 1863, maritime insurance rates had jumped from 1¼ percent of the value of the cargo to 4 percent. That cut significantly into the profits of every voyage even if the *Alabama* never moved into sight. Semmes himself professed to be amused by the reaction to his exploits and in the fall of 1862, after capturing the *Baron de Castine* off the U.S. coast, he decided to turn it into a cartel to relieve himself of his accumulated captives. Before sending her on her way, however, he charged the ship's master "to give my special thanks to Mr. [Abiel Abbot] Low of the New York Chamber of Commerce for the complimentary resolutions passed in regard to the Alabama." When the *Baron de Castine* arrived in New York Harbor and delivered this message, it triggered rumors that Semmes planned to steam into New York Harbor and attack the city.[19]

Semmes did seriously consider an attack on New York Harbor, but short on coal, he instead headed south to the West Indies. Unaware of this, New York merchants redoubled their requests to Lincoln to protect loyal trade. Mayor George Opdyke urged Lincoln to issue Letters of Marque as if privateers might succeed against the *Alabama* where the Navy had clearly failed. Unsurprisingly, Welles found such a suggestion insulting as well as misguided and he fought against it. Secretary of State William Henry Seward, himself a New Yorker, thought there was merit in the idea, however, and argued that the threat of a swarm of Yankee privateers would act as a brake on English misbehavior. Welles and Charles Sumner, the Chairman of the Senate Foreign Relations Committee, argued that U.S. privateers were just as likely to provoke a war with Britain as to modify her behavior, and in the end Lincoln declined to adopt the program.[20]

The alternative for New York merchants was to ship their goods in foreign vessels whose neutrality would exempt them from the ravages of Semmes and his fellow raiders. Seeing which way the trade winds were blowing, American ship owners began to re-register their ships under foreign flags. In 1860, two-thirds of all vessels

268 HARPER'S WEEKLY. [APRIL 25, 1863.

THE APPROACH OF THE BRITISH PIRATE "ALABAMA."

going in or out of New York Harbor flew the American flag; by 1863 three-quarters of all such shipping flew a foreign flag. On November 14, 1863, an observer in New York counted 176 ships in New York Harbor and made the following enumeration of their nationality: 93 flew the British flag; 20 flew the flag of the free city of Bremen; 10 flew the French flag. There were in addition, six Danes, six Hanoverians, six from Hamburg, four Prussian, three Belgian, three Norwegian, three Austrian, two Dutch, and one Swedish vessel. There were also nineteen American flag vessels, but they were becoming increasingly rare. James Gordon Bennett's *New York Herald* editorialized that it was "galling to the national pride that four or five fleet Anglo-rebel cruisers should be allowed to drive our commerce from the seas." Finally, in the summer of 1864, news arrived in New York that on June 19, the USS *Kearsarge,* commanded by John Winslow, had sunk the *Alabama* in a ship-to-ship duel off the coast of France near Cherbourg. Upon hearing the news, the New York Chamber of Commerce voted Winslow and his officers a cash bonus of $25,000.[21]

Some American flag vessels participated in a lucrative but questionable trade between New York and Matamoros, Mexico, across the Rio Grande River from Brownsville, Texas. It was evident to anyone who was paying attention that this was a mere subterfuge for trading with the enemy since goods shipped to Matamoros were immediately trans-shipped across the river into the Confederacy. Southerners had claimed from the outset that Yankees in general, and New Yorkers in particular, were so eager for profits that they would trade with the devil. Whether or not that was true, trade between New York and Matamoros increased dramatically during the war. Some twenty ships made the trip in 1862; seventy-two did so in 1863; and thirty-two in 1864. Significantly, when the war ended, so did this wartime trade.[22]

On the whole, however, New York's financial, manufacturing, and mercantile contributions to the Union war effort were invaluable. Moreover, in spite of pre-war fears, and the best efforts of rebel commerce raiders, the Civil War did as much to promote business activity in New York as to disrupt it. Two weeks before Appomattox, the *New York Sun* offered an editorial entitled "New York as Affected by the War." Recalling that Southerners had insisted that without the Southern markets, grass would grow in the streets of New York, the editors gleefully reported that the opposite was true.

> New York has not suffered, in a business point of view, in consequence of the rebellion. It is true that the city lost a large and lucrative trade by the secession of the Southern states, but it is also true that this loss has been made good by the vast increase of Northern and military trade since the commencement of the war. There never was a time in the history of New York when business

(opposite page) Winslow Homer (1836-1910). *The Approach of the British Pirate "Alabama."* Wood engraving, published in *Harper's Weekly,* April 25, 1863, 13 13/16 x 9 3/16 in (35.08 x 23.34 cm). PR 049

prosperity was more general, when the demand for goods was greater, and payments more prompt, than within the last two or three years. Manufacturers have been crowded with orders, dealers have had an abundance of customers, and every branch of legitimate trade has flourished. There have been virtually no suspensions [bankruptcies] of business houses, and there has been no cause for them … In short, New York has shown no evidence of business prostration … and to-day it stands more prosperous in every way than at the outbreak of the rebellion.[23]

NOTES

1. Quoted in Edwin G. Burrows and Mike Wallace, *Gotham: A History of New York City to 1898* (New York: Oxford University Press, 1999), 865.

2. Ibid.; Philip S. Foner, *Business & Slavery: The New York Merchants & the Irrepressible Conflict* (New York: Russell & Russell, 1941), 210–18; Ernest A. McKay, *The Civil War and New York City* (Syracuse: Syracuse University Press, 1990), 94; *New York Herald*, November 13, 1860.

3. Foner, *Business & Slavery*, 286–87.

4. Lincoln is quoted in Harold Holzer, *Lincoln at Cooper Union: The Speech that Made Abraham Lincoln President* (New York: Simon & Schuster, 2004), 214; Belmont is quoted in Foner, *Business & Slavery*, 289. See also Burrows and Wallace, *Gotham*, 872.

5. The state figures are from Frederick H. Dyer, ed., *A Compendium of the War of the Rebellion* (New York: Thomas Yoseloff, 1959), 1:11. The figure of 150,000 comes from the *New York Sun*, March 25, 1865. Almost certainly it includes immigrants who were recruited on the New York City docks the moment they came ashore, but even then it is an impressive figure. If half of the city's population of 800,000 was male, and half of them were of military age (18–45), that left a total of roughly 200,000 from which to draw soldiers, and if 150,000 of them served, it was a mobilization rate of 75 percent.

6. Philip Shaw Paludan, *A People's Contest: The Union and Civil War, 1861–1865* (New York: Harper & Row, 1988), 108; Sven Beckert, "The Making of New York's Bourgeoisie, 1850–1886" (Ph.D. diss., Columbia University, 1995), 149.

7. McKay, *The Civil War and New York City*, 109, 116, 122. When news arrived in New York in April 1865 that Richmond had fallen, gold prices fell 12 percent.

8. Emerson David Fite, *Social and Industrial Conditions in the North during the Civil War* (New York: Frederick Ungar Publishing, 1963), 127; McKay, *The Civil War and New York City*, 163, 217–19.

9. McKay, *The Civil War and New York City*, 220; Fite, *Social and Industrial Conditions*, 271–73; Burrows and Wallace, *Gotham*, 879.

10. Fite, *Social and Industrial Conditions*, 123–24.

11. Ibid., 128n.

12. Burrows and Wallace, *Gotham*, 873.

13. James West, *A Short History of the New York Navy Yard* (New York: U.S. Navy, 1941), 43–44.

14. E. A. Livingston, *President Lincoln's Third Largest City: Brooklyn and the Civil War* (New York: E.A. Livingston, 1994), 101.

15. Craig L. Symonds, *Lincoln and His Admirals: Abraham Lincoln, the U.S. Navy, and the Civil War* (New York: Oxford University Press, 2008), 134–37.

16. McKay, *The Civil War and New York City*, 224, 73; Livingston, *President Lincoln's Third Largest City*, 119.

17. Burrows and Wallace, *Gotham*, 873; *New York Times*, June 5, 1862 and September 29, 1862.

18. George W. Dalzell, *The Flight from the Flag: The Continuing Effect of the Civil War upon the American Carrying Trade* (Chapel Hill: University of North Carolina Press, 1940), 109.

19. Robert Greenhalgh Albion, *The Rise of New York Port* (New York: Charles Scribner's Sons, 1970), 412 (appendix XIX); Raphael Semmes, *Memoirs of Service Afloat during the War Between the States* (Secaucus, NJ: Blue & Gray Press, 1987), 492.

20. Symonds, *Lincoln and his Admirals*, 221–22.

21. *New York Herald*, November 18, 1863; Dalzell, *Flight from the Flag*, 244; Fite, *Social and Industrial Conditions*, 148, 148n.

22. Alan Nevins, *The War for the Union: The Organized War, 1863–1864* (New York: Charles Scribner's Sons, 1971), 369.

23. *New York Sun*, March 25, 1865, quoted in Fite, *Social and Industrial Conditions*, 150–51.

BLACK NEW YORK AND
THE LINCOLN PRESIDENCY

JAMES OLIVER HORTON

As the presidential election of 1860 approached, America faced the most dangerous political crisis in its history. More than any previous election, this contest revolved around increasing national tensions over slavery. For decades, New York blacks and their white allies had struggled to build the political abolition movement that became key to the state's support for the Republican Party and Abraham Lincoln's presidential victory.

After the Revolution, slavery became less significant in the North, but it grew more politically, socially, and economically powerful in the South. Most Northern states abolished slavery in the early years of nationhood, although many, like New York State, did so gradually. Thus, most African Americans from the North remained in slavery well into the early decades of the nineteenth century. In 1799 New York officials passed a measure that freed slaves born after July 4th of that year once they had served their master for a substantial term of work: twenty-five years for females and twenty-eight years for males. Then, in 1817, the New York state legislature voted to end all slavery in the state as of July 4, 1827.[1]

Meanwhile, the South sought to expand slavery into the western territories and Congress attempted to balance the number of free and slave states entering the Union. They agreed on a Missouri Compromise that balanced the statehood of free Maine in 1820 with that of slave Missouri in 1821 and restricted the expansion of slavery to regions south of Missouri's southern border. This balancing continued throughout the decades before the Civil War. Tensions between proslavery regions and antislavery regions continued to grow, however.[2]

As slavery declined in the North, African Americans formed supportive communities that aided their struggle against Southern slavery and its expansion. One

Alexander Gardner (1821–82). *Abraham Lincoln*, Washington, DC, August 9, 1863. Published in Meserve Historical Portraits. Gelatin silver copy of original albumen print, 3 ¼ x 2 ⅛ in (8.26 x 5.40 cm). PR 231

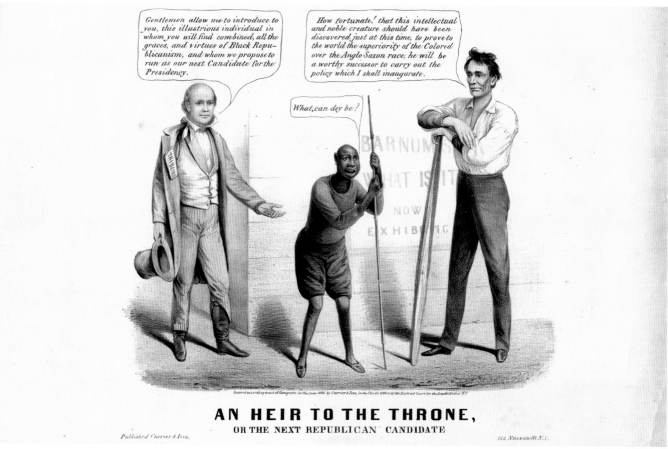

THE LINCOLN STATUE.
IN LINCOLN SQUARE, WASHINGTON, D.C.
Unveiled April 14th 1876.

The first contribution of $ 5, to the Statue Fund, was made the morning after the assassination of President Lincoln, by Charlotte Scott, a colored woman, of Marietta, Ohio, and the cost of the monument $ 17000, was paid by subscriptions of the colored people.

(left) Artist unknown. *The Lincoln Statue. In Lincoln Square, Washington, D.C., Unveiled April 14th 1876,* 1876. Lithograph, Currier & Ives, publisher, 12 ½ x 8 ⅞ in (31.75 x 22.54 cm). Gift of Henry O. Havemeyer, PR 052

(opposite page, top) Artist unknown. *"The Nigger" in the Woodpile,* 1860. Lithograph, Currier & Ives, publisher, 9 x 14 in (22.86 x 35.56 cm). PR 010

(opposite page, bottom) Artist unknown. *An Heir to the Throne, or The Next Republican Candidate,* 1860. Lithograph, Currier & Ives, publisher, 11 1/16 x 9½ in (28.10 x 24.13 cm). PR 010

(next page, left) "Anglo-African, Extra. Wendell Phillips on the War," 1861. N-YHS Library

(next page, right) "Frederick Douglass Paper," 1860. N-YHS Library

of the largest and most active was in New York City, where they established schools, churches, and a variety of social and political organizations. In 1827, the city's black leaders, including several powerful clergymen, established the country's first African American newspaper, *Freedom's Journal.* This publication, succeeded by others in the state, became the voice of Northern free black communities with agents and correspondents across the North and in Washington, DC.[3]

New York blacks found their publications particularly important for organizing their educational, mutual aid, and general political and social activities, including their abolitionist efforts. In the early 1830s they joined with other Northern free African Americans to convene a series of conventions that focused on issues of antislavery, equal rights, and racial justice. New York blacks held state conventions

ANGLO-AFRICAN, EXTRA.

Wendell Phillips on the War.

VOL. II. NO. 41. NEW YORK, APRIL 27, 1861. WHOLE NO. 93.

WENDELL PHILLIPS ON THE WAR.

Phonographic report by J. M. W. Yerrinton.

On Sunday last, April 21st, not less than four thousand people were crowded within the walls of the spacious Music Hall, in Boston, to listen to a Discourse on the War, by Wendell Phillips, Esq., before the Twenty-Eighth Congregational Society; and almost an equal number were excluded, because of the impossibility of finding even an inch of standing room. The platform was most profusely, yet tastefully decorated with the "stars and stripes," for the first time seeming to symbolize the cause of impartial freedom, under the extraordinary circumstances of the times. Other parts of the hall were also handsomely adorned. The desire to hear Mr. Phillips was of the gravest and intensest character. On entering the hall, he was greeted with hearty, irrepressible rounds of applause, which were frequently repeated during the delivery of his thrilling remarks. The following selection of Scripture, from the 50th and 51st chapter of Jeremiah, was first read by him, and produced a marked sensation, in consequence of its extraordinary applicability to the state of the times in our land. It was loudly cheered at its conclusion!

"The word that the Lord spake against Babylon, and against the land of the Chaldeans, by Jeremiah the prophet. Lo, I will raise, and cause to come up against Babylon, an assembly of great nations from the north country; and they shall set themselves in array against her; from thence she shall be taken: their arrows shall be as of a mighty expert man; none shall return in vain. And Chaldea shall be a spoil: all that spoil her shall be satisfied, saith the Lord. Put yourselves in array against Babylon round about: all ye that bend the bow, shoot at her, spare no arrows; for she hath sinned against the Lord. Shout against her round about; her foundations are fallen, her walls are thrown down; for it is the vengeance of the Lord: take vengeance upon her: as she hath done, do unto her.

A sound of battle is in the land, and of great destruction. The Lord hath opened his armory, and hath brought forth the weapons of his indignation: for this is the work of the Lord God of hosts in the land of the Chaldeans. Woe unto them! for their day is come, the time of their visitation.

Behold, I am against thee, O thou most proud, saith the Lord God of hosts: for thy day is come, the time that I will visit thee. And the most proud shall stumble and fall, and none shall raise him up: and I will kindle a fire in his cities, and it shall devour all round about him.

Thus saith the Lord of hosts, The children of Israel and the children of Judea were oppressed together; and all that took them captives held them fast, and refused to let them go. Their Redeemer is strong; the Lord of hosts is his name; he shall thoroughly plead their cause, that he may give rest to the land, and disquiet the inhabitants of Babylon.

A sword is upon the Chaldeans, saith the Lord, and upon the inhabitants of Babylon, and upon her princes, and upon her wise men. A sword is upon the liars, and they shall dote; a sword is upon her mighty men, and they shall be dismayed; a sword is upon their horses, and upon their chariots, and upon all the mingled people that are in the midst of her; and they shall become as women; for it is the land of graven images, and they are mad upon their idols. Thus the slain shall fall in the land of the Chaldeans, and they that are thrust through in her streets. For Israel hath not been forsaken, nor Judah of his God; though their land was fi[illegible] against the Holy One of Israel. Fl[illegible] of Babylon, and deliver every man his so[illegible] not cut off in her iniquity; for this is the time of the Lord's vengeance; he will render unto her a recompense. We would have healed Babylon, but she is not healed: forsake her, and let us go every one into his own country; for her judgment reacheth unto heaven, and is lifted up even to the skies.

One post shall run to meet another, and one messenger to meet another, to shew the king of Babylon that his city is taken at one end, and that the passages are stopped, and the reeds they have burned with fire, and the men of war are affrighted. For thus saith the Lord of hosts, the God of Israel, The daughter of Babylon is like a threshing-floor; it is time to thresh her. The violence done to me and to my flesh be upon Babylon, shall the inhabitant of Zion say; and, My blood upon the inhabitants of Chaldea, shall Jerusalem say. Then the heaven and the earth, and all that is therein, shall sing for Babylon: for the spoilers shall come unto her from the north, saith the Lord."

DISCOURSE OF MR. PHILLIPS.

"Therefore thus saith the Lord: Ye have not hearkened unto me in proclaiming liberty every one to his brother, and every man to his neighbor: behold, I proclaim a liberty for you, saith the Lord, to the sword, to the pestilence, and to the famine."—Jer. 34: 17.

Many times this winter, here and elsewhere, I have counselled peace—urged, as well as I knew how, the expediency of acknowledging a Southern Confederacy, and the peaceful separation of these thirty-four States. One of the journals announces to you that I come here this morning to retract those opinions. No, not one of them! (Applause.) I need them all—every word I have spoken this winter—every act of twenty-five years of my life, to make the welcome I give this war hearty and hot. Civil war is a momentous evil. It needs the soundest, most solemn justification. I rejoice before God to-day for every word that I have spoken counselling peace; and I rejoice with an especially profound gratitude, that for the first time in my anti-slavery life, I speak under the stars and stripes, and welcome the tread of Massachusetts men marshalled for war. (Enthusiastic cheering.) No matter what the past has been or said; to-day the slave asks God for a sight of this banner, and counts it the pledge of his redemption. (Applause.) Hitherto, it may have meant what you thought, or what I did; to-day, it represents Sovereignty and Justice. (Renewed applause.) The only mistake that I have made was in supposing Massachusetts wholly choked with cotton dust and cankered with gold. (Loud cheering.) The South thought her patience and generous willingness for peace were cowardice; to-day shows the mistake. She has been sleeping on her arms since '76, and the first cannon-shot brings her to her feet with the war-cry of the Revolution on her lips. (Loud cheers.) Any man who loves either liberty or manhood must rejoice at such an hour. (Applause.)

Let me tell you the path by which I, at least, have trod my way up to this conclusion. I do not acknowledge the motto, in its full significance, "Our country, right or wrong." If you let it trespass on the domain of morals, it is knavish and atheistic. But there is a full, broad sphere for loyalty; and no war-cry ever stirred a generous people that had not in it much of truth and right. It is sublime, this rally of a great people to the defence of what they think their national honor! A "noble and puissant nation rousing herself like a strong man from sleep, and shaking her invincible locks." Just now, we saw her "reposing, peaceful and motionless; but at the call of patriotism, she ruffles, as it were, her swelling plumage, collects her scattered elements of strength, and awakens her dormant thunders."

But how do we justify this last appeal to the God of Battles? Let me tell you how I do. I have always believed in the sincerity of Abraham Lincoln. You have heard me express my confidence in it every time I have spoken from this desk. I only doubted sometimes whether he were really the head of the government. To-day he is at any rate Commander-in-chief.

The delay in the action of Government has doubtless been necessity, but policy also. Traitors within and without made it hesitate to move till it had tried the machine of Government just given it. But delay was wise, as it matured a public opinion definite, decisive, and ready to keep step to the music of the Government march. The very postponement of another session of Congress till July 4th plainly invites discussion—evidently contemplates the ripening of public opinion in the interval. Fairly to examine public affairs, and prepare a community wise to coöperate with the Government, is the duty of every pulpit and every press.

Plain words, therefore, now before the nation goes mad with excitement, is every man's duty. Every public meeting in Athens was opened with a curse on any one who should not speak what he really thought. "I have never defiled my conscience from fear or favor to my superiors," was part of the oath every Egyptian soul was supposed to utter in the Judgment Hall of Osiris, before admission to heaven. Let us show, to-day, a Christian spirit as sincere and fearless. No mobs in this hour of victory, to silence those whom events have not converted. We are strong enough to tolerate dissent. That flag which floats over press or mansion at the bidding of a mob, disgraces both victor and victim.

All winter long, I have acted with that party which cried for peace. The anti-slavery enterprise to which I belong, started with peace written on its banner. We imagined that the age of bullets was over; that the age of ideas had come; that thirty millions of people were able to take a great question, and decide it by the conflict of opinions; and, without letting the ship of State founder, lift four millions of men into Liberty and Justice. We thought that if your statesmen would throw away personal ambition and party watchwords, and devote themselves to the great issue, this might be accomplished. To a certain extent, it has been. The North has answered to the call. Year after year, event by event, has indicated the rising education of the people,—the readiness for a higher moral life, the patience that waits for a neighbor's conversion. The North has responded to the call of that peaceful, moral, intellectual agitation which the anti-slavery idea has initiated. Our mistake, if any, has been that we counted too much on the intelligence of the masses, on the honesty and wisdom of statesmen as a class. Perhaps we did not give weight enough to the fact we saw, that this nation is made up of different ages; not homogeneous, but a mixed mass of different centuries. The North *thinks*—can appreciate argument—is the nineteenth century—hardly any struggle left in it but that between the working class and the money kings. The South *dreams*—it is the thirteenth and fourteenth century—baron and serf—noble and slave. Jack Cade and Wat Tyler loom over the horizon, and the serf rising calls for another Thierry to record his struggle. There the fagot still burns, which the Doctors of the Sorbonne called, ages ago, "the best light to guide the erring." There men are tortured for opinions, the only punishment the Jesuits were willing their pupils should look on. This is, perhaps, too flattering a picture of the South. Better call her, as Sumner does, "the Barbarous States." Our struggle, therefore, is no struggle between different ideas, but between barbarism and civilization. Such can only be settled by arms. (Prolonged cheering.) The Government have waited until its best friends almost suspected its courage or its integrity; but the cannon shot against Fort Sumter has opened the only door out of this hour. There were but two. One was Compromise; the other was Battle. The integrity of the North closed the first; the generous forbearance of nineteen States closed the other. The South opened this with cannon shot, and Lincoln shows himself at the door. (Prolonged and enthusiastic cheering.) The war, then, is not aggressive, but in self-defence, and Washington has become the Thermopylæ of Liberty and Justice. (Applause.) Rather than surrender it, cover every square foot of it with a living body (loud cheers); crowd it with a million of men, and empty every bank vault at the North to pay the cost. (Renewed cheering.) Teach the world once for all, that North America belongs to the stars and stripes, and under them no man shall wear a chain. (Enthusiastic cheering.) In the whole of this conflict, I have looked only at Liberty—only at the slave. Perry entered the battle of the Lakes, with "Don't give up the ship," floating from the masthead of the Lawrence. When with his fighting flag he left her crippled, heading north, and mounting the deck of the Niagara, turned her bows due west, he did all for one purpose,—to rake the decks of the foe. Acknowledge secession, or cannonade it, I care not which; but "Proclaim liberty throughout all the land unto all the inhabitants thereof." (Loud cheers.)

I said, civil war needs momentous and solemn justification. Europe, the world, may claim of us, that before we blot the nineteenth century by an appeal to arms, we shall exhaust every concession, try every means to keep the peace; otherwise, an appeal to the God of Battles is an insult to the civilization of our age; it is a confession that our culture and our religion are superficial, if not a failure. I think that the history of the nation and of the Government both, is an ample justification to our own times and to history for this appeal to arms. I think the South is all wrong, and the Administration is all right. (Prolonged cheering.) Let me tell you why. For thirty years, the North has exhausted conciliation and compromise. They have tried every expedient, they have relinquished every right, they have sacrificed every interest, they have smothered keen sensibility to national honor, and Northern weight and supremacy in the Union; have forgotten they were the majority in numbers and in wealth, in education and strength; have left the helm of Government and the dictation of policy to the Southern States. For all this, the conflict waxed closer and hotter. The Administration that preceded this was full of traitors and thieves. It allowed the arms, ships, money, military stores of the North to be stolen with impunity. Mr. Lincoln took office, robbed of all the means to defend the constitutional rights of the Government. He offered to withdraw from the walls of Sumter everything but the flag. He allowed secession to surround it with the strongest forts which military science could build. The North offered to meet in Convention her sister States, and arrange the terms of peaceful separation. Strength and right yielded everything—they folded their hands—waited the returning reason of the mad insurgents. Week after week elapsed, month after month went by, waiting for the sober second thought of two millions and a half of people. The world saw the sublime sight of nineteen millions of wealthy, powerful, united citizens allowing their flag to be insulted, their rights assailed, their sovereignty defied and broken in pieces, and yet waiting, with patient, brotherly, magnanimous kindness, until insurrection having spent its fury should reach out its hand for a peaceful arrangement. Men began to call it cowardice, on the one hand; and we, who watched closely the crisis, feared that this effort to be magnanimous would demoralize the conscience and the courage of the North. We were afraid that, as the hour went by, the virtue of the people, white-heat as it stood on the 4th day of March, would be cooled by the temptations, by the suspense, by the want and suffering that were stalking from the Atlantic to the valley of the Mississippi. We were afraid the Government would wait too long, and find, at last, that instead of a united people, they were deserted, and left alone to meet the foe.

All this time, the South knew, recognized, by her own knowledge of Constitutional questions, that the Government could not advance one inch towards acknowledging secession; that when Abraham Lincoln swore to support the Constitution and laws of the United States, he was bound to die under the flag on Fort Sumter, if necessary. (Loud applause.) They knew, therefore, that the call on the Administration to acknowledge the Commissioners of the Confederacy was a delusion and a swindle. I know the whole argument for secession. Up to a certain extent, I accede to it. But no administration that is not traitor, can ever acknowledge secession. (Cheers.) The right of a State to secede, under the Constitution of the United States—it is an absurdity; and Abraham Lincoln knows nothing, has a right to know nothing, but the Constitution of the United States. (Loud cheers.) The right of a State to secede, as a revolutionary right, is undeniable; but it is the nation that is to recognize that; and the nation offered, in broad convention, at the suggestion of Kentucky, to meet the question. The offer was declined. The Government and the nation, therefore, are all right. (Applause.) They are right on constitutional law; they are right on the principles of the Declaration of Independence. (Cheers.)

Let me explain this more fully, for this reason; because—and I thank God for it, every American should be proud of it—you cannot maintain a war in the United States of America against a constitutional or a revolutionary right. The people of these States have too large brains and too many ideas to fight blindly—to lock horns like a couple of beasts in the sight of the world. (Applause.) Cannon think in this 19th century; and you must put the North in the right—wholly, undeniably, inside of the Constitution and out of it—before you can justify her in the face of the world; before you can pour Massachusetts like an avalanche through the streets of Baltimore, (great cheering,) and carry Lexington and the 19th of April south of Mason and Dixon's Line. (Renewed cheering.) Let us take an honest pride in the fact that our Sixth Regiment made a way for itself through Baltimore, and were the first to reach the threatened Capital. In the war of opinions, Massachusetts has a right to be the first in the field.

I said I knew the whole argument for secession. Very briefly let me state the points. No government provides for its own death; therefore there can be no constitutional right to secede. But there is a revolutionary right. The Declaration of Independence establishes what the heart of every American acknowledges, that the people—mark you! THE PEOPLE—have always an inherent, paramount, inalienable right to change their governments, whenever they think—whenever *they* think, that it will minister to their happiness. That is a revolutionary right. Now, how did South Carolina and Massachusetts come into the Union? They came into it by a convention representing the people. South Carolina alleges that she has gone out by convention. So far, right. She says that when the *people* take the State rightfully out of the Union, the right to forts and national property goes with it. Granted. She says, also, that it is no matter that we bought Louisiana of France, and Florida of Spain. No bargain made, no money paid betwixt us and France or Spain could rob Florida or Louisiana of her right to remodel her government whenever the people found it would be for their happiness. So far, right. The People—mark you! South Carolina presents herself to the Administration at Washington, and says, "There is a vote of my convention, that I go out of the Union." "I cannot see you," says Abraham Lincoln. [Loud cheers.] "As President, I have no eyes but constitutional eyes; I cannot see you." [Renewed cheers.] He was right. But Madison said, Hamilton said, the Fathers said, in '89, "No man but an enemy of liberty will ever stand on technicalities and forms, when the essence is in question." Abraham Lincoln could not see the Commissioners of South Carolina, but the North could; the nation could; and the nation responded, "If you want a Constitutional Secession, such as you claim, but which I repudiate, I will waive forms—let us meet in convention, and we will arrange it." [Applause.] Surely, while one claims a right within the Constitution, it may without dishonor or inconsistency meet in convention—even if finally refusing to be bound by it. To decline doing so is only evidence of intention to provoke war. Everything under that instrument is peace. Everything under that instrument may be changed by a National Convention. The South says, "No!" She says, "If you don't allow me the Constitutional right, I claim the revolutionary right." The North responds—"When you have torn the Constitution into fragments, I recognize the right of THE PEOPLE of South Carolina to model their government. Yes, I recognize the right of the three hundred and eighty-four thousand white men, and four hundred and eighty-four thousand black men to model their Constitution. Show me one that they have adopted, and I will recognize the revolution. [Cheers.] But the moment you tread outside of the Constitution, the black man is not three-fifths of a man—he is a whole one" [Loud cheering.] Yes, the South has a right to secede; the South has a right to model her government; and the moment she shows us four million of black votes thrown even against it, I will acknowledge the Declaration of Independence is complied with, [loud applause]—that the PEOPLE, south of Mason's and Dixon's Line, have re-modeled their government to suit themselves: and our function is only to recognize it.

I say, the North had a right to assume this position. She did not. She had a right to ignore revolution until this condition was complied with; and she did not. She waived it. In obedience to the advice of Madison, to the long history of her country's forbearance, to the magnanimity of nineteen States, she waited: she advised the Government to wait. Mr. Lincoln, in his inaugural, indicated that this would be the wise course. Mr. Seward hinted it in his speech, in New York. The *London Times* bade us remember the useless war of 1776, and take warning against resisting the principles of Popular Sovereignty. The *Tribune*, whose unflinching fidelity and matchless ability make it, in this fight, "the white plume of Navarre," has again and again avowed its readiness to waive forms and go into Convention. We have waited. We said, "Anything for peace." We obeyed the magnanimous statesmanship of John Quincy Adams. Let me read you his advice, given at the "Jubilee of the Constitution," to the New-York Historical Society, in the year 1839: he says, Recognizing this right of the *people* of a State,—mark you, not a State: the Constitution knows no States; the right of revolution knows no States: it knows only THE PEOPLE. Mr. Adams says, "The PEOPLE of each State in the Union have a right to secede from the confederated Union itself.

Thus stands the RIGHT. But the indissoluble link of union between the people of the several States of this Confederated Nation is, after all, not in the *right*, but in the *heart*.

If the day should ever come (may Heaven avert it) when the affections of the people of these States shall be alienated from each other, when the fraternal spirit shall give way to cold indifference, or collisions of interest shall fester into hatred, the bands of political association will not long hold together parties no longer attracted by the magnetism of conciliated interests and kindly sympathies; and far better will it be for the people of the disunited States to part in friendship from each other, than to be held together by constraint. Then will be the time for reverting to the precedents which occurred at the formation and adoption of the Constitution, to form again a more perfect union, by dissolving that which could no longer bind; and to leave the separated parts to be reunited by the law of political gravitation to the center."

The North said "Amen" to every word of it. They waited. They begged the States to meet them. They were silent when the cannon-shot pierced the flag of the "Star of the West." They said "Amen," when the Government offered to let nothing but the bunting cover Fort Sumpter. They said "Amen," when Lincoln stood alone, without arms, in a defenceless Capital, and trusted himself to the loyalty and forbearance of thirty-four States.

The South, if the truth be told, *cannot* wait. Like all usurpers, they dare not give time for the people to criticise their title to power. War and tumult must conceal the irregularity of their civil course, and smother discontent and criticism at the same time. Besides, bankruptcy at home can live out its short term of possible existence only by conquest on land and piracy at sea. And, further, only by war, by appeal to popular frenzy, can they hope to delude the border States to join them. War is the breath of their life.

To-day, therefore, the question is, by the voice of the South, "Shall Washington or Montgomery own the continent?" And the North says, "From the gulf to the pole, the Stars and Stripes shall atone to four million of negroes whom we have forgotten for seventy years; and, before you break the Union, we will see that justice is done to the slave." [Enthusiastic and long continued cheers.]

There is only one thing that those cannon shot in the harbor of Charleston settled, and that is, that there never can be a compromise. [Loud applause.] We Abolitionists have doubted whether this Union really meant Justice and Liberty. We have doubted the honest intention of nineteen million of people. They have said, in answer to our criticism,—"We believe that the Fathers meant to establish justice. We believe that there are hidden in the Armory of the Constitution weapons strong enough to secure it. We are willing yet to try the experiment. Grant us time." We have doubted, derided the pretence, as we supposed. During these long and weary weeks, we have waited to hear the Northern conscience assert its purpose. It comes at last. [An impressive pause.] Massachusetts blood has consecrated the pavements of Baltimore, and those stones are now too sacred to be trodden by slaves. [Loud cheers.]

You and I owe it to those young martyrs, you and I owe it, that their blood shall be the seed of no mere empty triumph, but that the negro shall teach his children to bless them for centuries to come. [Applause.] When Massachusetts goes down to that Carolina fort to put the Stars and Stripes again over its blackened walls, [enthusiasm,] she will sweep from its neighborhood every institution that hazards their ever bowing again to the Palmetto. [Loud cheers.] All of you may not mean it now. Our fathers did not think in 1775 of the Declaration of Independence. The Long Parliament never thought of the scaffold of Charles the First, when they entered on the struggle; but having begun, they made thorough work. [Cheers.] It is an attribute of the Yankee blood—Slow to fight, and fight once. [Renewed cheers.] It was a holy war, that for Independence: this is a holier and the last—that for Liberty. [Loud applause.]

I hear a great deal about Constitutional liberty. The mouths of the Concord and Lexington guns have room only for one word, and that is Liberty. You might as well ask Niagara to chaunt the Chicago Platform, as to say how far war shall go. War and Niagara thunder to a music of their own. God alone can launch the lightning, that they may go and say, Here we are. The thunder-bolts of His throne abase the proud, lift up the lowly, and execute justice between man and man.

Now, let me turn one moment to another consideration. What should the Government do? I said "thorough" should be its maxim. When we fight, we are fighting for Justice and an Idea. A short war and a rigid one, is the maxim. Ten thousand men in Washington! it is only a bloody fight. Five hundred thousand men in Washington, and none dare come there but from the North. [Loud cheers.] Occupy St. Louis, with the millions of the West, and say to Missouri, "You cannot go out!" [Applause.] Cover Maryland with a million of the friends of the administration, and say, "We must have our Capital within reach. [Cheers.] If you need compensation for Slaves taken from you in the convulsion of battle, here it is. [Cheers.] Government is engaged in the fearful struggle to show that 89 meant Justice, and there is something better than life in such an hour as this." And, again, we must remember another thing—the complication of such a struggle as this. Bear with me a moment. We put five hundred thousand men on the banks of the Potomac. Virginia is held by two races, white and black. Suppose those black men flare in our faces the Declaration of Independence. What are we to say? Are we to send Northern bayonets to keep Slaves under the feet of Jefferson Davis? [Many voices, "no," "never."] In 1842, Gov. Wise, of Virginia, the symbol of the South, entered into argument with Quincy Adams, who carried Plymouth Rock to Washington. [Applause.] It was when Joshua Giddings offered his resolution stating his Constitutional doctrine that Congress had no right to interfere, in any event, in any way, with the Slavery of the Southern States. Plymouth Rock refused to vote for it. Mr. Adams said, (substantially,) "If foreign war comes, if civil war comes, if insurrection comes, is this beleagured Capital, is this besieged Government to see millions of its subjects in arms, and have no right to break the fetters which they are forging into swords? No; the war power of the Government can sweep this institution into the Gulf." [Cheers.] Ever since 1842, that statesman-like claim and warning of the North has been on record, spoken by the lips of her most moderate, wisest, coolest, most patriotic son. [Applause.]

When the South cannonaded Fort Sumpter the bones of Adams stirred in his coffin. [Cheers.] And you might have heard him, from that granite grave, at Quincy, proclaim to the nation, "The hour has struck! Seize the thunder-bolt God has forged for you, and annihilate the system which has troubled peace for seventy years!" [Cheers.] Do not say that it is a cold-blooded suggestion. I hardly ever knew Slavery go down in any other circumstances. Only once, in the broad sweep of the world's history, was any nation lifted so high that she could stretch her imperial hand across the Atlantic, and lift, by one peaceful word, a million of slaves into liberty. God granted that glory only to our mother land.

How did French Slavery go down? How did the French Slave-trade go down? When Napoleon came back from Elba, when his fate hung trembling in the balance, and he wished to gather around him the sympathies of the liberals of Europe, he no sooner set foot in the Tuilleries than he signed the edict abolishing the Slave-trade, against which the Abolitionists of England and France had protested for twenty years in vain. And the trade went down, because Napoleon felt that he must do something to gild the darkening hour of his second attempt to clutch the sceptre of France. How did the Slave-system go down? When, in 1848, the Provisional Government found itself in the Hotel de Ville, obliged to do something to draw to itself the sympathy and liberal feeling of the French nation, they signed an edict—it was the first from the rising republic—abolishing the death-penalty and Slavery. The storm which rocked the vessel of State almost to foundering, snapped forever the chain of the French slave. Look, too, at the history of Mexican and South American emancipation; you will find that it was, in every instance, I think, the child of convulsion.

That hour has come to us. So stand we to-day. The Abolitionist who will not now cry, when the moment serves, "Up, boys, and at them," is false to liberty. [Great cheering.] [A voice—"So is every other man."] Say not it is a hard lesson. Let him who fully knows his own heart and strength, and feels, as he looks down into his child's cradle, that he could stand and see that little nestling borne to Slavery, and submit—let him cast the first stone. But all you, whose blood is wont to stir over Naseby and Bunker Hill, will hold your peace, unless you are ready to cry with me—*Sic semper Tyrannis!* So may it ever be with Tyrants! [Loud applause.]

Why, Americans, I believe in the might of nineteen million of people. Yes, I know that what sowing machines and reaping machines and ideas and types and school-houses cannot do, the muskets of Illinois and Massachusetts can finish up. [Cheers.] Blame me not that I make every thing turn on liberty and the slave. I believe in Massachusetts. I know that free speech, free toil, school-houses, and ballot-boxes are a pyramid on its broadest base. Nothing that does not sunder the solid globe can disturb it. We defy the world to disturb us. [Cheers.] The little errors that dwell upon our surface, we have medicine in our institutions to cure them all. [Applause.]

Therefore there is nothing left for a New England man, nothing but that he shall wipe away the stain that hangs about the toleration of human bondage. As Webster said at Rochester, years and years ago, "If I thought that there was a stain upon the remotest hem of the garment of my country, I would devote my utmost labor to wipe it off." [Cheers.] To-day that call is made upon Massachusetts. That is the reason why I dwell so much on the Slavery question. I said I believed in the power of the North to conquer; but where does she get it. I do not believe in the power of the North to subdue two million and a half of southern men, unless she summons justice, God, and the negro to her side; [Cheers] and in that battle we are sure of this—we are sure to rebuild the Union down to the Gulf. [Renewed cheering.] In that battle, with that watchword, with those allies, the thirteen States and their children will survive—in the light of the world, a nation which has vindicated the sincerity of the Fathers of '87, that they bore children, and not pedlars, to represent them in the nineteenth century. [Repeated cheers.] But without that—without that, I know also, we shall conquer. Sumpter annihilated compromise. Nothing but victory will blot from history that sight of the Stars and Stripes giving place to the Palmetto. But without justice for inspiration, without God for our ally, we shall break the Union asunder; we shall be a confederacy, and so will they. This war means one of two things—Emancipation or Disunion. [Cheers.] Out of the smoke of the conflict there comes that—nothing else. It is impossible there should come anything else. Now, I believe in the future and permanent union of the races that cover this continent from the Pole down to the Gulf. One in race, one in history, one in religion, one in industry, one in thought, we never can be permanently separated. Your path, if you forget the black race, will be over the gulf of Disunion,—years of unsettled, turbulent, Mexican and South American civilization, back through that desert of forty years to the Union which is sure to come.

But I believe in a deeper conscience, I believe in a North more educated than that. I divide you into four sections. The first is the ordinary mass, rushing from mere enthusiasm to

"A battle whose great aim and scope
They little care to know,
Content like men-at-arms to cope,
Each with his fronting foe."

Behind that class stands another, whose only idea in this controversy is sovereignty and the flag. The seaboard, the wealth, the just-converted hunkerism of the country, fill that class. Next to it stands the third element, the people; the cordwainers of Lynn, the farmer of Worcester, the dwellers on the prairie—Iowa and Wisconsin, Ohio and Maine—the broad surface of the people who have no leisure for technicalities, who never studied law, who never had time to read any further into the Constitution than the first two lines—"Establish *Justice* and secure *Liberty*." They have waited long enough; they have eaten dirt enough; they have apologized for bankrupt statesmen enough; they have quieted their consciences enough; they have split logic with their Abolition neighbors long enough; they are tired of trying to find a place between the forty-ninth and forty-eighth corner of a Constitutional hair, [laughter;] and now that they have got their hand on the neck of a rebellious aristocracy, in the name of the PEOPLE, they mean to strangle it. That I believe is the body of the people itself. Side by side with them stands a fourth class—small, but active—the Abolitionists, who thank God that he has let them see his salvation before they die. [Cheers.]

The noise and dust of the conflict may hide the real question at issue. Europe may think, some of us may, that we are fighting for forms and parchments, for sovereignty and a flag. But really, the war is one of opinions: it is Civilization against Barbarism: it is Freedom against Slavery. The cannon shot against Fort Sumpter was the yell of pirates against the DECLARATION OF INDEPENDENCE: the war-cry of the North is its echo. The South, defying Christianity, clutches its victim. The North offers its wealth and blood in glad atonement for the selfishness of seventy years. The result is as sure as the throne of God. I believe in the possibility of Justice, in the certainty of Union. Years hence, when the smoke of this conflict clears away, the world will see under our banner all tongues, all creeds, all races—one brotherhood—and on the banks of the Potomac, the Genius of Liberty, robed in light, four-and-thirty stars for her diadem, broken chains under feet, and an olive-branch in her right hand. [Great applause.]

THE ANGLO-AFRICAN.

PROSPECTUS.

THE WEEKLY ANGLO-AFRICAN, to whose management the undersigned has recently succeeded, was started nearly two years ago, to afford a medium of communication whereby we, the people of color, might become better known to each other and to the community at large. It aimed to hold, as it were, a mirror before our people, wherein, seeing themselves reflected, they might detect and remedy their defects, or discover and improve their advantages.

In this endeavor it has, so far, met the approbation and patronage of our people, which it is our desire that it should continue to merit and attain. Therefore, in order to guard against misrepresentation and disarm prejudice, we take this occasion to assure our patrons and the public generally, that the aim of the paper will be in the future, as it has been in the past, the elevation and progress of the colored race. We shall endeavor to widen its field of vision and to extend its sphere of action, in order to ally our movements and identify our sympathies with the efforts of black men everywhere in their attempts to overthrow slavery, achieve their liberties and effect the complete rehabilitation of the race. To aid in the dissemination of the knowledge and the promotion of the culture necessary to accomplish this end, the Weekly Anglo-African will be devoted to a vigilant scrutiny and careful exposition of the condition and prospects, primarily, of the colored population of the United States, free and enslaved, and incidentally with that of the race abroad.

In the prosecution of this work, it will need, and earnestly solicits, the assistance of every well-wisher of our people, and all information and suggestions of a practical nature will be gratefully received.

It will endeavor to furnish reliable statistics relative to our moral, economic and social attitude: also, biographical sketches of distinguished men of color.

We intend to furnish a reliable "History of the Revolutions of Hayti," written by M. de St. Armand, a distinguished advocate and citizen of Port-au-Prince, translated expressly for the Anglo-African. It is now appearing in our columns. Subscribers can receive it from the commencement, if they so desire.

By the aid of intelligent correspondents, both at home and abroad, we hope to keep our readers advised on matters of local interest, as well as those of general import. We desire that this paper should be a reflex of the mature thought, and a proof of the mental ability of our people; and we hope by the aid of their good wishes and kind coöperation to make it instrumental in the overthrow of Slavery and the establishment of Liberty, Equality, and Fraternity.

Terms.

For one year, payable in advance,				$2 00
" six months,	"	"	"	1 00
" three "	"	"	"	50

Address GEORGE LAWRENCE, Jr.,
Publisher,
No. 48, Beekman St., New York.

WHAT THE WAR IS—NO COMPROMISE!

Let it be clearly understood by men of all parties, what the war is—not a war of aggression, or of its own seeking, on the part of the National Government, but purely of self-defence and for SELF-PRESERVATION—a war not to subjugate THE PEOPLE of the South, but to crush a desperate and traitorous SLAVE OLIGARCHY, who despise popular rights, and who have not dared to submit the Constitution of their new Confederacy to the verdict of Southern voters—a war for the illimitable extension and unending existence of a system which turns millions of God's rational creatures into beasts and merchandize, and for the overthrow of all free institutions, and the subversion of the Declaration of Independence, on the part of the conspirators! Surely, all honest, upright, patriotic citizens can have but one opinion about it. Surely, never before could a people, in taking up arms to defend all that is dear to them, and to put down a tyrannical usurpation, more appropriately use the words of the immortal Burns:—

"Who would be a traitor-knave?
Who would fill a coward's grave?
Who so base as be a slave?
Let him turn, and flee!

Lay the proud USURPERS low!
Tyrants fall in every foe!
LIBERTY'S IN EVERY BLOW!
LET US DO OR DIE!"

Frederick Douglass' Paper.

DEVOTED TO THE RIGHTS OF ALL MANKIND, WITHOUT DISTINCTION OF COLOR, CLASS, OR CLIME.

VOL. XIII.--NO. 27.   ROCHESTER, N. Y., JUNE 15, 1860.   WHOLE NO. 650.

FREDERICK DOUGLASS' PAPER
IS PUBLISHED EVERY FRIDAY MORNING,
At No. 25, Buffalo Street, (opposite the
Arcade,) Rochester N. Y.

TERMS OF SUBSCRIPTION.

Single copies, one year, (invariably in advance,) $1 50 ; Five copies, $5 00.

Postage to all in Monroe County, free ; to
any part of New York State, payable in advance,
3 cents a quarter ; to any part of the U. S., a cent.

HOW THE MAHOMEDANS VIEW SLAVERY IN THIS COUNTRY.

We commend the following, which we copy from the N. Y. Tribune, to the Pro-Slavery Churches of our country :

The following story was not told from the platform at any recent meeting of the American Board of Commissioners for Foreign Missions. It would, nevertheless, be wholesome for sundry doctors of divinity to take heed to it, especially if they be members of the societies named, to which societies it is respectfully dedicated.

There are missionaries in Syria, many of them. Not a few are Americans, and the success of the latter has been 'most encouraging.' The Roman Catholics are not gratified with this rapid advance toward Protestantism, and desire to check it. Knowing that Syrian convicts have 'a conscience' which is apt to strike a Tractarian as ludicrously tender upon certain points, the Roman Catholic goes to them and says : Preachers from America come here to convert you, as they pretend, to the 'true faith of Jesus Christ, and tell you of the freedom in that free and liberal country. We will tell you to what Protestantism and freedom lead, and then tell us whether even the Moslems in Turkey would enact such 'iniquitous laws.' Then he translates to his attentive hearers certain passages from American and English journals, wherein the fact is made painfully clear that such a thing as human bondage does exist in America. On one occasion, four or five respectable natives called upon an American, and desired him to translate into their language a paragraph which some one had marked for them in the London Times. It was a bit narrating how the free colored people of several Southern and South Western States were driven by the law from their homes, on pain of being reduced to slavery, if they remained. To the rather callous moral cuticle of an American, this gave no sharp bite ; it was to him, we may suppose, rather a mild case of the system and its incidents. But the Syrians thought otherwise. As they listened, they held their breath ; then whispered each to the other : 'Is he the priest told us,' and for a moment kept silence. Then, as if thinking the whole affair might be attempted, one of them prepared to administer a most solemn oath—one, too, that may have had a sarcasm in it : 'Now, on the oath of an Englishman, do you believe these things to be true.' Being assured that they were even so, they at once took a voluntary pledge of total abstinence from the American chapel and books, even from all things American, lest they be allied with American Slavery. The unfortunate man who had acted as translator tried to explain, that America had a North as well as a South, and that there was a deep and indignant sorrow even in that land for these things. 'Let those of the North,' said they, 'go home and convert those of the South before they come to preach to the South. Even the Turks never did such things as these.'

It was the remark of an Italian friar, a remark gleefully uttered, that all the priests sent forth by the Propaganda at Rome could not have struck so heavy a blow at Protestantism in Syria, as the American news touching Slavery.

HYATT IN PRISON.

During the late excursion of Ohio Editors, while in the city of Washington some of them who had not the fear of man and prejudice before their eyes, visited Thaddeus Hyatt, in 'the common jail.' The editor of the Ashtabula Sentinel thus speaks of his visit and of his impression of the principle which Mr. Hyatt represents :

When in Washington recently, we called upon Mr. Hyatt in his prison, and received from him his version of his case. Much has been said of him ; and very much that we cannot but regard as unjust. To appreciate his position it must be understood and seen from a stand point, which we acknowledge to be high, and which very few take. Mr. H. has gone to prison for an abstract principle, and one that is vital to the preservation of our liberty. He is making a stand against what he sees to be tyranny, and a dangerous tyranny, because insidious, and likely to work great wrongs unrebuked, for the reason that it requires but small concessions to establish its precedents—as in this case. Mr. Hyatt says he knows nothing about John Brown that is not unwilling to testify before a proper tribunal. But he denies that the Senate has any right to require his testimony ; and he insists the constitution does not confer such powers upon them, as they have assumed to exercise. This is the stand he makes for the Principle, and that only. They have him in their power and are crushing him without mercy. He knows that he can be released immediately upon telling the little that he knows which will hurt no one, but he says this will be giving up to the principle and forming a precedent, under which more tyranny may be perpetrated. Those who ridicule him and talk of his cheap martyrdom (if susceptible) might be shamed to bear him state his case and his views of it. With his health and great pecuniary interests at stake, and the miserable quarters he occupies, his martyrdom is far from cheap. We make no pretensions to the nerve he manifests, nor do we suppose we would stand up as he does ; but, we must honor him for courage and devotion to the principle that few men know any thing about.

—The Senate has passed a resolution to adjourn on the 18th inst.

THE BARBARISM OF SLAVERY.

SPEECH

OF

HON. CHARLES SUMNER,

ON THE

BILL FOR THE ADMISSION OF KANSAS AS A FREE STATE.

In the United States Senate, June 4th, 1860.

Mr. President—Undertaking now, for the first time after a silence of more than four years, to address the Senate on this important subject, I should suppress the emotion natural on such an occasion if I did not declare on the threshold my gratitude to that Supreme Being through whose benign care I am enabled, after much suffering and many changes, once again to resume my duties here and to speak for the cause which is so near my heart. To the honored Commonwealth, whose representative I am, and also to my immediate associates in this body, with whom I enjoy the fellowship which is found in thinking alike concerning the republic, I owe thanks which I seize this moment to express for the indulgence shown me throughout the protracted seclusion enjoined by medical skill ; and I trust that it will not be thought unbecoming in me to put on record here, as an apology for leaving my seat so long vacant, without making way, by resignation, for a successor, that I acted under the illusion of an invalid, whose hopes for restoration to his natural health constantly triumphed over his disappointments.

When last I entered into this debate, it became my duty to expose the crime against Kansas, and to insist upon the immediate admission of that Territory as a State of this Union, and thus forthwith forbidding slavery. Time has passed ; but the question remains. Resuming the discussion precisely where I left it, I am happy to avow that toil or moderation, which, it is said, may venture even to fix the boundaries of wisdom itself. I have no personal grief to utter ; only a barbarous egotism could intrude these into this chamber. I have no personal wrongs to avenge ; only a barbarous nature could attempt to wield that vengeance which belongs to the Lord. The years that have intervened and the tombs that have been opened since, I speak, bare their voices too, which I cannot fail to hear. Besides, what am I—what is any man among the living or among the dead compared with the question before us ? It is this, sir, which I shall discuss, and I open the argument with that new elevation wherewith this grief, if such it may be called, stands forth in painful light. Search history and you cannot find its parallel. The slave-trade is bad ; but even this enormity is petty compared with that elaborate contrivance by which, in a Christian age and within the limits of a republic, all forms of constitutional liberty were perverted ; by which all the rights of human nature were violated, and the whole country was held trembling on the edge of civil war ; while all this large exuberance of wickedness, detestable in itself, becomes tenfold more detestable when its origin is traced to the madness for slavery. The fatal partition between freedom and slavery, known as the Missouri Compromise ; the subsequent overthrow of this partition, and the seizure of all by slavery ; the violation of plighted faith ; the conspiracy to force slavery at all hazards into Kansas ; the successive invasions by which all security there was destroyed, and the electoral franchise itself was trodden down ; the sacrilegious seizure of the very polls, and, through pretended forms of law, the imposition of a foreign Legislature upon this Territory ; the acts of this Legislature, fortifying the usurpation, and, among other things, establishing test oaths, calculated to disfranchise actual settlers, friendly to freedom, and securing the privileges of the citizen to actual strangers friendly to slavery ; the whole crowned by a statute, 'the be-all and the end-all' of the whole usurpation—through which slavery was not only recognized on this beautiful soil, but made to bristle with a code of death such as the world has rarely seen ; all these I have fully exposed on a former occasion. And yet the most important part of the argument was, at that time, left untouched ; I mean that which is found in the character of slavery. This natural sequel, with the permission of the Senate, I propose now to supply. Motive is to crime as soul to body ; and it is only when we comprehend the motive that we can truly comprehend the crime. Here the motive is found in slavery and the rage for its extension. Therefore, by logical necessity, must slavery be discussed—not indirectly, timidly, and sparingly, but directly, openly, and thoroughly. It must be exhibited as it is ; alike in its influence and in its animating character, so that not only its outside but its inside may be seen.

This is no time for soft words or excuses—All such are out of place. They may turn away wrath ; but what is the wrath of man ? This is no time to abandon any advantage in the argument. Senators sometimes announce that they resist slavery on political grounds only, and remind us that they say nothing of the moral question. This is wrong. Slavery must be resisted not only on political grounds, but on all other grounds, whether social, economical or moral. Ours is no holiday contest, nor is it any strife of rival factions—of white and red races—of theatric Neri and Bianchi ; but it is a solemn battle between right and wrong—between good and evil. Such a battle cannot be fought with rose-water. There is austere work to be done, and freedom cannot consent to fling away any of her weapons. If I were disposed to shrink from this discussion, the boundless assumptions now made by Senators on the other side would not allow me. The whole character of slavery as a pretended form of civilization is put directly in issue, with a pertinacity and a hardihood which banish all reserve on this side. In these assumptions, Senators from South Carolina naturally take the lead. Following Mr. Calhoun, who pronounced 'slavery the most safe and stable basis for free institutions in the world,' and Mr. McDuffie, who did not shrink from calling it 'the corner stone of the republican edifice,' the Senator from South Carolina (Mr. Hammond) insists that 'its forms of society are the best in the world' ; and his colleague (Mr. Chesnut) takes up the strain. One Senator from Mississippi (Mr. Davis) adds that slavery 'is but a form of civil government for those who are not fit to govern themselves' ; and his colleague (Mr. Brown) openly vaunts that it 'is a great moral, social and political blessing—a blessing to the slave and a blessing to the master.' One Senator from Virginia (Mr. Hunter) in a studied vindication of what he is pleased to call the social system of the slaveholding States, 'exalts slavery as 'the normal condition of human society'—'beneficial to the non-slave owner as it is to the slave owner'—'best for the happiness of both races' ; and, in enthusiastic advocacy, declares 'that the very keystone of the mighty arch, which by the concentrated strength is able to sustain our social superstructure, consists in the black marble block of African slavery. Knock that out,' he says, 'and the mighty fabric, with all that it upholds, topples and tumbles to its fall.' These were his very words, uttered in debate here ; and his colleague (Mr. Mason,) who has never hesitated where slavery was in question, has proclaimed that it is 'ennobling to both master and slave'—a word which, so far as the slave was concerned, he changed, on a subsequent day to 'elevating,' assuming still that it is 'ennobling to the master—which is simply a new version of an old assumption, by Mr. McDuffie, of South Carolina, that 'slavery supersedes the necessity of an order of nobility.'

Thus, by various voices, is the claim made for slavery, which is put forward defiantly as a form of civilization—as if its existence were not plainly inconsistent with the first principles of anything, that can be called civilization—except by that figure of speech in classical literature, where a thing takes its name from something which it has not, as the dreadful fates were called merciful because they were without mercy. And pardon the allusion, if I add, that, listening to these sounding words for slavery, I am reminded of the hundred extravagance related by that remarkable traveler in China, the late Abbe Huc, of a gloomy hole in which he was lodged, pestered by mosquitoes and exhaling noisome vapors, where light and air entered only by a single narrow aperture, but styled by Chinese pride the Hotel of the Beatitudes. It is natural that Senators, thus insensible to the true character of slavery, should evince an equal insensibility to the true character of the constitution.

Such are the two assumptions—the first an assumption of fact, and the second an assumption of constitutional law, which are now made without apology or hesitation. I meet them both. To the first I oppose the essential barbarism of slavery in all its influences, whether high or low, as Satan is Satan still, whether towering in the sky or squatting in the toad. To the second I oppose the unanswerable, irresistible truth, that the Constitution of the United States nowhere recognizes property in man.—These two assumptions naturally go together. They are 'twins' suckled by the same wolf—They are the 'couple' in the present slave hunt. And the latter cannot be answered without exposing the former. It is only when slavery is exhibited in its truly hateful character that we can fully appreciate the absurdity of the assumption, which, in defiance of the express letter of the constitution, and without a single sentence, phrase or word upholding human bondage, yet foists into this blameless text the barbarous idea that man can hold property in man.

On former occasions I have discussed slavery only incidentally ; in unfolding the principle that 'slavery is sectional and freedom national ; in exposing the 'unconstitutionality of the Fugitive Slave bill ; in vindicating the prohibition of slavery in the Missouri Territory ; in exhibiting the imbecility throughout the Revolution of the slave States, and especially of South Carolina ; and lastly, in unmasking the crime against Kansas. On all these occasions, where I have spoken at length, I have said too little of the character of slavery, partly because other topics were presented, and partly from a disinclination which I have always felt to press the argument against those whom I knew to have all the sensitiveness of a sick man. But God be praised, this time has passed, and the debate is now lifted from details to principles. Grander debate has not occurred in our history ; rarely in any history ; nor can this debate close or subside except with the triumph of Freedom.

First Assumption.—Of course I begin with the assumption of fact. It was the often quoted remark of John Wesley, who knew well what he wrote, as also have to rude hearts, that slavery was 'the sum of all villainies.' The phrase is pungent ; but it would be rash in any of us to criticize the testimony of that illustrious founder of Methodism, whose ample experience of slavery in Georgia and the Carolinas, seems to have been all condensed in this sententious judgment. Language is feeble to express all the enormity of this institution, which is now vaunted as itself a form of civilization, 'ennobling' at least to the master, if not to the slave. Look at it whatever light you will, and it is always the uncodier, the 'bare bones,' and the shame of discovery ; resting not merely in the abstract, as is often admitted by its apologists, but wrong in the concrete also, and possessing no single element of right. Look at it in the light of principles, and it is nothing less than a huge insurrection against the eternal law of God, involving in its pretensions the denial of all human rights, and also the denial of that divine law in which God himself is manifest, thus being practically the grossest lie and the grossest Atheism. Founded in violence, sustained only by violence, such a wrong must by a sure law of compensation blast the master as well as the slave ; blast the lands on which they are a part ; blast the community which does not forbid the outrage ; and the longer it exists and the more complexity it prevails, must its blasting influences penetrate the whole social system. Barbarous in origin ; barbarous in its law ; barbarous in all its pretensions ; barbarous in the instruments it employs ; barbarous in consequences ; barbarous in spirit ; barbarous wherever it shows itself ; slavery must breed barbarians, while it develops everywhere alike in the individual, and in the society of which he forms a part, the essential elements of barbarism. In this character it is now conspicuous before the world. In undertaking now to expose the barbarism of slavery, the whole broad field is open before me. There is nothing in its character, its manifold wrong, its wretched results, and especially in its influence on the class who claim to be 'ennobled' by it, that will not fall naturally under consideration.

I know well the difficulty of this discussion involved in the humiliating truth with which I begin. Senators on former occasions in revealing their sensibility, have even protested against any comparison between what were called the 'two civilizations,' meaning the two social systems produced respectively by freedom and by slavery. The sensibility and the protest are not unnatural, though mistaken.—'Two civilizations !' Sir, in this nineteenth century of Christian light there can be but one civilization, and this is where freedom prevails. Between slavery and civilization there is an essential incompatibility. If you are for the one, you cannot be for the other, and just in proportion to the embrace of slavery is the divorce from civilization. That slave-masters should be disturbed when this is exposed, might be expected. But the assumptions now so boastfully made, while they may not prevent the sensibility, yet surely exclude all ground of protest when these assumptions are exposed. Nor is this the only difficulty. Slavery is a bloody touch-me-not, and everywhere in sight now blooms the bloody flower. It is on the wayside as we approach the national Capitol ; it is on the marble steps which we mount ; it flaunts on this floor. I stand now in the house of its friends. About me, while I speak, are its most sensitive guardians, who have shown in the past how much they are ready either to do or not to do where slavery is, or oddly here, with which I have been honored by a generous and enlightened people, if I could hesitate. Idolatry has been often exposed in the presence of idolaters, and hypocrisy has been chastised in the presence of Scribes and Pharisees. Such examples may give encouragement to a Senator who undertakes in this presence to expose slavery ; nor can any language, directly responsive to the assumptions now made for this barbarism, be open to question. Slavery can only be painted in the sternest colors ; but I cannot forget that nature's sternest painter has been called the best.

The barbarism of slavery appears, first, in the character of slave masters, and secondly, in the character of slavery itself. Under the first head we shall naturally consider (1) the law of slavery and its origin, and (2) the practical results of slavery, as shown in a comparison between the free States and the slave States. Under the second head we shall naturally consider (1) slave masters as shown in the law of slavery ; (2) slave masters in their relations with slaves, here glancing at their three brutal instruments ; and (3) slave masters in their relations with each other, with society, and with government ; and (4) slave masters in their unconsciousness. The way will then be prepared for the consideration of the assumption of constitutional law.

I. In presenting the character of slavery, there is little for me to do, except to allow slavery to paint itself. When this is done, the picture will need no explanatory words.

(1.) I begin with the Law of Slavery and its Origin, and here its barbarism paints itself in its own chosen definition. It is simply this : Man, created in the image of God, is divested of his human character, and declared to be a 'chattel'—that is, a beast, a thing or article of property. That this statement may not seem to be put forward without precise authority, I quote the statutes of three different States, beginning with South Carolina, whose voice for Slavery always has an unerring distinctiveness. Here is the definition supplied by this State—

'Slaves shall be deemed, held, taken, reputed, and adjudged in law, to be chattels personal in the hands of their owners and possessors, and their executors, administrators and assigns, to all intents, constructions, and purposes whatsoever.'—[2 Brev. Dig. 229.

And here is the definition supplied by the Civil Code of Louisiana :—

'A slave is one who is in the power of a master to whom he belongs. The master may sell him, dispose of his person, his industry, and his labor. He can do nothing, possess nothing, nor acquire anything, but what must belong to his master.'—[Civil Code, Art. 35.

In similar spirit, the law of Maryland thus indirectly defines a slave as an article :—

'In case the personal property of a ward shall consist of specific articles, such as slaves, working beasts, animals of any kind, the Court, if it deem it advantageous to the ward, may at any time pass an order for the sale thereof.'—[Statutes of Maryland.

Not to occupy time unnecessarily, I present a summary of the pretended law defining slavery in all the slave States, as made by a careful writer, Judge Stroud, in a work of juridical as well as philanthropic merit :—

'The cardinal principle of slavery—that the slave is not to be ranked among sentient beings, but among things—as an article of property—a chattel personal—obtains as undoubted law in all of these (slave) States.'—[Stroud's Law of Slavery, p. 22.

Out of this definition, as from a solitary germ, which in its pettiness might be crushed by the hand, towers our Upas tree and all its gigantic poison. Study it, and you will comprehend the whole monstrous growth.

Sir, look at its plain import, and see the relation which it establishes. The slave is held simply for the use of his master, to whose behests his life, liberty and happiness are devoted, and by whom he may be bartered, leased, mortgaged, bequeathed, invoiced, shipped as cargo, stored as goods, sold on execution, knocked off at public auction ; and even staked at the gaming table on the hazard of a card or a die ; all according to law. Nor is there anything within the limit of life, inflicted on a beast which may not be inflicted on the slave. He may be marked like a hog, branded like a mule, yoked like an ox, hobbled like a horse, driven like an ass, sheared like a sheep, maimed like a cur, and constantly whipped like a brute ; all according to law. And should his teeth be taken out, what is the remedy ? The law of slavery, imitating that rule of evidence which in barbarous days and barbarous countries prevented a Christian from testifying against a Mahomedan, openly pronounces the incompetency of the whole African race—whether bond or free—to testify in any case against a white man, and, thus having already surrendered the slave to all possible outrage, crowns its tyranny by excluding the very testimony through which the bloody cruelty of the slave master might be exposed. Thus in its law does slavery paint itself ; but it is only when we look at details, and detect its essential elements—five in number—all inspired by a single motive, that its character becomes completely manifest.

Foremost, of course, in these elements, is the impossible pretension, where barbarism is lost in impiety, by which man claims property in man. Against such arrogance the argument is brief. According to the law of nature, written by the same hand that placed the planets in their orbits, and, like them, constituting a part of the eternal system of the universe, every human being has a complete title to himself direct from the Almighty. Naked he is born ; but this birthright is inseparable from the human form. A man may be poor in this world's goods, but he owns himself.—No war or robbery, ancient or recent, entitled him ; no middle passage, no change of clime, no capture, no purchase money, no transmission from hand to hand no matter how many times, and no matter at what price can debase this indefeasible God given franchise. And a Divine mandate, strong as that which guards life, guards liberty. Even at the very morning of creation, when God said, 'Let there be light,' and there was light, man was not then made, nor was he the chattel giving to man dominion over the fish of the sea, and over the fowl of the air, and over every living thing that moveth upon the earth :

—that right we hold
By His donation ; but man over men
He made not lord ; such title to himself
Reserving, human left from human free.

Slavery tyrannically assumes a power which Heaven denied, while, under its barbarous necromancy, borrowed from the source of evil, a man is changed into a chattel—a person is withered into a thing—a soul is shrunk into merchandise. Say, sir, in your madness, that you own the sun, the stars, the moon ; but do not say that you own a man, endowed with a soul that shall live immortal, when sun, and moon, and stars have passed away.

Secondly. Slavery paints itself again in its complete abrogation of marriage, recognized as a sacrament by the church, and recognized as a contract wherever civilization prevails.—Under the law of slavery no such sacrament is respected, and no such contract can exist. The ties that may be formed between slaves are all subject to the selfish interests or more selfish lust of the master, whose license knows no check. Natural affections which have come together are rudely torn asunder ; nor is this all. Stripped of every defence, the chastity of a whole race is exposed to violence, while the result is recorded in the tell tale faces of children, glowing with their master's blood, but doomed for their mother's skin to slavery, through all descending generations.—The Senator from Mississippi (Mr. Brown) is galled by the comparison between slavery and polygamy, and winces. I hail this sensibility as the sign of virtue. Let him reflect, and he will confess that there are many disgusting elements in slavery which are not present in polygamy, while the single disgusting element of polygamy is more than present in slavery. By the license of polygamy one man may have many wives, all bound to him by the marriage tie, and in other respects protected by law. By the license of slavery, a whole race is delivered over to prostitution and concubinage, without the protection of any law. Sir, is not slavery barbarous ?

Thirdly. Slavery paints itself again in its complete abrogation of the parental relation, which God in his benevolence has provided for the nurture and education of the human family, and which constitutes an essential part of civilization itself. And yet, by the law of slavery—happily beginning to be modified in some places—this relation is set at naught, and in its place is substituted the arbitrary control of the master, at whose mere caprice the helpless children, such as the Saviour called to him, though clasped by a mother's arms, may be swept under the hammer of the auctioneer. Sir, is not slavery barbarous ?

Fourthly. Slavery paints itself again in closing the gates of knowledge, which are also the shining gates of civilization. Under its plain, unequivocal law, the bondman may, at the unrestrained will of his master, be shut out from all instruction, while, in many places, merciful to relate, the law itself, by cumulative provisions, positively forbids that he shall be taught to read. Of course, the slave cannot be allowed to read, for to his soul would then expand in larger air, while he saw the glory of the North Star, and the helping truth that God, who made iron, never made a slave ; for he would then become familiar with the Scriptures, with the Decalogue still speaking in the thunders of Sinai ; with that ancient text, 'He that stealeth a man and selleth him, or if he be found in his hands, he shall surely be put to death ;' with that other text, 'Masters, give unto your servants that which is just and equal ;' with that great story of Redemption, when the Lord raised the slave born bondman to deliver his chosen people from the house of bondage ; and with that sublimer story, where the Saviour died a cruel death, that all men, without distinction of race, might be saved, leaving to mankind commandments which, even without his example, makes slavery impossible. Thus, in order to fasten his manacles upon the slave, you fasten other manacles upon his soul. Sir, is not slavery barbarous ?

Fifthly. Slavery paints itself again in the appropriation of all the toil of its victims, excluding them from that property in their own earnings which the law of nature allows and civilization secures. The fundamental injustice of this pretension is lost in its meanness. It is robbery and petty larceny under the garb of law ; and even its meanness is lost in the absurdity of its associate pretension that, through this miserable, thus despoiled of all his earnings, is saved from poverty, and that for his own good slavery is made ; while imitating a Christian from testifying against a Mahomedan, openly pronounces the incompetency of the whole African race—whether bond or free—to testify ; Alas ! by such a fallacy is a whole race pauperised. And yet this transaction is not without illustrative example. A solemn poet, whose verse has found favor, pictures a creature who—

—With one hand put
A penny in the urn of poverty,
And with the other took a shilling out.
—Pollock's Course of Time, Book VIII, 622.

And a celebrated traveller through Russia, more than a generation ago, describes a kindred spirit, who, while on his knees before an altar of the Greek church, devoutly told his beads with one hand, and, with the other deliberately picked the pocket of a fellow sinner by his side. Not admiring these instances, I cannot cease to deplore a system which has much of both, while, under an affectation of charity, it sordidly takes from the slave all the fruits of his bitter sweat, and thus takes from him the mainspring to exertion. Tell me, sir, is not slavery barbarous ?

Such is slavery in its five special elements of barbarism, as recognized by law ; first, assuming that man can hold property in man ; secondly, abrogating the relation of husband and wife ; thirdly, abrogating the parental relation ; fourthly, closing the gates of knowledge ; and fifthly, appropriating the unpaid labor of another. Take away these elements, sometimes called 'abuses,' and slavery will cease to exist ; for it is these very elements which constitute slavery. Take away any one of them, and the abolition begins. Now when I present slavery for judgment, I mean no slight evil, with regard to which there may be a reasonable difference of opinion, but I mean this five-fold embodiment of 'abuse'—this ghastly quincunx of barbarism—each particular of which, if considered separately, must be denounced at once with all the ardor of an honest soul, while the five fold combination must awake a five-fold denunciation. But this five-fold combination becomes still more hateful when its single motive is considered. The Senator from Mississippi (Mr. Davis) says that it is 'but a form of civil government for those who are not fit to govern themselves.' The Senator is mistaken. It is an outrage where 'n different pretension all concur in one single object, looking only to the profits of the master, and constituting its ever present motive power, which is simply to compel the labor of fellow men, without wages ! If the offence of slavery were less extended ; if it were confined to some narrow region ; if it had less of grandeur in its proportions ; if its victims were counted by tens and hundreds, instead of millions, the five-headed enormity would find little indulgence. All would rise against it, while religion and civilization would lavish their choicest efforts in the general warfare. But what is wrong when done to one man cannot be right when done to many. If it is wrong thus to degrade a single soul—if it is wrong thus to degrade a man, Mr. President—it cannot be right to degrade a whole race. And yet this is denied by the barbarous logic of slavery, which, taking advantage of its own wrong, claims immunity because its usurpation has assumed a front of audacity that cannot be safely attacked. Such is American slavery, as defined by existing law, stands forth as the greatest organized barbarism on which the sun now shines. It is without a single peer. Its author, after making it, broke the die.

If curiosity carries us to the origin of this law—and here I approach a topic often considered in this chamber—we shall confess again its barbarism. It is not derived from the common law, that fountain of liberty ; for this law, while unhappily recognizing a system of servitude, known as villenage, secured to the bondman privileges unknown to the American slave ; protected his person against mayhem ; protected his wife against rape ; gave to his marriage equal validity with the marriage of his master, and surrounded his offspring with generous presumptions of freedom, unlike that rule of yours by which the servitude of the mother is necessarily stamped upon the child. It is not derived from the Roman law, that fountain of tyranny, for two reasons—first, because this law, in its better days, when its early rigors were spent—like the common law itself—secured to the bondman privileges unknown to the American slave—in certain cases of cruelty secured him from his master—prevented the separation of parents and children, also of brothers and sisters—and even protected him in his marriage relation ; and secondly, because the thirteen colonies were not derived from any of those countries which recognized the Roman law. Of course, the slave cannot be allowed to read, for to his soul would then expand in larger air, while he saw the glory of the North Star ; nor is it derived from the Mahomedan law ; for under the mild injunctions of the Koran, a benignant servitude, unlike yours, has prevailed—where the lash is not allowed to lacerate the back of a female ; where no knife or branding iron is employed upon any human being ; where the master is expressly enjoin-

THE

LINCOLN

CATECHISM

WHEREIN THE

Eccentricities & Beauties of Despotism

ARE FULLY SET FORTH.

A Guide to the Presidential Election of 1864

J. F. FEEKS, PUBLISHER,

No. 26 ANN STREET, N. Y.

---

12   THE LINCOLN

LESSON THE THIRD.

I.

Do loyal leaguers believe in the Ten Commandments?

They do.

II.

What are the Ten Commandments?

Thou shalt have no other God but the negro.

Thou shalt make an image of a negro, and place it on the Capitol as the type of the new American man.

Thou shalt swear that the negro shall be the equal of the white man.

Thou shalt fight thy battles on the Sabbath day, and thy generals, and thy captains, and thy privates, and thy servants, shall do all manner of murders, and thefts as on the other six days.

Thou shalt not honor nor obey thy father nor thy mother if they are Copperheads; but thou shalt serve, honor and obey Abraham Lincoln.

Thou shalt commit murder—of slaveholders.

Thou mayest commit adultery—with the contrabands.

Thou shalt steal—everything that belongeth to a slaveholder.

Thou shalt bear false witness—against all slaveholders.

Thou shalt covet the slave-holder's man-servant and his maid-servant, and shalt steal his ox and his ass, and everything that belongeth to him.

For on these commandments hang all the law and the honor of loyal leaguers.

CATECHISM.

III.

Do loyal leaguers believe the teachings of t gospel?

They do.

IV.

What does the gospel teach?

That we shall hate those who believe not with u and persecute those who never wronged us.

V.

What else does the gospel teach?

That we shall resist evil, and that we shall ove come evil with evil.

VI.

What does the gospel say of peace-makers?

That they shall be accursed.

VII.

Whose children are the peace-makers?

The children of the devil.

VIII.

Do Loyal Leagues believe in the Sermon on t Mount?

They do.

IX.

Repeat the Sermon on the Mount.

Blessed are the proud and the contractors, theirs is the kingdom of greenbacks.

Blessed are they that do not mourn for them th are murdered in the abolition war, for they shall comforted with office.

Blessed are the haughty, for they shall inherit sh plasters.

Artist unknown. *The Lincoln Catechism, Wherein the Eccentricities & Beauties of Despotism are Fully Set Forth,* 1864. Pamphlet; lithograph, J. F. Feeks, publisher. Gilder Lehrman Collection (GLC08632)

that met regularly and sent representatives to meetings of the Negro Convention Movement. The New York convention strongly supported the Liberty Party, an abolitionist political party organized in western New York in 1839. At its first national convention held in Albany, New York in the spring of 1840, the Liberty Party nominated James G. Birney, a Kentucky-born slaveholder-turned-abolitionist, as its candidate for U.S. president. Birney had been prosecuted in Ohio for sheltering a fugitive slave, giving him solid credentials with African Americans. John T. Raymond, a black Baptist minister attended the party convention and black newspapers endorsed the party's entire national slate, comparing Birney to the current Democratic President, Martin Van Buren. The *Colored American* saw Birney as "decidedly a better man in every possible respect to be President of the United States."[4]

Although the Liberty Party attempted to broaden its appeal to include class issues that attracted poor whites, it remained committed to antislavery. Jermain Wesley Loguen, a fugitive slave from Tennessee, who became pastor of a small black church in Bath, New York, became one of the party's most effective stump speakers. Party leaders found him so impressive that they allowed him to use his speeches to raise money for his church. Loguen incorporated stories about his years

FREEDOM TO THE SLAVES
Proclaimed January 1st 1863, by ABRAHAM LINCOLN, President of the United States.
"Proclaim liberty throughout All the land unto All the inhabitants thereof." ____ LEV. XXV. 10

Artist unknown. *Freedom to the Slaves...*, ca. 1865. Lithograph, Currier & Ives, publisher. 11 ¾ x 8 ⅝ in (29.85 x 21.90 cm). PR 052

Artist unknown. *Northern Coat of Arms*, 1864. Lithograph, 11 ¼ x 9 ¼ in (28.60 x 23.50 cm). Gift of Daniel Parish, Jr., PR 010

NORTHERN COAT OF ARMS.

in slavery into his party message, winning him many admirers. Of his presentation in Cortland, New York, one white observer wrote, "No prayer ever made in Cortland melted the people like that."[5]

Despite the enthusiastic support of African Americans and white abolitionists for the Liberty Party, the Whigs and Democrats controlled the White House for the next twenty years, from the election of 1840 until the 1860 election of Lincoln, the first Republican president. During this period as slavery expanded its political power, its opponents, black and white, became more militant in their

Kurz & Allison. *Storming Fort Wagner*, 1890. Chromolithograph. Library of Congress, LC-USZC4-507

(opposite page) Artist unknown. *Freedom to the Slave*, ca. 1863. Verso: text of "original version of the John Brown Song." Hand-colored lithograph, 9 ½ x 12 in (24.13 x 30.48 cm). William Gladstone Collection

attacks. In 1841 David Ruggles, an African American printer and journalist in New York City, announced plans for a convention of free blacks to be held in Buffalo, New York. In his article, published in Boston's radical abolitionist newspaper, the *Liberator*, he railed against what he called the "storm of colonization." He strongly condemned plans, advocated by some conservative-to-moderate antislavery advocates, to encourage the ending of American slavery by sending African Americans to the West African colony of Liberia, established by the American Colonization Society with federal financial assistance during the early 1820s. Then, he called for direct action against slavery, urging, "Rise brethren, rise! Strike for freedom or die slaves." He continued, "In our cause, mere words are nothing—action is everything."[6]

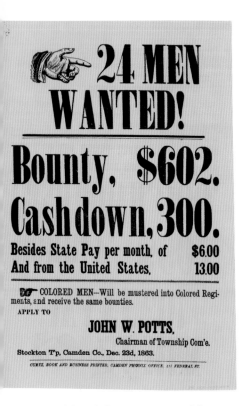

EXECUTION OF GORDON THE SLAVE-TRADER, NEW YORK, FEBRUARY 21, 1862.—[SEE PAGE 150.]

(above) "24 Men Wanted!" 1863. Letterpress poster, Curtz, printer. 15 ½ x 10 ³⁄₁₆ in (39.35 x 25.88 cm) PR 055

(right) Artist unknown. "Execution of Gordon the Slave Trader." Wood engraving, published in *Frank Leslie's Illustrated Newspaper*, February 21, 1862. *E171.L63

In the spring of 1843, the Negro Convention meeting in Buffalo took an equally strong antislavery stand that troubled many of even the most radical white abolitionists. On the second day of the convention, Henry Highland Garnet addressed the gathering with a rousing call to action. Garnet, who had been enslaved in Maryland, escaped to New York City where he attended the African Free School. While there, he became the leader of a group of African American students who vowed that after their education was completed, they would, "go South, start an insurrection and free our brethren in bondage."[7] In his speech to the convention, Garnet called for just such action. Conventioneers sat entranced by his words and his style. They suspended the time rules to allow him to speak for almost one and one-half hours.[8] Garnet proclaimed that black people had been patient long enough. "We have hoped in vain," he told the gathering. "However much you and all of us may desire it, there is not much hope of Redemption without the shedding of blood. If you must bleed, let it all come at once—rather, *die freemen, than live to be slaves.*" Now, he said, was the time for action.[9]

Slavery remained a major national issue through the 1840s and 1850s, becoming even more complex after the 1845 American victory in the Mexican War brought vast areas of the southwest under American control. National efforts at compromise in 1850 brought California into the Union as a free

(above) Photographer unknown. *Fred[erick]. Douglass (1817–95)*, undated. Albumen print, carte-de-visite, 3 ½ x 2 ⅛ in (8.89 x 5.40 cm). Gift of Mr. Rodman Gilder. PR 011

(left) Edwin White (1817–77). *Thoughts of Liberia, Emancipation*, 1861. Oil on canvas, 18 x 21 in. The Robert L. Stuart Collection, on permanent loan from the New York Public Library (S-200)

state and outlawed the slave trade in Washington, DC. It also left these southwestern territories open to slavery if American settlers so desired. In addition, this Compromise of 1850 established the harshest national fugitive slave provision ever written into American law. It provided virtually no rights to accused fugitives and severely punished anyone who assisted them or failed to aid in their capture.

The New York State Vigilance Committee, a group committed to the protection of fugitives, organized a major protest convention in opposition to this new law. The meeting was held in Cazenovia village, a well-known abolitionist center in the western area of the state known as the "Burned Over District," because of the fires of evangelical reform which were said to have burned over the region. More than two thousand people met in an orchard to hear fiery abolitionist speeches. Among those attending were a substantial number of fugitive slaves. Frederick Douglass, who escaped from Maryland in 1838, chaired the proceedings. By the time of the Cazenovia meeting he had become one of the most respected abolitionist speakers in the nation and editor of *North Star*, a weekly newspaper which he published in Rochester, also centered in the Burned Over District of western New York.[10]

Douglass's reaction to the new fugitive slave law serves as an instructive example of its impact on the African American and the abolitionist community. He had not voted to support Garnet's call for full-scale slave rebellion at the 1843 Buffalo Negro convention, largely because he feared such a public resolution might encourage violence against all blacks by police and military authorities. After the

View of Transparency

IN FRONT OF HEADQUARTERS OF SUPERVISORY COMMITTEE FOR RECRUITING COLORED REGIMENTS,

Chestnut Street, Philadelphia,

IN COMMEMORATION OF EMANCIPATION IN MARYLAND, NOVEMBER 1, 1864.

COME AND JOIN US BROTHERS.
PUBLISHED BY THE SUPERVISORY COMMITTEE FOR RECRUITING COLORED REGIMENTS
1210 CHESTNUT ST. PHILADELPHIA.

passage of the 1850 Fugitive Slave Law, however, he became much more outspoken. "The only way to make the fugitive slave law a dead letter," he argued, was "to make a few dead slave catchers."[11]

This willingness to use violence to protect fugitives became more widespread. The first fugitive to be captured and returned to slavery under the new law was Baltimore fugitive James Hamlet, apprehended in New York City in September of 1850. At a mass meeting protesting Hamlet's capture, an African American speaker urged the crowd to action. "My colored brethren, if you have not swords, I say to you, sell your garments and buy one. ..." Ultimately, Hamlet was freed without violence as New Yorkers raised $800 to purchase his freedom. A crowd of 5,000 well wishers celebrated when he returned to the city as a free man.[12]

In early October of 1851, while the Liberty Party was holding its New York State Convention in Syracuse, the police arrested a fugitive known as Jerry who worked as a barrel maker in the town. African Americans were determined to rescue him. Jermain Loguen addressed the Syracuse black community urging that they

Artist unknown. *Come and Join Us Brothers*, ca. 1863–64, Hand-colored lithograph, P. S. Duval & Son, lithographer; Supervisory Committee for Recruiting Colored Regiments, publisher, 10 ⅜ x 13 ¹¹⁄₁₆ in (26.35 x 34.77 cm). PR 068

(opposite page) Artist unknown. *View of Transparency in Front of Headquarters of Supervisory Committee for Recruiting Colored Regiments*, 1864. Hand-colored wood engraving, Ringwalt and Brown, printers, 11 ½ x 8 ½ in (29.21 x 21.60 cm). PR 068

Artist unknown. *Colored Pickets on Duty, near Dutch Gap*, ca. 1863. E. & H. T. Anthony & Co., publisher. Stereograph, 3 ⅛ x 6 ¼ in (7.94 x 15.88 cm). PR 164

Charles H. Rockwell, from an earlier daguerreotype. *"Old" John Brown*, 1859. Retouched photograph, D. Francis Bacon, publisher, 8 ⁵⁄₁₆ x 6 in (21.11 x 15.24 cm). PR 052

seek the assistance of the antislavery men of the Liberty Party. "Now is the time to try the spunk of white men," he argued, "I want to see whether they have courage only to make speeches and resolutions when there is no danger. Let us be here at nightfall, and if white men won't fight, let fugitives and black men smite down Marshals and Commissioner—anybody who holds Jerry—and rescue him or perish." At the appointed hour, church bells rang out, calling together a huge interracial crowd that freed Jerry and eventually transported him to the safety of Canada, injuring at least one deputy marshal in the process.[13]

These and other dramatic developments during this critical decade figured prominently in the selection of the field of presidential candidates in the 1860 election. In 1854, Congress adopted the Kansas Nebraska Act, which organized the Midwestern territory in preparation for construction of a transcontinental railroad. This highly controversial measure removed the regional restrictions imposed on slavery by the Missouri Compromise, infuriating all those opposed to slavery's expansion. No longer was it limited to the areas south of Missouri. This new measure allowed slavery's extension northward, into the Kansas and Nebraska territories, if a majority of voters there wanted it. Lincoln, who by 1854 had largely returned to his law practice after a brief political career in Illinois, strongly opposed slavery's continued expansion. His reaction to this measure sponsored by his Illinois political rival Stephen A. Douglas, fueled his

THE COLORED VOLUNTEER.

Thomas Nast (1840–1902). *The Colored Volunteer*, 1863. Lithograph, Currier and Ives, publisher. 15 ⁹⁄₁₆ x 13 ⅛ in (39.50 x 33.30 cm). PR 068

political reentry. Lincoln became one of the early members of the new Republican Party formed in 1854 from a broad coalition of political groups seeking to contain slavery.[14]

Meanwhile, proslavery and antislavery forces, each attempting to control the politics of the region, met in bloody conflict in the area which soon took on the name, "Bleeding Kansas." John Brown, a radical abolitionist from Connecticut, led antislavery troops into battle, executed at least five proslavery supporters, and became infamous in the South. Bleeding Kansas was a part of the explosion of violence that made the Compromise of 1850 increasingly untenable and moved the nation closer to civil war.

In New York all these developments exacerbated tensions already elevated by the new fugitive slave law of 1850. Even before the passage of that law abolitionists had organized groups to protect fugitive slaves seeking aid and protection in the state. In 1835, David Ruggles helped to organize the New York Vigilance Committee to shield fugitives from the slave catchers who roamed the streets of New York City hoping to collect rewards by capturing runaways. Ruggles also sheltered and assisted Frederick Douglass in his escape from slavery.[15]

Fugitives, however, were not the only blacks threatened by slave catchers. In his biography, *Twelve Years a Slave*, Solomon Northup, a New York free-born African American wrote of being kidnapped in 1841 and enslaved in Louisiana for twelve years before his wife secured his freedom with the aid of New York officials. Since the new fugitive slave law provided almost no right of defense for an accused fugitive, Northup's story, published in 1853, raised great concern among black New Yorkers and their white abolitionist allies. Abolitionists grew even more determined to protect fugitives. Still, during these insecure times, some blacks fled the state, resulting in a 8 percent decline in New York's African American population between 1850 and 1855. New York City lost 15 percent of its black population during the same period.[16]

For those African Americans who continued to live in New York, life remained complicated and often quite difficult. Throughout the state, blacks faced widespread discrimination in everything from public accommodations and transportation to education and social activities. Workplace discrimination was especially disruptive, limiting most of their occupational choices to those at the bottom of the wage scale. Although there were a few black professionals in the state, the vast majority who could find work were unskilled workers. In these jobs black workers competed largely with immigrants, in particular the poor unskilled immigrants who left Ireland in large numbers in the wake of the great potato famine of 1845. In the 1850s, only about 5½ percent of New York City's blacks

PRESENTATION OF COLORS TO THE 20TH U. S. COLORED INFANTRY, COL. BARTRAM, AT THE UNION LEAGUE CLUB HOUSE, N. Y., MARCH 5.—PAGE 7

held skilled jobs. White dockworkers forced the exclusion of most blacks from jobs on the docks. When, during the longshoremen's strike of 1855, management used a few blacks as strikebreakers, the situation exploded. Ultimately, the docks remained the haven of white workers.[17]

Despite the discrimination they faced, African Americans in New York State and New York City were able to establish communities built around churches, mutual aid societies, educational establishments, cultural institutions, and political organizations. These were the essential elements of community that sustained black New Yorkers, helping them to deal with the racial injustice prevalent throughout the North.[18]

Black New Yorkers also faced a complex and precarious situation in terms of their general citizenship rights. As they moved toward freedom during the early decades of the nineteenth century, their rights as potentially free citizens of New York became a topic of debate and concern among state officials. From the earliest years of the Revolution, a discussion of voting rights was part of New York's preparation for statehood. Its constitution of 1777 provided that any adult male with the equivalent of $50 in real property could vote for assemblymen or state representatives while those with the equivalent of $250 could vote for state senators

Artist unknown. "Presentation of Colors to the 20th U. S. Colored Infantry." Wood engraving, published in *Frank Leslie's Illustrated Newspaper*, March 26, 1864. *E171.L63

(opposite) *Presentation Address of the Ladies of the City of New York to the Officers and Men of the Twentieth United States Colored Troops*, 1863. Broadside. SY [1863–5]-22

and the governor. That provision was challenged by those New Yorkers who argued that voting was a natural right built into the status of citizenship and should be provided without regard to personal wealth or property holding.[19]

Some white New Yorkers grew increasingly concerned about the joint consequences of the state's property holding voting requirements and its plan for general emancipation. Since provisions did not specifically limit the franchise by race, as African Americans emerged from slavery, many might become property holders and thus qualified voters in the state. By 1820, New York's more than 39,000 blacks represented only 3 percent of the state's population, but their vote might be significant should, as most whites assumed, they vote as a block. This concern held sway in the state constitutional constitution of 1821, when delegates removed property requirements for white men. Simultaneously, they maintained and even increased requirements for black men, effectively barring almost all from the franchise.[20] As of 1825, only 298 New York African Americans held enough property to vote. Some legislators defended their actions by claiming that this new race-based franchise law might provide an incentive for blacks, emerging from slavery after 1827 to work hard and acquire property.[21]

Immediately, African Americans in New York organized to press for equal voting rights. As they supported the activities of the Liberty Party and other anti-slavery political efforts, they acquired the aid of white abolitionist allies. In 1846 Gerrit Smith, a wealthy white political abolitionist, announced his intention to provide land grants to temperate blacks of good character as a means of qualifying them as voters in New York State. He was assisted by black activists James McCune Smith and Charles B. Ray, who eventually distributed more than three thousand land titles for parcels of forty-to-sixty acres each. This act qualified thousands of new black voters.

The presidential election of 1860 was a complex and anxiety-producing event for the nation at large. It followed the violent decade that culminated with a Supreme Court decision in the 1857 Dred Scott case, which ruled that African Americans were not citizens of the United States and that the federal government had no right to outlaw slavery from the territories. Then, in 1859, white abolitionist John Brown and his interracial force attacked the federal arsenal at Harpers Ferry, Virginia to gather weapons to equip a Southern slave rebellion.[22]

The South felt threatened by what many saw as a far-ranging abolitionist threat evidenced by the support for John Brown's raid from prominent Northern abolitionists and influential businessmen. The Southern branch of the Democratic Party was determined that the president elected to office in 1860 must be devoted to the protection of slavery. Therefore, when the party chose Illinois Senator Stephen A. Douglas as its presidential nominee, Southern Democrats rebelled. They did not trust Douglas on the slavery question. In protest, they formed a new Southern

(opposite page) W. Roberts. *Proclamation of Emancipation By the President of the United States of America,* 1864. Engraving and lithograph with letterpress, C. A. Alvoid, printer, R. A. Dimmick, publisher, 22 ³⁄₁₆ x 17 ¼ in (56.36 x 43.82 cm). PR 068

PROCLAMATION OF EMANCIPATION

1861 — 1863

By the President of the United States of America.

Whereas, On the Twenty-Second day of September, in the year of our Lord one thousand eight hundred and sixty-two, a Proclamation was issued by the President of the United States, containing, among other things the following, to wit:

"That on the first day of January, in the year of our Lord one thousand eight hundred and sixty-three, all persons held as Slaves within any State or designated part of a State, the people whereof shall then be in rebellion against the United States, shall be then, thenceforth, and **FOREVER FREE,** and the EXECUTIVE GOVERNMENT OF THE UNITED STATES, including the military and naval authorities thereof, WILL RECOGNIZE AND MAINTAIN THE FREEDOM of such persons, and will do no act or acts to repress such persons, or any of them, in any efforts they may make for their actual freedom.

"That the Executive will, on the first day of January aforesaid, by proclamation, designate the States and parts of States, if any, in which the people thereof respectively shall then be in rebellion against the United States, and the fact that any State, or the people thereof shall on that day be in good faith represented in the Congress of the United States by members chosen thereto at elections wherein a majority of the qualified voters of such State shall have participated, shall, in the absence of strong countervailing testimony be deemed conclusive evidence that such State and the people thereof are not then in rebellion against the United States."

Now, therefore, I, ABRAHAM LINCOLN, PRESIDENT OF THE UNITED STATES, by virtue of the power in me vested as Commander-in-Chief of the Army and Navy of the United States in time of actual armed Rebellion against the authority and government of the United States, and as a fit and necessary war measure for suppressing said Rebellion, do, on this first day of January, in the year of our Lord one thousand eight hundred and sixty-three, and in accordance with my purpose so to do, publicly proclaim for the full period of one hundred days from the day of the first above-mentioned order, and designate, as the States and parts of States wherein the people thereof respectively are this day in rebellion against the United States, the following, to wit: ARKANSAS, TEXAS, LOUISIANA (except the Parishes of St. Bernard, Plaquemines, Jefferson, St. John, St. Charles, St. James, Ascension, Assumption, Terre Bonne, La Fourche, St. Mary, St. Martin, and Orleans, including the City of Orleans), MISSISSIPPI, ALABAMA, FLORIDA, GEORGIA, SOUTH CAROLINA, NORTH CAROLINA, AND VIRGINIA (except the forty-eight counties designated as West Virginia, and also the counties of Berkeley, Accomac, Northampton, Elizabeth City, York, Princess Ann, and Norfolk, including the cities of Norfolk and Portsmouth), and which excepted parts are for the present left precisely as if this Proclamation were not issued.

And by virtue of the power and for the purpose aforesaid, I do order and declare that **ALL PERSONS HELD AS SLAVES** within said designated States and parts of States ARE, AND HENCEFORWARD **SHALL BE FREE!** and that the Executive Government of the United States, including the Military and Naval Authorities thereof, will RECOGNIZE AND MAINTAIN THE FREEDOM of said persons.

And I hereby enjoin upon the people so declared to be free, to abstain from all violence, UNLESS IN NECESSARY SELF-DEFENCE, and I recommend to them that in all cases, when allowed, they LABOR FAITHFULLY FOR REASONABLE WAGES.

And I further declare and make known that such persons of suitable condition will be received into the armed service of the United States, to garrison forts, positions, stations, and other places, and to man vessels of all sorts in said service.

And upon this act, SINCERELY BELIEVED TO BE AN ACT OF JUSTICE, warranted by the Constitution, upon military necessity, I invoke the considerate judgment of mankind, and the gracious favor of ALMIGHTY GOD.

In testimony whereof I have hereunto set my name, and caused the seal of the United States to be affixed.

Done at the CITY OF WASHINGTON, this first day of January, in the year of our Lord one thousand eight hundred and sixty-three, and of the Independence of the United States the eighty-seventh.

[L. S.]

By the President.

William B. Seward
Secretary of State.

A. Lincoln

Edward Lamson Henry
(1841–1919). *Presentation of Colors
to the First Colored Regiment of New
York by the Ladies of the City in Front of
the Old Union League Club, Union
Square, New York City, in 1864,* 1869.
Oil on canvas, 14 ½ x 18 ¾ in
(36.83 x 47.63 cm). The Union
League Club, New York City

(opposite page) Artist unknown.
*Major Martin R. Delaney U.S.A.
Promoted on the Battle Field for Bravery,*
undated. Hand-colored
lithograph, Joseph Hoover,
publisher, 21 x 16 ¾ in (53.34 x
42.55 cm). PR 052

Democratic Party, nominating John C. Breckinridge of Kentucky as their presidential candidate. They found Breckinridge, who was then Vice President under Democratic President James Buchanan, far more acceptable on the slavery issue.

As the agitation over slavery became increasingly disruptive of national politics in 1860, threats by radicals in the Deep South to withdraw their regions from the United States raised great fear in the nation. Some border state politicians, hoping to quiet the issue, formed the Constitutional Union Party. This new compromise party nominated John Bell of Tennessee for U.S. president with Edward Everett of Massachusetts as his running mate for vice president. Although their candidates' selection was calculated to bridge the widening political gap in national politics, their attempt failed when the Republicans nominated Abraham Lincoln. Although Lincoln opposed the spread of slavery, he stated publicly that he recognized the constitutional right of slaveholders in the South to maintain and protect their human property. Still, Southerners regarded him as an abolitionist tool. They were sure that Republican power in the White House would endanger slavery.

Most Northern Democrats knew better, but they used Southern charges that Lincoln was an abolitionist to their political advantage. They sought to appeal to the immigrant vote and to inflame Northern fears that abolitionist influence in

Published by Joseph Hoover 712 Sansom Str Philad.a

MAJOR MARTIN R. DELANY U. S. A.

PROMOTED ON THE BATTLE FIELD FOR BRAVERY.

the Republican Party would lead to a racial confrontation as newly freed Southern blacks "invaded" the North.

Although black New Yorkers bristled at these Democratic political arguments, many were ambivalent about the Republican nomination of Lincoln. Surely he was better on slavery and other racial issues than the other candidates. Yet, he had made some disturbing public statements that raised questions about his racial beliefs. Just two years earlier, during his 1858 run for the U.S. Senate seat in Illinois, Lincoln had made racially charged statements, defending himself from the accusations of his opponent, Stephen A. Douglas. During the Senatorial debates of that year, Douglas had claimed that Lincoln believed in "a perfect equality between the [N]egroes and white people," even going so far as to charge that he favored interracial marriage. Lincoln made clear his stand for white supremacy: "I am not, nor ever have been, in favor of bringing about in any way the social and political equality of the white and black races." Then he spoke directly to Douglas's interracial marriage accusation. "I do not understand that because I do not want a [N]egro woman for a slave I must necessarily want her for a wife. My understanding is that I can just leave her alone."[23]

These statements and his willingness to engage in the telling of racially disparaging "darky jokes" convinced many blacks that Lincoln was not to be trusted as an advocate for racial justice. Further complicating their assessment was his support of colonization, the program that would remove free African Americas from America. Many blacks concurred with Thomas Hamilton's editorial in New York City's *Weekly Anglo-African* that a Lincoln-led federal government might only represent "the fag end of a series of pro-slavery administrations."[24]

No matter their misgivings, however, African Americans generally found Lincoln far more acceptable than the other choices for the 1860 presidency. The issue of slavery played a significant role in forming the field of candidates. All but Lincoln were committed to not only protecting slavery in the South, but also to allowing its expansion into the territories of the West, the region most Americans saw as the nation's future. Thus, given the slate of candidates, for the state's few African Americans voters, Lincoln seemed the only favorable choice. This impression was strengthened by a lecture he delivered in New York City early in the election year.

On February 27, 1860, a capacity crowd of 1,500 gathered at Cooper Union to attend Lincoln's lecture sponsored by the Young Men's Republican Union. In this one and one-half- hour speech, the longest of his political career, Lincoln examined the intentions of the Constitutional founders in establishing the authority of the federal government. In so doing, he leveled an attack on the Supreme Court ruling in the Dred Scott case that in addition to denying African American citizenship, ruled that the federal government had no power to prohibit

N.H Babcock.   G.Foster. W.H.Shelton. A.Foster.   C.J.Bulkley.   Servant.

slavery in the western territories. Lincoln asserted in powerful, yet simple and direct terms that the federal government did indeed have the right to regulate slavery and to limit its extension. This speech was an overwhelming success, exciting the audience and bringing many to their feet in approval. In the following day's *New York Tribune*, editor Horace Greeley commented, "No man ever before made such an impression on his first appeal to a New York audience"[25]

For most New York voters, however, the field was more competitive. Although neither Breckenridge nor Bell received support, the race was no runaway victory for Lincoln, who carried the election but received less than 40 percent of the national vote. He carried New York with 53.7 percent of the popular vote, but Douglas placed a reasonably close second with 46.3 percent of the state vote. As if to complicate matters, in addition to selecting a president, New York voters in 1860 were presented with a resolution to provide equal voting rights for the state's

Studio of Mathew B. Brady (ca. 1823–96). *Brady's Incidents of the War, Harper's Ferry and Vicinity, Virginia, 22nd Regiment NYSNG*, 1862. Albumen print, 10 ⅝ x 13 ⅝ in (26.99 x 34.61 cm). Gift of Louisa H. Clarke, Charles M. Ward, Henry Marion Ward, and William F. Ward, 1942, PR 164

Abraham Lincoln to Robert
Lincoln, July 14, 1863. Lincoln
Presidential Library, Springfield,
IL. Worried that his son—en
route to Washington from
Harvard—is caught in the New
York City draft riots, Lincoln
writes to Robert: *"Why do I hear no
more of you?"*

Washington. D. C.. July 14   1863

Rob't. T. Lincoln
New. York.
5th Av. Hotel—
Why do I hear no more
of you.?,

A. Lincoln

African Americans.[26] This volatile addition to the choices New Yorkers were
called upon to make seemed to play into the hands of the state's Democratic
efforts to alarm immigrant voters to what was presented as the potential dangers
of black political power. The resolution failed with almost 64 percent of voters
opposing it.

At a free suffrage convention in New York City, African Americans protested,
basing "our claim upon the principle of human freedom and equality—That
instrument [The Declaration of Independence] of which Americans are justly
proud."[27] With the election of Lincoln to the presidency, those principles were
about to be challenged in a civil war. When war broke out in the spring of 1861,
the migration of blacks from New York City, which had continued through the
1850s, came to a halt. Instead, blacks formed military clubs to ready themselves
to serve the nation in what they determined would ultimately be a war to end
slavery. African Americans in other Northern communities had formed similar
militia groups during the mid-1850s. In his first inaugural address, Lincoln had
assured slaveholders that he had no intention of interfering with the institution
in the places where it currently existed. The slaveholding South did not believe
him, however, and acted to defend slavery from what they assumed was a federal
attack. Yet when African Americans volunteered for U.S. military service, they
were turned down and told that this was a "white man's war" being waged only
to save the Union.

Partly in response to the human cost of the war, Lincoln changed this policy
with his Emancipation Proclamation in January 1863. The proclamation declared
free all slaves in the possession of those still in rebellion against the United States
and authorized the recruitment of African American troops into the U.S. military.
Black soldiers at all ranks received less pay, however, than their white counterparts.
This injustice angered African Americans who protested even as they prepared
themselves to answer Lincoln's call.[28] Federal war policy also angered many

working class whites. Their protest led to an explosion of racial violence in New York City. In March 1863, a new federal draft law targeting adult male citizens exempted those who could afford $300 to pay a substitute. This exemption of the wealthy outraged many working-class whites. Draftees were to be determined by a lottery, the first of which was held on Saturday, July 11, 1863. Reaction was swift and violent, resulting in a bloody draft riot, which quickly became a race riot. From July 13 to 16, the mob attacked blacks, lynching eleven, and destroying the Colored Orphan Asylum on Fifth Avenue.

This draft riot drove a great number of blacks from the city. Many joined the war effort, however, after Lincoln's proclamation made that possible. In February and April 1864, military commanders organized three black infantry units at Riker's Island and Hart's Island in New York harbor. These units saw significant combat in various regions of the South until honorably discharged and mustered out in the fall of 1865.[29] Despite continuing efforts, however, equal voting rights for New York blacks were not achieved until after the Civil War with the ratification of the Fifteenth Amendment to the U.S. Constitution in March 1870.[30]

Thus, life for African Americans in New York during the years of the Lincoln administration was strained and complex. Despite their misgivings about many of Lincoln's racial statements, blacks understood that he had done more to end slavery than any president before him. They were deeply saddened by his assassination in Washington by Southern sympathizer and actor John Wilkes Booth in April 1865 as the war ended. Their mourning turned to anger when New York's City Common Council voted to exclude blacks from Lincoln's funeral procession as it passed through the city. Frederick Douglass addressed a black crowd at the Cooper Union, denouncing the decision and calling it "the most disgraceful and scandalous proceeding ever exhibited by people calling themselves civilized."[31]

The pressure continued and intensified, with local African Americans and many of their white allies gaining support from Republican officials in Washington. Finally, the City Council relented, allowing some two thousand blacks to participate, although at the rear of the funeral procession. Lincoln's legacy was complex indeed. Under his administration, slavery had been severely weakened, and although the Thirteenth Amendment to the Constitution abolishing it altogether was not fully ratified until after his death, Lincoln had strongly supported it during his last days as president. While most blacks understood the limitations of the Emancipation Proclamation, his efforts on behalf of the constitutional destruction of the institution that had held millions of African Americans in bondage for more than two and a half centuries made him, for generations to come, the Great Emancipator.

NOTES

1   Leslie M. Harris, *In the Shadow of Slavery: African Americans in New York City, 1826–1863* (Chicago: University of Chicago Press, 2003).

2   The slave state of Arkansas joined the Union in 1836 followed by the free state of Michigan in 1837. Florida and Texas joined as slave states in 1845, balanced by Iowa in 1846 and Wisconsin in 1848, both free states.

3   James Oliver Horton and Lois E. Horton, *In Hope of Liberty: Culture, Community and Protest Among Northern Free Blacks, 1700–1860* (New York: Oxford University Press, 1997).

4   *Colored American*, April 18, 1840.

5   Catherine M. Hanchett, "Agitators for Black Equality and Emancipation: Cortland County, 1837–1855," (unpublished paper, n.d.), 91, on file at the Cortland Historical Society, Cortland, New York.

6   *Liberator*, August 13, 1841.

7   Alexander Crummell, *The Eulogy on Henry Highland Garnet, D.D.* (Washington, DC, 1882), 25

8   "Minutes of the National Convention of Colored Citizens, Held in Buffalo, 1843," in *Minutes of the Proceedings of the National Negro Conventions, 1830–1864*, ed. Howard Holman Bell (New York: Arno Press and the New York Times, 1969), 13.

9   Henry Highland Garnet, *Walker's Appeal, With a Brief Sketch of his Life, And Also Garnet's Address to the Slaves of the United States of America* (New York: J. H. Tobitt, 1848), 90–96.

10   Milton C. Sernett, *North Star Country: Upstate New York and the Crusade for African American Freedom* (Syracuse, NY: Syracuse University Press, 2002).

11   James Oliver Horton and Lois E. Horton, *Black Bostonians: Family Life and Community Struggle in the Antebellum North*, rev. ed. (New York: Holmes & Meier, 1999), 135.

12   Harriet A. Jacobs, *Incidents in the Life of a Slave Girl*, ed. Jean Fagan Yellin (Cambridge, MA: Harvard University Press, 1987 [1894]), 289, n5.

13   Jermain Wesley Loguen, *The Rev J. W. Loguen, As A Slave and As a Freeman: A Narrative of Real Life* (Syracuse, New York: J.G.K. Truair & Co., 1859), 302.

14   Members of the Liberty Party were among those who formed the Republican Party. Others included Know-Nothings, Whigs, Free Soilers, and some Northern Democrats.

15   Frederick Douglass, *Narrative of the Life of Frederick Douglass, An American Slave, Written by Himself* [1849], ed. and intro. David W. Blight (Boston: Bedford/St. Martin's, 2003).

16   Solomon Northup, *Twelve Years a Slave* (Buffalo: Derby, Orton, and Mulligan, 1853); Phyllis F. Field, *The Politics of Race in New York: the Struggle for Black Suffrage in the Civil War Era* (Ithaca: Cornell University Press, 1982), 36; Harris, *In the Shadow of Slavery*, 275. The New York State black population declined to 45,286 by 1855 and in New York City to 11,740.

17   Harris, *In the Shadow of Slavery*, 264–65.

18   Horton and Horton, *In Hope of Liberty*.

19   Field, *Politics of Race in New York*.

20   Lois E. Horton, "From Class to Race in Early America: Northern Post-Emancipation Racial Reconstruction," *Journal of the Early Republic* 19 (Winter 1999): 629–49; Charles Wesley, "Negro Suffrage in the Period of Constitution-Making, 1787–1865," *Journal of Negro History* 32, no. 2 (April 1947): 143–68; Leo H. Hirsch, "The Free Negro In New York," in "The Negro In New York, 1783–1865," *Journal of Negro History* 16, no. 4 (October 1931): 415–53.

21   Field, *Politics of Race in New York*, 36–37.

22   James Oliver Horton and Lois E. Horton, *Slavery and the Making of America* (New York: Oxford University Press, 2005). In 1859 the area in which Harpers Ferry is located was still part of Virginia. It became West Virginia in 1863 in order to remain part of the Union as Virginia seceded.

23   Fourth Debate with Stephen A. Douglas at Charleston, Illinois September 18, 1858, quoted

in James Oakes, *The Radical and the Republican: Frederick Douglass, Abraham Lincoln, and the Triumph of Antislavery Politics* (New York: W. W. Norton, 2007), 122.

24 *Weekly Anglo-African,* March 17, 1860.

25 Harold Holzer, *Lincoln at Cooper Union: The Speech That Made Abraham Lincoln President* (New York: Simon & Schuster, 2006), 157.

27 David N. Gellman and David Quigley, eds., *Jim Crow New York: A Documenatry History of Race and Citizenship, 1777–1877* (New York: New York University Press, 2003), 273.

28 A white private was paid $13 per month, $3 of which was provided as a uniform allowance. A black private was paid $10 per month minus $3 deducted for uniforms.

29 Frank Smith, ed., *Book of Names: United States Colored Troops* (Washington, DC: African American Civil War Memorial Freedom Foundation & Museum, 2007).

30 See Field, *Politics of Race In New York.*

31 Philip S. Foner, *History of Black Americans: From the Compromise of 1850 to the End of the Civil War* (Westport, CT: Greenwood Press, 1983), 449–50.

THE LINCOLN IMAGE:
MADE IN NEW YORK

HAROLD HOLZER

O N J U L Y 13, 1863, as anti-draft riots enveloped New York, threatening both the private property and physical safety of its pro-Union citizens, one particularly angry mob of marauders broke into a brownstone on Lexington Avenue between Forty-fourth and Forty-fifth streets. As the alarmed families of its pro-Lincoln residents, clothing dealer John Dowdey and coach manufacturer William L. Turner, took flight, intruders broke into every room of their dwellings. Before they set the homes on fire, "costly pianos were smashed to atoms with bludgeons and pickaxes," a newspaper reported, "stones were hurled through mirrors ... furniture was tossed from the windows ... [and] all the appliances of homes of comfort were ruthlessly, wantonly destroyed."[1]

Among the casualties that night were images. One eyewitness to the terror watched in astonishment as "elegant pictures" were "torn from the walls, and after having been cut and destroyed, hurled into the street." Photographs were ripped from their albums, or seized from parlor tables, and "stereoscopes were cast out into the crowd" below. And then, the onlooker reported this remarkable incident: "One fellow appeared at a window with a picture of the President, spat on it, split it over his knee and hurled it into the street, where it was quickly trampled into atoms."[2] Here is the only known testimony in the entire literature of Lincoln iconography describing an act of violence directed against a Lincoln image. And it occurred in New York.

Aside from this remarkable story, precious little evidence exists to detail, much less explain, the precise use to which their owners put popular prints of Abraham Lincoln during the Civil War.[3] Scholars since have either disputed or elaborated on historian Robert Philippe's convincing 1980 speculation that political pictures

Mathew B. Brady (ca. 1823–96). *Abraham Lincoln*, Washington, DC, January 8, 1864. Published in Meserve Historical Portraits. Albumen silver print from glass negative, 3 ¼ x 2 ⅛ in (8.26 x 5.40 cm). PR 231

became far more meaningful than mere home decorations, evolving into "heirs of the sacred picture" by attaining honored places in the American family parlor.⁴ That makes it doubly ironic that this rare Draft Riot report, from a city that arguably provided the public with more Lincoln images than any other metropolis, attests neither to their production nor veneration, but to their desecration. As Philippe and other historians have accurately commented, political graphics testified powerfully to their owners' political beliefs—and, evidently, to their violent opposition as well.

We have no way of knowing precisely which Lincoln images perished on that turbulent July night. But we do know that the act of iconoclasm that terrorized Lexington Avenue was hardly enough to inhibit local publishers from churning out additional Lincoln portraits in the months and years to come, or to discourage Lincoln's admirers from purchasing them. These pictures were created to pay tribute to the president as an emancipator, to supply banners and posters for his 1864 re-election campaign, and then in 1865 to hail him as a martyred hero. During these periods of particularly high demand for Lincoln imagery—just as for those that had come earlier (triggered by his first White House campaign and his unexpected post-election decision to alter his appearance by growing whiskers)—New York printmakers produced a veritable gallery of mass-produced pictures for every taste, every budget, and notably, for every political persuasion. And, as the rioters' actions in 1863 show, they were capable of stirring a highly emotional response.

The one group that brought little emotion to the enterprise were the picture-makers themselves. For while New York's engravers and lithographers may have helped introduce Lincoln to America, they did not do so out of political sympathy with the man or his cause. Their motivation was strictly commercial: to satisfy consumer demand and profit from the public hunger for his image, as well as for those of his opponents. New York-made Lincoln prints—engravings and lithographs, both reverential and comic alike—testify not to Lincoln's popularity in the city, but to the robust publishing industry that flourished here and found a ready national market for its products.

Lincoln himself was no stranger to New York City. On February 27, 1860, he enjoyed an enormous success here with a lecture at Cooper Union that transformed him practically overnight into a serious contender for the Republican presidential nomination. *New York Tribune* editor Horace Greeley, who reprinted the full text of the address the next morning, was not alone in declaring of that oratorical triumph: "No man ever before made such an impression on his first appeal to a New-York audience."⁵

Importantly, that original "impression" was further, and even more widely, disseminated, not in words alone, but through pictures. That is principally because Mathew Brady took Lincoln's photograph earlier the same day at his Broadway

Artist unknown. *Brady's New Daguerreotype Saloon, New York*, 1853. Wood engraving, published in *The Illustrated News*, June 11, 1853. 5 ⅞ x 9 ⁹⁄₁₆ in (14.92 x 24.29 cm). PR 020

gallery (see frontispiece to book, page ii), making sure first to tug up his subject's shirt collar to conceal his long, scrawny neck, and to move his camera back in order to capture the subject's imposing physique. The result proved so flattering, and so widely reproduced during the presidential campaign to come, that Brady convincingly claimed later that it "was the means of his election."[6] Lincoln himself, on his second introduction to the photographer the following February, agreed, at least according to Brady's own recollection, that the Cooper Union picture had indeed helped make him president.[7] In fact, during the rowdy 1860 presidential campaign, during which the Republican candidate, true to period tradition, stayed at home and did no campaigning of his own, such images had "appeared" in his place as surrogates: affixed to walls, toted at rallies and parades, and distributed in bulk by political clubs for home display.

Testifying to the infant nature of the photography medium itself, it should be noted that the Brady original, famous as it later became as an illustration in biographies and history books, actually made surprisingly little impact at the outset as an independent image. Five weeks after the New York sitting, copies had apparently still not been circulated nationally. When a Poughkeepsie admirer wrote in April to ask Lincoln for his most recent photographic portrait, the candidate had to admit: "I have not a single one now at my control," adding: "I think you can easily get one at New-York. While I was there I was taken to one of the places where they get up such things, and I suppose they got my shaddow [sic], and can multiply copies indefinitely."[8] The truth is, they could *not*. The mass-produced little photographs that came to be known as *cartes-de-visite* would not be introduced to America until early the next year—*after* the presidential campaign had ended.[9] But as he had done throughout his career, the entrepreneurial Brady did make

Artist unknown, after a photograph by Mathew B. Brady. "Hon. Abraham Lincoln, Born in Kentucky, February 12, 1809." Wood engraving, published in *Harper's Weekly*, November 10, 1860. 15 ¾ x 11 in (40.01 x 27.94 cm). Gift of Harry T. Peters, PR 052

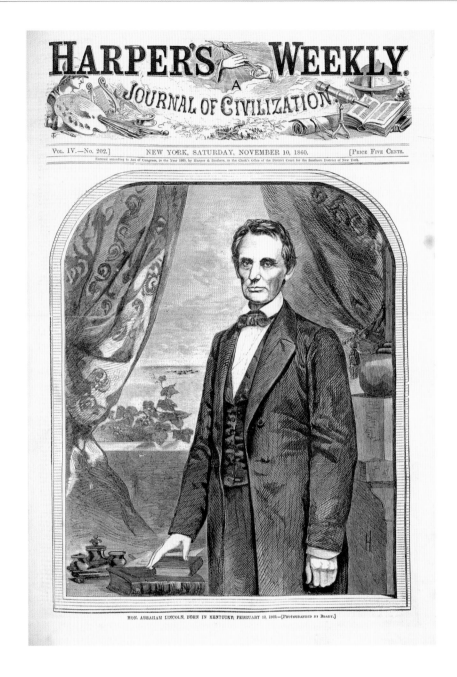

certain that his Lincoln portrait did achieve wide circulation—by partnering with many local publishers to ensure its adaptation, reproduction, and wide circulation in other media.

Then, as now, New York City could claim to be the publishing center of the nation. Not only did it boast some of the country's most influential daily newspapers —Greeley's *Tribune,* the *New York Times, Evening Post, World,* and *Herald* among them—a survey of newspapers listed in city directories in the New-York Historical Society shows a total of 174 New York dailies, weeklies, and monthlies in operation there on the eve of the 1860 presidential campaign.[10] New York was home, too, to a number of illustrated weekly papers that brought portraits and caricatures into American homes on a regular basis. The heavyweight periodicals,

Frank Leslie's Illustrated Newspaper, Vanity Fair, and *Harper's Weekly,* were augmented by smaller, but inventive publications like the *New-York Illustrated News, Comic Monthly, Frank Leslie's Budget of Fun, Nick Nax, Merryman's Monthly, Momus, Yankee Notions,* and *Phunny Phellow.*[11]

All the picture weeklies published woodcut portraits of Lincoln in 1860 to introduce him both to New York and to a nationwide readership curious about the dark horse candidate's appearance and political views. They issued derisive caricatures as well, humorously exaggerating Lincoln's great height and frontier roots, and assailing him as a covert friend of the African American. As *Leslie's,* in particular, made clear to its readers and advertisers, such papers prided themselves on avoiding "political bias" that might lead to their "utter exclusion from the whole South." *Leslie's* boasted: "Our Artists and Correspondents are cordially received in the South, and *in our columns alone* will be found correct representations of what is daily transpiring in that section of the country."[12] It was no wonder that these New York-based weeklies published more Lincoln lampoons than straightforward portraits.

The rush of Lincoln images began in May, once Lincoln unexpectedly won the Republican presidential nomination, unleashing the first outpouring of demand for his pictures. Within days, *Harper's* issued a woodcut based on Brady's Cooper Union photograph, with buffalo visible grazing in the background, a none-too-subtle reference to the nominee's western roots.[13] Artists rushed out lampoons showing Lincoln wearing homespun and clutching frontiersman's tools. With such emblematic pictures in mind, the *New York Times* criticized the earliest representations of Lincoln "in various picturesque attitudes as a rail-splitter and as a guider of oxen" to be "very silly, and we cannot help thinking very useless." Voters would not be persuaded, it warned, by an emphasis on "the exploits of 'Honest Old Abe' with a maul and a wedge."[14] The *Times* could not have been more wrong.

Not that such admonitions dissuaded the picture makers. Nor were newspaper illustrations the only means at Brady's disposal to promulgate his Lincoln image. New York housed not only the country's premier photographers and newspapers, but also its most prolific publishers of separate sheet popular prints—the kind of display items that so incensed the rioters three years later. These engravers and lithographers thrived in the small two- and three-story buildings huddled along Nassau, Fulton, Ann, and Howard Streets in the shadow of Newspaper Row, not far from City Hall. By the midpoint of the Civil War, New York housed a staggering number of firms engaged in the picture trade: twenty-three card engravers, fifty-three general engravers, six bank note engravers, four map engravers, nine stencil engravers, thirteen "historical engravers," fifteen envelope makers, thirty-five wood engravers, and forty-five lithographers—along with affiliated businessmen who published their art or supplied their industry, one hundred ninety-five printers, seven printing-press makers, and four importers of lithographic stones.[15]

THE RAIL CANDIDATE.

Artist unknown. *The Rail Candidate*, 1860. Lithograph, Currier & Ives, publisher, 9¾ x 14 ⅞ in (24.77 x 37.28 cm). PR 010

Among the most successful of all the picture-makers were the storied lithographers Nathaniel Currier and James Merritt Ives of Nassau Street, who grandly—but justifiably—advertised their shop as "The Grand Central Depot for Cheap and Popular Pictures." During the Civil War, Currier & Ives was the sole printmaker in the city business directory to list itself under a singular new category: "print publisher."[16] No one disputed its claim. The firm published hundreds of hand-colored images of pretty girls, adorable pets, calamities and disasters, epic historic events, bucolic landscapes, genre scenes—and with these, both flattering political portraiture and acidic political caricature. Its medium-folio prints sold for but twenty cents each, with attractive discounts available in bulk (three dollars for fifty prints), postage extra.[17] Seizing on the hometown Brady photograph as a model, Currier & Ives created handsome introductory Lincoln portraits as well as pro- and anti-Lincoln campaign cartoons, many showing an axe- or rail-toting Lincoln wearing informal, open-neck shirts, yet with a face often modeled on Brady's elegant original photograph.[18]

Such cartoons could be rude, crude, occasionally racist, and were seldom displayed at home, but rather distributed at campaign headquarters and rallies, and probably pasted mischievously onto neighborhood walls and fences. That they also

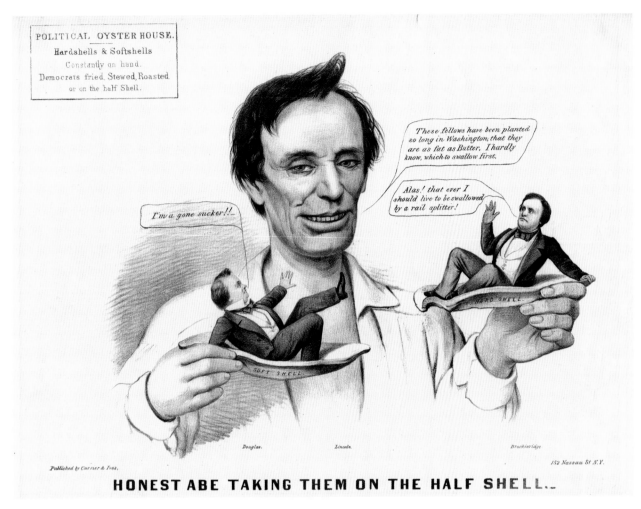

HONEST ABE TAKING THEM ON THE HALF SHELL.

inhabited shop windows on the best New York boulevard was acknowledged by an 1860 visitor from England. Filing a dispatch for Charles Dickens's weekly, *All the Year Round*, the British correspondent reported:

> All the way up Broadway the windows of the palatial shops are full of election caricatures. Yankee Notions shows us a rowdy in a silk hat, and boots over his trousers, taking boxing lessons ready for polling-day. Nick Nax presents us with Abe Lincoln spouting from a platform of rails, under which grins a half-concealed [slave]. ... At the print-shops we see [Currier & Ives's] lithographs of Douglas being flogged by his mother for associating with the naughty "[Kansas-] Nebraska Bill," and on the other side of the door-post, a gaunt Abraham Lincoln trying top ford the Potomac and get into a very small "White House."[19]

Lacking such period accounts, early scholars of period printmaking too often argued erroneously that Currier & Ives "played no inconsiderable part in the election of Mr. Lincoln," forgetting that such firms also issued assaultive cartoons like the ones described above.[20] Competitors did likewise, though we still tend primarily to recall and reprint the portraiture. In the latter category, local

Artist unknown. *Honest Abe Taking Them on the Half Shell*, 1860. Lithograph, Currier & Ives, publisher, 14 ¼ x 9 ¹⁄₁₆ in (36.20 x 23.02 cm). PR 010

"UNCLE SAM" MAKING NEW ARRANGEMENTS.

Published by Currier & Ives. 152 Nassau St N.Y.

engravers Edward H. Ensign, Erastus C. Bridgman, and Thomas C. Fanning, whose headquarters was on William Street, adapted the Brady photograph in color and placed it within a rural setting complete with the now-ubiquitous buffalo roaming outside. John Chester Buttre of Franklin Street issued yet another version, advertising it as "The Dime Picture of Abraham Lincoln," which he promoted as "Beautifully engraved on steel, and printed on the finest enamel card … neatly enclosed in an envelope, ready for delivery, or to send by mail," advising: "Every member of the LINCOLN CLUBS throughout the United States should possess a copy of this little gem."[21]

Before long so many of these adaptations had flooded the marketplace that New York engraver Alexander Hay Ritchie, whose firm occupied space at 442 Broadway, wrote directly to the Republican candidate to propose something less redundant. "We would use Brady's likeness," wrote Ritchie, "were it not that it has been already extensively copied & caricatured & we wish something different." Could not the candidate "get an Ambrotype or Daguerreotype taken by one of the best operators as near you as may be convenient?"[22] Apparently he could not. Bowing to opportunity over originality, Ritchie had little choice but to issue his own adaptation of the same image he had hoped to replace, though at least Lincoln's assistant private secretary John Hay later judged "Ritchie's reproduction of Brady's photograph the Cooper one the best thus far."[23]

To his credit, one New York print publisher did invest considerable time and money to create something altogether new. In early June, William H. Schaus & Co. of 749 Broadway paid the young artist Thomas Hicks to travel all the way to Springfield, Illinois to paint a new portrait of Lincoln that could be made into a fresh campaign lithograph. Hicks's oil on canvas turned out to be the first painting for which the candidate ever sat, and when it was brought back East lithographer Leopold Grozelier promptly copied it for a large and handsome print. "We have at last a respectful likeness of Lincoln," one newspaper declared after seeing it. "It is a splendid lithograph from the painting by Hicks… a good picture. There seems to have been a vigorous rivalry among portraitists and cartoonists in making Lincoln appear the ugliest of living men. Some of them show a coarse wrinkled personage, who does not look as if a gleam of good nature or common sense ever disturbed him. In Hicks' portrait, we have a more pleasing as well as a more accurate painting." Lincoln himself laughingly agreed with at least half of this assessment. "I think the picture has a somewhat pleasanter expression than I usually have," he told the artist, "but that, perhaps is not an objection."[24]

In a return to reliance on Brady's irresistible "Cooper Union" model, mapmaker Henry H. Lloyd of Howard Street—specialists in large wood-engraved posters on cheap paper, which, in their various iterations, featured both Democratic and Republican candidates—issued several "political charts" showing not only the rival aspirants for national office but also providing the texts of the party platforms, as well as vital statistical data about the sharply divided Northern and Southern states. Such publications offered more than propaganda—they all but supplied voters with educations. That they influenced viewers is documented by one of the most famous of all Lincoln stories. As it happened, the little girl who first wrote to Lincoln suggesting he grow a beard to improve his appearance—Grace Bedell of upstate Westfield, New York—was inspired to compose her letter after seeing

A. Lincoln

J[ohn]. C[hester]. Buttre (1821–93), engraver, after photograph by Mathew B. Brady (ca. 1823–96). A[braham]. Lincoln, 1860. Steel engraving, 11 ⅝ x 8 ½ in (29.53 x 21.6 cm). PR 052

(next page) Advertisement for works published by J. C. Buttre, 1860. Harold Holzer Collection

PORTRAITS AND SKETCHES

OF THE

Hon. J. C. BRECKINRIDGE

AND THE

Hon. JOSEPH LANE.

IN ONE NEAT 8vo. PRICE 25 CTS.

IT CONTAINS

TWO PORTRAITS BEAUTIFULLY ILLUSTRATED ON STEEL, FACTS IN THE LIFE
OF EACH, THE NATIONAL DEMOCRATIC PLATFORM , THE
CINCINNATI PLATFORM, AND

THE CONSTITUTION OF THE UNITED STATES.

Published by J. C. BUTTRE,

48 FRANKLIN STREET, NEW-YORK.

Copies sent by mail, postage prepaid, on receipt of the price.

AGENTS WANTED.

THE DIME PICTURE

OF

Hon. ABRAHAM LINCOLN,

Beautifully engraved on steel, and printed on the finest enamel
card, about 4 x 6 inches in size. It is neatly enclosed in an envelope, ready for delivery, or to send by mail.

Every member of the LINCOLN CLUBS throughout the United
States should possess a copy of this little gem.

It is sent free by mail on receipt of the price,

ONE DIME.

Engraved and Published by J. C. BUTTRE,

48 Franklin Street, New-York.

☞ A GOOD PICTURE FOR AGENTS TO SELL.

ABRAHAM LINCOLN.

THE STANDARD PORTRAIT—NOW READY.

PAINTED FROM LIFE, AT THE WHITE HOUSE, IN 1864,

BY F. B. CARPENTER.

And Magnificently reproduced on Steel, in Line and Stipple,

BY F. HALPIN.

SIZE OF SHEET, 24 BY 30 INCHES.

For *six months* MR. CARPENTER was an inmate of the WHITE HOUSE, studying the *countenance* and *character* of President Lincoln. His great painting,

"The First Reading of the Emancipation Proclamation,"

engraved upon Steel by A. H. RITCHIE, of which engraving thousands have been sold, with an increased demand since the reduction in price by the undersigned; and his book, "SIX MONTHS AT THE WHITE HOUSE," attest the closeness of his intercourse with Mr. Lincoln and the fidelity of his study. Carpenter's "Lincoln" must soon become a household word. It is

THE FAVORITE PORTRAIT OF THE LINCOLN FAMILY.

The following distinguished persons were painted from life by Mr. Carpenter: Millard Fillmore, Franklin Pierce, John Tyler, Wm. L. Marcy, Wm. H. Seward, Lewis Cass, Salmon P. Chase, Sam Houston, Edwin M. Stanton, Gideon Welles, Schuyler Colfax, Edward Bates, Caleb Cushing, Montgomery Blair, John C. Fremont, Horace Greeley, Gov. Myron H. Clark, Judge Stephen J. Field, Dr. Lyman Beecher, Henry Ward Beecher, Rev. Drs. Cox, Field, Storrs, Bacon, Bushnell, John Pierpont, and many others.

From the Publisher of the "New York Tribune."

I well remember the occasion of Mr. Lincoln's sitting to you, at which I was present. * * * Mr. Lincoln then made this remark: "I feel that there is more of me in this portrait than in any representation which has ever been made." I think these were his very words.

Truly yours,   SAMUEL SINCLAIR.

From MRS. LINCOLN.

F. B. CARPENTER: *My Dear Sir—* * * * I write you to-day to thank you for the most perfect likeness of my beloved husband that I have ever seen. The resemblance is so accurate in Mr. Halpin's engraving that it will require far more calmness than I can now command to have it placed continually before me. * * * Very truly your friend,   MARY LINCOLN.

From MR. ROBERT T. LINCOLN.

MR. F. B. CARPENTER: *My Dear Sir—*I received your letter and engraving several days ago, and I beg you to excuse my delay in acknowledging your kindness. Mr. Halpin has had most extraordinary success in engraving your portrait of my father, and has made the best likeness that I have seen. I do not know that I can express my idea of it better than by saying that I am perfectly satisfied with it as a likeness. Mr. Marshall made a very good picture, but there is something unsatisfactory about it which I can not explain, and I would have no hesitation in choosing between the two. Mr. Fuller, one of the gentlemen in whose office I am studying, who was an old personal friend of my father, was about purchasing Marshall's portrait, but on seeing this, immediately said that yours was the one he wanted. Speaking on the subject a day or two afterward, he said that your picture left a satisfied impression on his mind, which Marshall's, though pleasing while he was looking at it, did not. I mention this to show what is thought of your engraving by the only one of my father's personal friends who has seen it. * * * Please accept my thanks, and my heartiest wishes for the success which your work merits.   Very sincerely yours,   ROBERT T. LINCOLN.

From HON. WM. H. HERNDON, *for twenty years Mr. Lincoln's law-partner.*

MR. F. B. CARPENTER: *My Dear Sir—* * * * I received per express, yesterday morning, your admirable and exquisite engraving by Halpin. When I opened the box and unrolled the portrait, Mr. Lincoln *flashed* on me as never from picture. As a portrait—a likeness—it is Lincoln. His head rests naturally, easily, symmetrically on his shoulders; his hair parted upon

Thomas Hicks (1823–90). *Portrait of Abraham Lincoln*, 1860. Oil on canvas, 24 ⁹⁄₁₆ x 19 ½ in (62.39 x 49.53 cm). Chicago History Museum

(previous page) Advertisement for engraving of Abraham Lincoln portrait by F. B. Carpenter, ca. 1865. Harold Holzer Collection

one of Lloyd's posters, *The National Republican Chart*, at a local fairgrounds. Though Lloyd's advertisements for the twenty-five-cent broadside boasted of "Life-Like Portraits…in a vignette of log rails," and predicted that "200,000 Republicans" (later two *million!*) would buy it and be inspired to vote for Lincoln,[25] Grace Bedell concluded that it made the nominee's face appear too "thin."

After cutting out Lincoln's portrait as a keepsake, Grace wrote to tell him: "If you … let your whiskers grow … You would look a great deal better. … All the ladies like whiskers and they would tease their husband's [sic] to vote for you and then you would be President."[26] This was another New York invitation Lincoln usefully accepted, though he first wrote Grace a famous letter to the contrary. "As to the whiskers," he asked her, "never having worn any, do you not think people

Leopold Grozelier, after Thomas Hicks, *Hon. Abraham Lincoln*, 1860. W. H. Schaus, publisher. Lithograph, 26 ⅞ x 20 ⅝ in (54.46 x 41.59 cm). PR 052

would call it a piece of silly affect[at]ion if I were to begin it now?"[27] Yet within a month, once elected to the White House, the "silly piece of affectation" was seen sprouting from his face. Thus, a New York-made image actually inspired Lincoln to *change* that image and transform himself from the rugged frontiersman whose inspiring rise from poverty helped him win the presidency, into an avuncular statesman who now appeared more capable of leading the nation through the worst crisis of its history.

In the end, of course, votes speak louder than both words and pictures. In 1860, the same year he allegedly won the hearts of New York City at Cooper

Grace Bedell to Abraham Lincoln, October 15, 1860. Burton Historical Collection, Detroit Public Library. *"I have got 4 brothers and part of them will vote for you any way and if you let your whiskers grow I will try and get the rest of them to vote for you you would look a great deal better for your face is so thin...."*

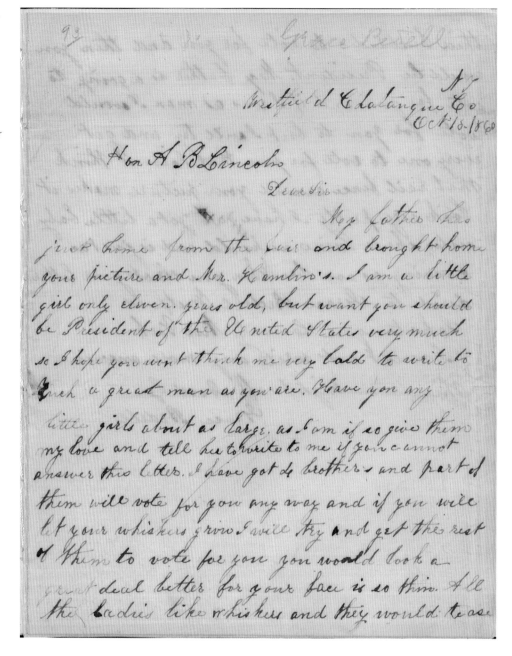

Union, and the attention of New York printmakers soon thereafter, the city overwhelmingly rejected Lincoln on Election Day. Democrat Stephen A. Douglas beat him by 24,000 votes in Manhattan, by 5,000 in Brooklyn, and by 2,500 in Westchester.[28] Ironically, Lincoln fared much better upstate, where he had never spoken a word. But there, a rugged adaptation of a tousle-haired Lincoln in an 1857 Chicago-made photograph had been adapted for a sheet music cover by publishers Blodgett & Bradford in Buffalo; it was reproduced as a portrait by Illinois engraver Thomas Doney and published by William Pate of 16 Burling Slip in Manhattan. Lincoln evidently liked this image, though his wife objected to "the disordered condition of the hair."[29] Excusing himself as a "very indifferent judge" of his own portraits, Lincoln nevertheless wrote the engraver to declare

their husbands to vote for you and then you would be President. My father is a going to vote for you and if I was a man I would vote for you to but I will try and get every one to vote for you that I can I think that rail fence around your picture makes it look very pretty I have got a little baby sister she is nine weeks old and is just as cunning as can be. When you direct your letter diret to Grace Bedell Westfield Chatauque County New York I must not write any more answer this letter right off Good bye

Grace Bedell

the "picture (I know not the artistic designation) … a very excellent one."[30]

Perhaps the lopsided vote on Election Day helps explain Lincoln's apparent reluctance to return to New York City once president. After his inauguration, the greatest figure of the Civil War would never make another public appearance in the Union's largest state. But before he assumed office, the train carrying Lincoln to Washington for his swearing-in did pause at Grace Bedell's tiny village on February 16, 1861. There, Lincoln devoted his very first speech in New York State as president-elect to acknowledging her influence on his very visible image transformation:

Some three months ago, I received a letter from a young lady here…she advised

160   HARPER'S WEEKLY.   [MARCH 9, 1861.

THE FLIGHT OF ABRAHAM.
(As Reported by a Modern Daily Paper.)

(1.) THE ALARM.

"On Thursday night, after he had retired, Mr. LINCOLN was aroused, and informed that a stranger desired to see him on a matter of life and death. * * * A conversation elicited the fact that an organized body of men had determined that Mr. LINCOLN should never leave the City of Baltimore alive. * * * Statesmen laid the plan, Bankers indorsed it, and Adventurers were to carry it into effect."

(2.) THE COUNCIL.

"Mr. LINCOLN did not want to yield, and his friends cried with indignation. But they insisted, and he left."

(3.) THE SPECIAL TRAIN.

"He wore a Scotch plaid Cap and a very long Military Cloak, so that he was entirely unrecognizable."

(4.) THE OLD COMPLAINT.

"Mr. LINCOLN, accompanied by Mr. SEWARD, paid his respects to President BUCHANAN, spending a few minutes in general conversation."

me to let my whiskers grow, as it would improve my personal appearance; acting partly upon her suggestion, I have done so; and now, if she is here, I would like to see her.[31]

Of course, she *was* there—along with most of her village. Excited onlookers located Grace and urged her toward the tracks. Lincoln stepped from his train, and "gave her several hearty kisses … amid … yells of delight from the … crowd."[32] It was an auspicious New York debut for the president-elect. But when he reached the pro-Democratic state capital, he received a rather chillier reception—which one eyewitness actually attributed to the robust circulation of his engravings and lithographs. "Lincoln, tired, sunburned, adorned with huge whiskers," journalist Henry Villard observed, "looked so unlike the hale, smooth shaven, red-cheeked individual who is represented upon the popular print … that it is no wonder that the people did not recognize him until his extreme height distinguished him unmistakably."[33]

Reaching Manhattan the next day, February 19, 1861, Lincoln was greeted more coldly still by a smaller-than-expected crowd, notwithstanding his triumphant Cooper Union experience the year before. Eyewitness Walt Whitman remembered feeling mortified by the absence of what he called "the glad exulting thunder-shouts of countless unloos'd throats of men." On the other hand, the poet was relieved that no "outbreak or insult" had occurred, for as he put it, Lincoln "possess'd no personal popularity in New York and not much political." Besides, as Whitman contended, probably with a bit of hyperbole, "many an assassin's knife and pistol lurked in hip or breast pocket" that New York day.[34]

Behind this frigid New York welcome lay even colder frost. At a City Hall reception the next morning, Lincoln felt compelled to announce: "There is nothing that can ever bring me willingly to consent to the destruction of the Union, under which not only the commercial city of New York, but the whole country has acquired its greatness."[35] As the president-elect well knew, Mayor Fernando Wood had been encouraging the metropolis to secede and become an international port so it could maintain profitable trade with the slave states. It was remembered that Lincoln responded privately to this news by drawling: "I reckon that it will be some time before the front door sets up housekeeping on its own terms."[36] None of this tension was visible in the wood-engravings published in *Harper's Weekly* and the *New York Illustrated News*: depictions of his arrival at the Astor House, his maiden speech from the hotel's second-floor balcony, and his visit to City Hall for the reception with the Mayor. Just as Lincoln predicted, New York indeed remained part of the State. Printmakers like Currier & Ives meanwhile heralded Lincoln's recent image metamorphosis by publishing allegedly "new" prints of the be-whiskered leader, more often than not outdated campaign portraits with guesswork

(opposite page) Artist unknown. "The Flight of Abraham. (As Reported by a Modern Daily Paper.)" Wood engraving, published in *Harper's Weekly*, March 9, 1861. 10 ¹³⁄₁₆ x 9 ⁹⁄₁₆ in (27.46 x 24.29 cm). PR 010

Artist unknown. *Abraham Lincoln*, undated. Engraving, John Chester Buttre, publisher, 29 ⅝ x 22 ⁵⁄₁₆ in (75.25 x 55.67 cm). PR 052

beards haphazardly superimposed.[37]

Lincoln's sudden transformation from clean-shaven politician to bewhiskered president found perhaps its most bizarre representation in an extraordinary New York print that had come of the presses of William Pate's publishing house more than a decade earlier. Back in 1850, Pate issued a timely print entitled *Union* that celebrated that year's historic Congressional compromises on slavery, and paid

Artist unknown. *Abraham Lincoln*, undated. Mezzotint, John Chester Buttre, publisher, 25 ¹¹⁄₁₆ x 18 ¹¹⁄₁₆ in (65.25 x 47.47 cm). Gift of Samuel V. Hoffman, PR 052

tribute to its authors, including Henry Clay, Daniel Webster, and John C. Calhoun. Ten years later, during the 1860 presidential campaign, Pate burnished out the face of the now-deceased (not to mention unmarketable) Calhoun and replaced the old secessionist's portrait with that of Republican presidential candidate Lincoln, now shown incongruously dressed in Calhoun's flowing robes and inexplicably posing alongside his late hero, Clay. Now, another year later in 1861,

Pate produced one final incarnation of the hopelessly outdated print, with Lincoln now bearded, and new heroes of the period replacing other forgotten visages from the past. The mere fact that the ahistorical print re-emerged in this third state offers strong visual testimony that popular demand for Lincoln images remained high during the secession winter, and that New York publishers again fed the hunger. In the case of the Pate engraving, iconography yielded to exigency as a print that once celebrated compromise on slavery now re-emerged to honor a new president who opposed it.

Lincoln's line-in-the-sand opposition to measures that might have saved the Union, but at the cost of extending and preserving slavery, had consequences for both the nation and the president's image. In April 1861, just two months after the inauguration, Confederate forces bombarded and seized Fort Sumter. In response to Lincoln's subsequent call for troops, New York quickly raised volunteers and sent them south to defend Washington. Parading down Broadway, the Seventh Regiment marched beneath the very flag of Fort Sumter, recently brought to the city for inspiration, and igniting a mania for flags, pictures of flags, and pictures of soldiers carrying flags.[38]

Then, understandably, images of the Union's new military commanders achieved the kind of popularity that Lincoln's had enjoyed in the months leading up to war. That is not to say that secession and rebellion inhibited the New York printmakers' opportunistic quest for every audience still within their reach. The local lithography firm of Jones & Clark, for example, saw no compelling patriotic reason *not* to issue an 1861 portrait of Jefferson Davis, the first president of the Confederacy, and might cheerfully have produced others had not the Southern market eventually been cut off from Northern publishers. Similarly, *Leslie's* proudly published what it called "Our first portrait of the President" just five days after Lincoln's inauguration. The portrait was not of Lincoln, however, but of the new chief executive of the "Southern Confederacy"—Davis.[39] Finally, the only engraving Lincoln is ever known to have autographed, a tiny Cooper Union adaptation he carried with him from Springfield in his carpetbag, reconfirmed this governing commercial impulse with particular sting. The print had come off the presses of the American Bank Note Company. But during the early months of the Civil War the same firm went on to produce currency for the enemy: the Confederate States of America.[40] The bank note company was headquartered in New York.

War notwithstanding, printmakers were reluctant to surrender commercial opportunity. Only rarely did politics trump business. One exception occurred during the 1864 presidential election campaign, when New York printmakers returned to the Lincoln theme with a vengeance—sometimes literally—with some of the most antagonistic graphic attacks of the decade, tempered, of course, by flattering portraiture. Currier & Ives and most other local firms, predictably, issued their

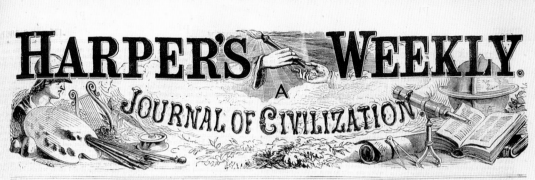

HARPER'S WEEKLY.
A JOURNAL OF CIVILIZATION.

VOL. V.—No. 218.]   NEW YORK, SATURDAY, MARCH 2, 1861.   [PRICE FIVE CENTS.

Entered according to Act of Congress, in the Year 1861, by Harper & Brothers, in the Clerk's Office of the District Court for the Southern District of New York.

ABRAHAM LINCOLN, THE PRESIDENT ELECT, ADDRESSING THE PEOPLE FROM THE ASTOR HOUSE BALCONY, FEBRUARY 19, 1861.—[SEE NEXT PAGE.]

Artist unknown. *Printing-House Square*. Hand-colored lithograph, Endicott & Co., printer, Baker & Godwin, publisher, 17 9/16 x 25 7/8 in (44.61 x 65.72 cm). PR 020

customary straightforward portraits and campaign posters, along with equally convincing tributes to Lincoln's Democratic opponent, George B. McClellan. Similarly, their cartoons of the period might just as earnestly portray a gigantic Lincoln regarding the tiny McClellan as a "little joke," or lionize McClellan as a unifier trying to keep Lincoln and Jefferson Davis from tearing apart a map of the nation. Currier & Ives alone copyrighted three 1864 campaign cartoons in the space of just three days in early October.[41] This and most other New York firms remained relentlessly devoted not to politics but to profits, producing prints that appealed to all tastes and biases.

But in 1864, uniquely, the marketplace alone did not dictate the production of images. For the first time, New York's anti-Republican press also directly organized a politically motivated pictorial campaign against Lincoln. Hitherto, even the most vitriolic attacks had been leavened by similar criticism of his rivals from the very same publishers. Now the *New York World*—which the Union Army had earlier shut down for alleged disloyalty, earning for Lincoln its further and permanent enmity—issued both pamphlets and pictures alleging that the president favored the explosively radical concept of racial integration and equality.[42]

With particular venom, a *World*-affiliated publisher, Bromley & Co., produced a lithograph entitled *Miscegenation*, in which Lincoln was depicted respectfully bowing to a mixed-race couple to indicate the dawn of a dangerous new era in which African Americans would achieve positions in society equal to those of whites. In an advertising brochure touting the picture, Bromley boasted of this "capital hit" that: "It represents society as it is to be in the era of 'Equality and Fraternity.' Lincoln, [antislavery Massachusetts Senator Charles] Sumner, Greeley, a female Lecturer, and a large number of 'colored ladies and gentlemen,' with white drivers and servants, show what society is to be in the millennium of Abolitionism." (Unladylike ladies were staples of mid-nineteenth-century popular prints; suffrage pioneers were considered as dangerously radical as abolitionists, and often morphed into free love advocates.) Copies of the *Miscegenation* caricature, bragged the publisher, would make "excellent campaign documents."[43] Accordingly, the print sold for twenty-five cents apiece, but at a discounted sixteen dollars for one hundred copies, intended for bulk distribution to Democratic campaign organizations.[44]

The inspiration for the *World's* attack, Lincoln's Emancipation Proclamation, might have inspired compelling rebuttal graphics, but surprisingly generated only a few print reproductions from any Northern city. The rarity of Emancipation pictures dating to 1863 or 1864 strongly suggests that the theme of freedom was at first considered too controversial to grace the homes of even the most progressive white patrons. Rare indeed was the 1864 campaign print that went even further and alluded directly to future prospects for racial equality.

One remarkable exception was produced by New Yorker Matthew W. Siebert at his shop on the corner of Centre and Reade Streets. A self-described "German Steam Job Printer," Siebert's previous specialties were "Posters, Show Cards, Billheads, Checks, Receipts, Drafts, Cards, Circulars, Price Currents, Statements,

James Frothingham (1786–1864). *Diogenes his lantern needs no more. An honest man is found!* 1865. Etching; stipple engraving, Woodcock & Harvey Engraving Co. 15 ½ x 12 in (39.37 x 30.48 cm). National Portrait Gallery, Smithsonian Institution, NPG.79.161

Artist unknown. *Political Caricature No. 2. Miscegenation or the Millennium of Abolitionism*, 1864. Lithograph, G.W. Bromley & Co., publisher, 12 ⅝ x 20 ⅝ in (32.07 x 52.39 cm). PR 010

Custom-House Entries, [and] Bills of Lading."[45] In 1864 he graduated to presidential campaign caricature, entitling his impressive two-panel pro-Republican cartoon—the city's Germans remained firmly behind the president—*Union and Liberty! and Union and Slavery!* The cartoon's first panel celebrated Lincoln for befriending a white working man while in the background, white and black children go to school together; the second panel imagined Lincoln's Democratic opponent, McClellan, consorting with Jefferson Davis as slave auctions resume in the wake of Democratic victory.[46] The print presaged a true image transfiguration for Lincoln, but by and large he did not live to see its full realization.

Thanks to one intrepid New York artist, however, Lincoln did at least begin to understand the transcendent future power of his image as an emancipator. In early 1864, painter Francis B. Carpenter secured sittings with the president to paint a canvas depicting the historic first reading of the Emancipation Proclamation before the Cabinet. Carpenter worked in the White House for six months, observing Lincoln closely and eventually writing an important memoir of his experience.[47] More importantly, he produced a scene that, however static it may appear to the modern eye, achieved breathtaking popularity as an engraving. Hailed as a "Great National Picture," A. H. Ritchie's handsome adaptation,

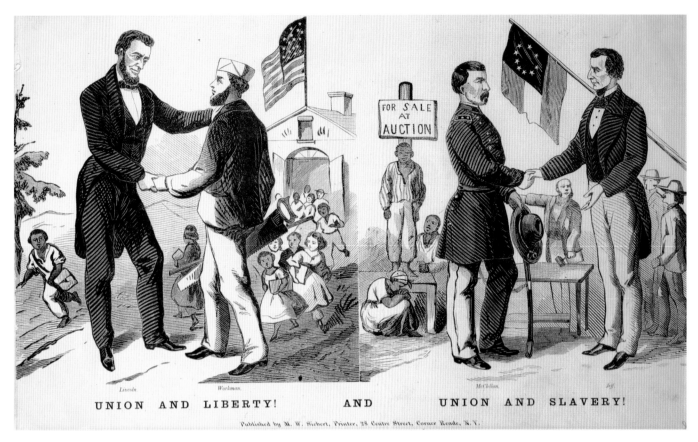

Lincoln.   Workman.   McClellan.   Jeff.

UNION AND LIBERTY!   **AND**   **UNION AND SLAVERY!**

Published by M. W. Siebert, Printer, 28 Centre Street, Corner Reade, N. Y.

issued in 1866 by Derby & Miller of Spruce Street, arguably became the most popular Lincoln print ever issued, though precise sales records for this and most other titles did not survive.[48] We do know, however, that in 1871 a New York newspaper optimistically purchased the five-year old steel plate for a staggering $8,000; and that its original publisher claimed in the 1880s that 30,000 prints had been produced altogether.[49] Lincoln himself enthusiastically signed on to pre-order the first $50 artist's proof, but because of production delays he did not live to secure his copy. Nevertheless the picture more than lived up to one New York newspaper's prediction that it would "take its place among the pictures which the people hang upon their walls to commemorate one of the great acts in the nation's history."[50]

After Lincoln's assassination, New York paid tribute to the slain president's memory at a series of funerals that re-traced in reverse, but far more emotionally, the route of the inaugural journey four years earlier—as detailed in Michael Kammen's chapter in this book. Comparing the frosty Manhattan welcome of 1861—when Lincoln was both "scoffed and scowled" upon—to the "love and veneration" which greeted his return in death, the *New York Herald* said of that grand Manhattan funeral: "Yesterday witnessed the *real* triumphal march of Abraham Lincoln; for he had conquered the prejudices of all hordes and classes. ... Better for his fame that it should come thus late than too soon."[51] Prints not only helped pave the way for Lincoln's transfiguration, but vastly extended the audience for the local funeral spectacles.

Artist unknown. *Union and Liberty! And Union and Slavery!* 1864. Wood engraving, Martin W. Siebert, publisher, 11 ⅞ x 20 ⅞ in (sight) (30.16 x 53.02 cm). PR 055

(next page) Francis Bicknell Carpenter (1830–1900). Portrait study of Abraham Lincoln for *The Emancipation Proclamation*, 1864. Oil on canvas, 33 ¾ x 28 in (85.73 x 71.12 cm). The Union League Club, New York City

Francis Bicknell Carpenter (1830–1900). Portrait studies for *The Emancipation Proclamation*, 1864. Oil on canvas. (clockwise from top left) *Edwin McMasters Stanton (1814–69)*, 35 ¼ x 28 ¼ in (89.54 x 71.76 cm); *Gideon Welles (1802–78)*, 35 ½ x 28 in (90.17 x 72.39 cm); *William Henry Seward (1801–72)*, 35 x 28 in (88.90 x 72.39 cm); *Edward Bates (1793–1869)*, 35 x 28 ½ in (88.90 x 71.12 cm); *Montgomery Blair (1813–83)*, 35 x 28 in (88.90 x 72.39 cm); *Salmon P. Chase (1808–73)*, 35 x 28 in (88.90 x 72.39 cm). The Union League Club, New York City

From life by
F.B.Carpenter
1864.

Eng.d by F. Halpin
N.Y.

THE FIRST READING OF THE EMANCIPATION PROCLAMATION BEFORE THE CABINET.

For his growing number of admirers here, and elsewhere, New York firms produced dozens of new engravings and lithographs: depictions of Lincoln's murder, deathbed, and funeral; memorial portraits, images showing him, however unrealistically, in the comforting company of his wife and children; and belated tributes to Lincoln as emancipator and preserver of the Union. These now portrayed the once-partisan figure heroically smashing the shackles of enslaved African Americans (in an 1865 Currier & Ives lithograph) or occupying an imagined afterworld alongside the founder of the republic, George Washington (examples of the "apotheosis" genre were issued by Currier & Ives, Kimmel & Forster, and other New York firms). Wood engraver John W. Orr of Nassau Street acknowledged—and attempted to profit from—the late president's historic role as an orator by issuing a portrait surrounded by "Golden Sayings of Abraham Lincoln." And H. H. Lloyd returned to the Lincoln theme with a mourning scene showing a distraught Columbia grieving at the martyr's tomb, above the words: "Lincoln. Ours the Cross, His the Crown."[52] Critical lampoons were now but a fading memory.

The depictions of the assassination itself proved particularly newsworthy, and judging alone from the number of surviving copies in public and private collections, highly popular. Currier & Ives alone issued no fewer than three different

Alexander Hay Ritchie (1822-95), after Francis Bicknell Carpenter (1830–1900). *The First Reading of the Emancipation Proclamation Before the Cabinet*, 1866. Engraving, 25 11/16 x 36 in (65.25 x 91.44 cm). Gift of Mrs. Harold E. Hoyt, PR 052

(opposite page) F[rancis]. B[icknell]. Carpenter (1830–1900). *Abraham Lincoln*, undated. Engraving, F[rederick]. H. Halpin, publisher, 16 15/16 x 12 7/8 in (43.02 x 32.70 cm). Gift of Henry O. Havemeyer, PR 052

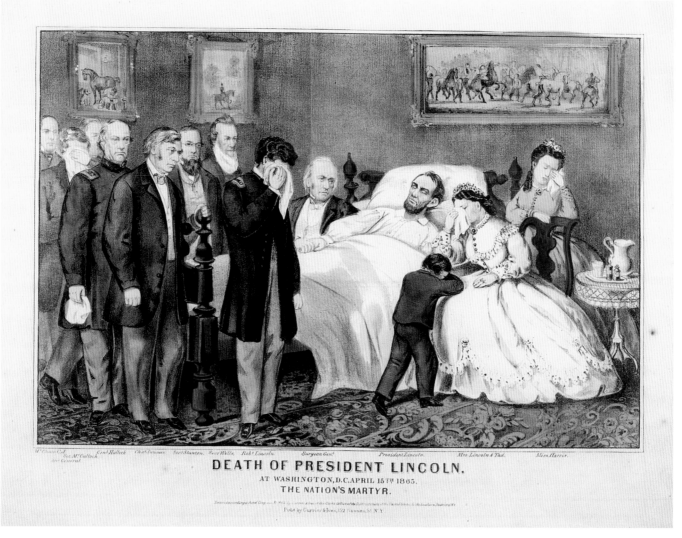

DEATH OF PRESIDENT LINCOLN.
AT WASHINGTON, D.C. APRIL 15TH 1865.
THE NATION'S MARTYR.

Artist unknown. *Death of President Lincoln*, 1865. Lithograph, Currier & Ives, publisher, 11 ¾ x 15 ¹¹⁄₁₆ in (29.85 x 39.85 cm). PR 052

versions of the scene at Lincoln's deathbed, presenting a rotating cast of onlookers reflecting both national curiosity and a rigid sense of propriety—which dictated the inclusion of Vice President Andrew Johnson among the teary-eyed eyewitnesses, for example, even though his visit had been so perfunctory he had hardly been noticed. Reflecting the powerful public demand for visualizations of the tragedy, Currier & Ives created, printed, and copyrighted its assassination and deathbed lithographs in just nine days—a breathtakingly fast response in the 1860s.[53] The next step after death was deification, and popular prints not only illustrated, but undoubtedly influenced, Lincoln's second rise as well.

For more expensive tastes, A. H. Ritchie published a mammoth engraving showing twenty-six eyewitnesses surrounding the Lincoln deathbed, with the tiny bedroom in which Lincoln breathed his last miraculously transformed into a capacious chamber fit for a king. The two-by-three-foot print sold for $20–$30 for signed artist's proofs—and Ritchie introduced it with a costly promotional campaign, publishing a brochure filled with endorsements from eyewitnesses to Lincoln's final moments. One of them, former Quartermaster General

Entered according to Act of Congress, A.D. 1865, by Currier & Ives, in the Clerk's Office of the District Court of the United States, for the Southern District of N.Y.

THE BODY OF THE MARTYR PRESIDENT, ABRAHAM LINCOLN.
LYING IN STATE AT THE CITY HALL, N.Y. APRIL 24TH & 25TH 1865.

Published by Currier & Ives, 152 Nassau St. NY.

Artist unknown. *The Body of the Martyr President, Abraham Lincoln. Lying in State at the City Hall, N.Y. April 24th & 25th 1865*, 1865. Lithograph, Currier & Ives, publisher, 11 11/16 x 8 1/8 in (29.69 x 20.64 cm). Gift of Daniel Parish Jr., PR 052

(following pages, left) Artist unknown. *Golden Sayings of Abraham Lincoln*, 1865. Hand-colored wood engraving, D. P. Mann & Co., engraver, 20 3/8 x 16 7/8 in (51.75 x 42.86 cm). PR 052

(following pages, right) John Sartain (1808–97). *Abraham Lincoln, the Martyr, Victorious.*, 1866. Mezzotint, W. H. Hermans, publisher, 18 1/4 x 14 in (46.36 x 35.56 cm). Gift of O. T. Barck Sr., PR 052

GOLDEN SAYINGS of ABRAHAM LINCOLN.

I am sure I bring a heart true to the work. For the ability to perform it, I must trust in that Supreme Being who has never forsaken this favored land, through the instrumentality of this great and intelligent people. Without that assistance I shall surely fail; with it I cannot fail.

I hold that, in contemplation of universal law, and of the Constitution, the Union of these States is perpetual.

I have never had a feeling, politically, that did not spring from the sentiments embodied in the Declaration of Independence. I have pondered over the toils that were endured by the officers and soldiers of the army who achieved that Independence. I have often inquired of myself what great principle or idea it was that kept this Confederacy so long together. It was not the mere matter of the separation of the Colonies from the mother land, but that sentiment in the Declaration of Independence which gave liberty, not alone to the people of this country, but, I hope, to the world, for all future time. It was that which gave promise that in due time the weight would be lifted from the shoulders of all men. This is the sentiment embodied in the Declaration of Independence. Can this Country be saved upon that basis? If it can, I will consider myself one of the happiest men in the world if I can help to save it. If it cannot be saved upon that principle it will be truly awful. But if this country cannot be saved without giving up that principle, I was about to say, I would rather be assassinated on this spot than surrender it.

This nation, under God, shall have a new birth of freedom, and government of the people, by the people, and for the people, shall not perish from the earth.

If the Almighty Ruler of Nations, with his eternal truth and justice, be on your side of the North, or on yours of the South, that truth and that justice will surely prevail, by the judgment of this great tribunal of the American people.

Our common country is in great peril, demanding the loftiest views and boldest action to bring a speedy relief. Once relieved, its form of government is saved to the world; its beloved history and cherished memories are vindicated, and its happy future fully assured and rendered inconceivably grand.

It is true that, while I hold myself, without mock modesty, the humblest of all individuals that have ever been elevated to the Presidency, I have a more difficult task to perform than any one of them. You have generously tendered me the united support of the great Empire State. For this, in behalf of the nation—in behalf of the present and future of the nation—in behalf of civil and religious liberty for all time to come, most gratefully do I thank you.

A house divided against itself cannot stand. I believe this Government cannot endure permanently half slave and half free. I do not expect the Union to be dissolved—I do not expect the house to fall, but I do expect it will cease to be divided. It will become all one thing or all the other.

Let us resolve that the martyred dead shall not have died in vain.

ABRAHAM LINCOLN,
Sixteenth President of the United States.
BORN, 1809. DIED, 1865.

The struggle of to-day is not altogether for to-day; it is for a vast future also. With a reliance on Providence, all the more firm and earnest, let us proceed in the great task which events have devolved upon us.

No human counsel hath devised, nor hath any mortal hand worked out these great things. They are the gracious gifts of the Most High God, who, while dealing with us in anger for our sins, hath nevertheless remembered mercy.

If slavery is not wrong, nothing is wrong. I cannot remember when I did not so think and feel.

With malice toward none, with charity for all, with firmness in the right as God gives us to see the right, let us strive on to finish the work we are in, to bind up the nation's wounds and care for him who shall have borne the battle and for his widow and his orphans; to do all which may achieve and cherish a just and lasting peace among ourselves and with all nations.

Whatever shall tend to turn our thoughts from the unreasoning and uncharitable passions, prejudices and jealousies incident to a great national trouble such as ours, and to fix them on the vast and long-enduring consequences, for weal or for woe, which are to result from the struggle, and especially to strengthen our reliance on the Supreme Being for the final triumph of the right, cannot but be well for us all.

I cannot but know what you all know, that without a name, perhaps without a reason why I should have a name, there has fallen upon me a task such as did not rest even upon the Father of his country, and so feeling I cannot but turn and look for the support without which it will be impossible for me to perform that great task. I turn, then, and look to the great American people, and to that God who has never forsaken them.

A duty devolves upon me which is, perhaps, greater than that which has devolved upon any other man since the days of Washington. He never would have succeeded except for the aid of Divine Providence, upon which he at all times relied. I feel that I cannot succeed without the same Divine aid which sustained him, and on the same Almighty Being I place my reliance for support.

As a private citizen the Executive could not have consented that these institutions shall perish; much less could he, in betrayal of so vast and so sacred a trust as these free people have confided to him. He felt that he had no moral right to shrink, or even to count the chances of his own life, in what may follow. In full view of his great responsibility he has so far done what he has deemed his duty.

I repeat the declaration made a year ago, that while I remain in my position, I shall not attempt to retract or modify the emancipation proclamation, nor shall I return to slavery any person who is free by the terms of that proclamation, or by any of the acts of Congress. If the people should, by whatever mode or means, make it an executive duty to re-enslave such persons, another, and not I, must be the instrument to perform it.

Entered according to Act of Congress, in the year 1865, by D. P. MANN & Co., in the Clerk's Office of the District Court of the United States for the Southern District of New York.

D. P. MANN & CO., Proprietors, Oneida, N. Y.

J. W. ORR & CO., Engravers and Printers, No. 96 Nassau Street, New York.

ABRAHAM LINCOLN, THE MARTYR.
VICTORIOUS.

Artist unknown. *Ours the Cross His the Crown*, ca. 1865. Hand-colored wood engraving, H.H. Lloyd & Co., publisher, 17 ½ x 11 ¹³⁄₁₆ in (44.45 x 30.00 cm). PR 052

Published by H. H. LLOYD & CO., 21 John Street, New York.

(opposite page) William Edgar Marshall (1837–1906). *Abraham Lincoln*, 1864. Oil on canvas, 21 ¾ x 16 ¼ in (55.25 x 41.28 cm). Gift of Mrs. Oscar Marshall and her children, 1926.4

(pages 162–163) Advertisement for Marshall's Line Engraving of President Lincoln. Letter from the artist to the publishers, 1866. SY 1866 no. 123

Montgomery Meigs, expressed the hope "that the engraving may well have a place in thousands of American homes."[54] But judging from the rarity of surviving copies, these ambitions likely went unfulfilled, perhaps because the print was simply too big, too expensive, and too late: it appeared three long years after the tragedy and the huge burst of audience interest it sparked.

Yet for months after the assassination, competition for market supremacy in the realm of Lincoln sanctification remained fierce, and the city's picture publishers responded vigorously. At one point the publishers of three handsome, but seemingly benign, New York-made Lincoln engravings—modeled after paintings

Prints 5.
Proofs 10
Artists Proofs $20.
By subscription only.

Agents will soon wait Canvass the city.

Marshall's Line Engraving of President Lincoln.

PUBLISHED BY TICKNOR & FIELDS, BOSTON. *163 Bleecker St. N.Y.*

Letter from the Artist to the Publishers.

NEWARK, July 25th, 1866.

MESSRS. TICKNOR & FIELDS:

DEAR SIRS. — I send you with this a proof of my engraved portrait of President LINCOLN, upon which I have been engaged so long — engraved as you are aware after my own painting. As a work of art, I submit it to yourselves and to the public on its merits. That it is a truthful portrait of MR. LINCOLN, as he appeared in his calm and thoughtful moments, I have the assurance of many who were intimately connected with him during his whole official career, as well as the testimony of others who enjoyed his acquaintance for many years. On this point I would ask your attention to the opinions of MR. SUMNER, MR. STANTON, MR. TRUMBULL, and MR. COLFAX, contained in the letters which I enclose.

The execution of this portrait has been a pleasant labor to me during the many months I have been engaged upon it; and in executing it, I have endeavored not merely to gratify a professional ambition in producing a work of art, but I have sought so far as could be done in one picture, to represent MR. LINCOLN as he was, and as he will be known in the pages of history and biography.

MR. LINCOLN's countenance was a very peculiar one, presenting not only plainness of features but great diversity of expression. Its changeableness was remarkable, passing in a moment from the expression of sadness or even despondency, to that of the utmost good humor. A person seeing him under but one of his various expressions could form but a feeble conception of him. I am not aware that I ever saw a face, the features of which demanded such attentive study. It were easy enough to catch a single expression, to depict him in one of his moods, but such a representation would necessarily be an imperfect or unsatisfactory one to all who had seen him under different aspects, as well as wanting in truthfulness of general representation. To avoid this imperfect representation, I sought a knowledge of him from other sources than the features and expressions of his countenance. I read attentively his various speeches, letters, messages, &c., and I also studied the various biographies of him which have been written; and also I have been favored with many reminiscences of him by people who knew him intimately. This was before I commenced work upon the canvas, and I fancy this familiarity with [his] life, enabled me to form in some measure an idea of what a true portrait should represent. I shall [not] attempt to say just what I conceived the character of MR. LINCOLN to be; or to state just wh[at I] intended to represent in the portrait, further than to remark that I felt justified in bringing into pro[mi]nence, through his plain features, in a not unwonted expression, those higher qualities for which he w[as] and always will be distinguished. If in this attempt I have succeeded in producing a portrait satisfacto[ry] to those who knew MR. LINCOLN well, and at the same time one that will enable those who nev[er] knew him to see what manner of man he was, I shall feel that my labors have not been in vain.

Very truly yours,

WM. E. MARSHALL.

TESTIMONIALS.

(From ROBERT T. LINCOLN.)

CHICAGO, Sept. 25, 1866.

W. E. MARSHALL, Esq.: SIR: I have seen a copy of your engraving of my father's portrait, published by Ticknor & Fields, and I take pleasure in testifying to its excellence as a likeness. I cannot suggest any improvement.

Yours very truly,

ROBERT T. LINCOLN.

(From MR. HERNDON, Mr. Lincoln's Law Partner in Springfield, Illinois.)

SPRINGFIELD, ILL., Sept. 26, 1866.

MESSRS. TICKNOR & FIELDS: SIRS: I have known President LINCOLN for a period of quite thirty years — twenty years of which, he and myself were law partners in this city. It has been my pleasure to study the man, physically and mentally, especially since 1854, when he fairly commenced looming up in the nation. I have seen and been with him in every mood, and under almost all conditions of human life, and his form and features are deeply impressed on my memory. Mr. Wm. E. Marshall's engraved portrait of him has been shown me, published by your house, and I have studied the picture sufficiently long to form an opinion of it. If art is the expression of an idea embodied in fact, which at once translates itself to the intelligent observer, then this picture is a work of the highest art. The organs and features of the face are almost exact — are true to nature. In this portrait the artist has caught Mr. LINCOLN in kindness, tenderness and reflection combined — and in my humble judgment, this is the best portrait of Mr. LINCOLN I have seen. As a work of art, it will take its proper place among the finest in America. Those who have never had the pleasure of seeing the original, may rest assured that the expression of organ, and feature, and mood of the man are well caught, expressed and preserved. I am pleased to know you are soon to make the picture public through its, I hope, universal sale.

Yours truly,

W. H. HERNDON.

(From the Mayor of Springfield, Ill.)

SPRINGFIELD, ILL., Sept. 26, 1866.

To all who desire a correct likeness of our late President, I would commend that so successfully produced by Mr. Wm. E. Marshall, and published by Messrs. Ticknor & Fields. As a life-likeness, it is far superior to any I have seen.

A long intimacy with President LINCOLN, has fixed his likeness firmly upon my memory, and in this engraving see truth in every line.

J. T. BRADFORD.

(From Judge TREAT, of Springfield, Ill.)

SPRINGFIELD, ILL., Sept. 28, 1866.

I HAVE examined the engraving of ABRAHAM LINCOLN, recently published by Ticknor & Fields. It is an accurate likeness of Mr. LINCOLN.

S. H. TREAT.

(From Judge LOGAN, of Springfield, Ill.)

SPRINGFIELD, ILL., Sept. 26, 1866.

GENTLEMEN: I have examined the engraved likeness of President LINCOLN, by Mr. Wm. E. Marshall. I have had -four years of intimate acquaintance with President LINCOLN, and have his features well impressed on my mind. think the engraving represents with great accuracy, not only the features but also the expression of his countenance.

STEPHEN T. LOGAN.

MESSRS. TICKNOR & FIELDS.

(From SENATOR SUMNER.)

SENATE CHAMBER, 17th July, 1866.

MY DEAR SIR: I congratulate you upon your success in the engraved portrait of President LINCOLN. As a work art, it will take its place among those rare productions not to be forgotten. As a portrait, it will always be valued presenting the original in his most interesting expression, where gentleness and sympathy unite with strength. I think .t I cannot err in predicting for it general favor among all who love art, or venerate the name of our Martyred President. am sure that many will look upon it with grateful enthusiasm.

Very faithfully yours,

WILLIAM E. MARSHALL, Esq.

CHARLES SUMNER.

by William Edgar Marshall, John Littlefield, and Francis B. Carpenter respectively—battled each other through audacious advertising campaigns that not only claimed that each product was the most faithful to the revered original, but routinely assailed the competing works as inferior.[55] Littlefield's canvas was universally hailed as "a superb work of art," claimed its publisher. Marshall's would "be sought out for two hundred years hence," historian George Bancroft countered on behalf of its rival. And no less expert a judge than Lincoln's widow Mary was enlisted to call the Carpenter picture the "most perfect likeness of my husband, that I have ever seen."[56] Such was the degree of public interest in Lincoln images that all three engravings found an audience.

In life, the supposedly modest and self-deprecating Lincoln had nonetheless sat for a surprising number of photographers and artists, including Carpenter, whose two great canvases, *First Reading of the Emancipation Proclamation* and *The Lincoln Family in 1861*,[57] inspired definitive popular prints of Lincoln, both as statesman and family man. But even Lincoln might have been surprised by the flood of graphic arts that greeted his martyrdom, and the bare-knuckles commercial competition it unleashed.

"New York never before saw such a day," the *Herald* had written of the outpouring of public grief expressed at the Lincoln funeral here.[58] Neither had Abraham Lincoln. But reflected through the medium of popular prints, made in New York for a national audience, his fellow Americans could "see" Lincoln as an emancipator, martyr, and secular saint for many years to come.

NOTES

1   *New York Daily News*, July 14, 1863. The author is indebted to researcher Avi Mowshowitz for his work in uncovering this report.

2   Ibid.

3   Historian Mark E. Neely Jr. has reported several hitherto-unknown examples of partisans using campaign prints. See Neely, *The Boundaries of American Political Culture in the Civil War Era* (Chapel Hill: University of North Carolina Press, 2006).

4   Robert Philippe, *Political Graphics: Art as a Weapon* (New York: Abbeville Press, 1980), 172.

5   *New York Tribune*, February 28, 1860.

6   Quoted in Francis B. Carpenter, *Six Months at the White House with Abraham Lincoln: The Story of a Picture* (New York: Hurd & Houghton, 1866), 46–47.

7   George Alfred Townsend, "Still Taking Pictures," *New York World*, April 12, 1891, quoted in Mary Panzer, *Mathew Brady and the Image of History* (Washington: Smithsonian Institution Press, 1997), 224.

8   Lincoln to Harvey Eastman, April 7, 1860, in *The Collected Works of Abraham Lincoln*, ed. Roy P. Basler (New Brunswick: Rutgers University Press, 1953–55), 4:39–40.

9   See William C. Darrah, *Cartes de Visite in Nineteenth Century Photography* (Gettysburg, PA: William C. Darrah, 1981), 4.

10 *New York City Register* (New York: H. Wilson, 1859), 28–29, 31, 33–35, 41.

11 The most comprehensive list is to be found in Gary L. Bunker, *From Rail-Splitter to Icon: Lin-*

coln's Image in Illustrated Periodicals, 1860–1865 (Kent, OH: Kent State University Press, 2001), 374–76.

12 Frank Leslie's Illustrated Newspaper, February 23, 1861. The date this front-page notice appeared is significant: seven Southern states had already seceded from the Union, and Lincoln had arrived in Washington for his inauguration, yet this New York weekly was still boasting of its "unparalleled" Southern reach, and warning against the "present disastrous state of the political and business prospects of the country."

13 Harper's Weekly, May 26, 1860 and Frank Leslie's Illustrated Newspaper, October 20, 1860. Harper's re-published the Brady-inspired engraving on November 10.

14 New York Times, June 9, 1860.

15 Wilson's Business Directory of New York City (New York: John F. Trow, 1863), 145–47, 266–67, 376–79.

16 Ibid., 376.

17 Currier & Ives catalogue reprinted in C. Carter Smith, Currier & Ives: A Catalogue Raisonnée (Detroit: Gale Research, 1984), xl–xli.

18 The firm issued at least sixteen 1860 campaign cartoons, including such titles as: The Impending Crisis, The "Irrepressible Conflict," or the Republican Barge in Danger, The Great Exhibition of 1860 (showing Lincoln as a gymnast), The Rail Candidate, The Republican Party Going to the Right House, and The National Game. Three "Outs" and One "Run" (this time depicting Lincoln as a baseball player wielding a log rail of his own making as a bat). All the originals are in the Prints & Photographs Division, Library of Congress. See Bernard C. Reilly, American Political Prints, 1776–1876: A Catalog of the Collections in the Library of Congress (Boston: G. K. Hall, 1991), 438–52.

19 All the Year Round, April 13, 1861, quoted in Matthew Noah Vosmeier, "'Election-Time in America': An Englishman's View of Popular Politics During the 1860 Campaign," Lincoln Lore 1832 (October 1991): 2. The Currier & Ives cartoons to which the correspondent referred were probably: Stephen Finding His Mother, which mocked the Democratic candidate for using his mother's illness as an excuse to travel (and campaign) East (the print showed his mother to be Columbia, who makes him see "stars" by flogging him with "stripes" (a cat o'nine tails) as Uncle Sam looks on; and Political 'Blondins' Crossing Salt River, although there is no White House in this lithograph. The reporter may have confused it with two similar prints from the weekly newspapers: The Perilous Voyage to the White House, which appeared in Frank Leslie's Budget of Fun on October 15, 1860, or Shaky. Daring Transit on the Perilous Rail, Mr. Abraham Blondin de Lave Lincoln, in Vanity Fair, June 9, 1860. See Reilly, American Political Prints, 446; Bunker, From Rail-Splitter to Icon, 40, 52.

20 Rufus Rockwell Wilson quoted in Harold Holzer, Lincoln Seen and Heard (Lawrence: University Press of Kansas, 2000), 112.

21 Portraits and Sketches of the Lives of All the Candidates for the Presidency and Vice-Presidency for 1860, Comprising Eight Portraits Engraved on Steel. . . (New York: J. C. Buttre, 1860), back matter. Buttre went on to produce a full-length mezzotint portrait of Lincoln as well, 19 x 26 inches, which he sold for $3 for plain proofs and $5 for India proofs; and an "exquisite picture" of The Early Home of Abraham Lincoln as it Now Stands, for 25 cents.

22 Ritchie & Co. to Lincoln, June 28, 1860, Abraham Lincoln Papers, Library of Congress.

23 John Hay to Francis B. Carpenter, January 22, 1865, John Hay Papers, John Hay Library, Brown University.

24 Harold Holzer, Gabor S. Boritt, and Mark E. Neely Jr., The Lincoln Image: Abraham Lincoln and the Popular Print (New York: Charles Scribner's Sons, 1984), 50; Thomas Hicks in Reminiscences of Lincoln by Distinguished Men of His Time, ed. Allen Thorndike Rice (New York: North American Review, 1888), 602. The Hicks original is now in the collection of the Chicago Historical Society.

25 New York Times, June 9, 1860 and June 12, 1860.

26 Grace Bedell to Lincoln, October 15, 1860, in Basler, *Collected Works of Abraham Lincoln*, 4:130.

27 Lincoln to Grace Bedell, October 19, 1860, Ibid.

28 *New York Tribune Almanac for the Years 1838 to 1864, Inclusive...* (New York: The New York Tribune, 1868), 41.

29 Lincoln to James Babcock, September 13, 1860, in Basler, *Collected Works of Abraham Lincoln*, 4:114.

30 Lincoln to Thomas Doney, July 30, 1860, Ibid., 89. For further discussion of these prints, see Holzer, Boritt, and Neely, *The Lincoln Image*, 22–25.

31 Remarks at Westfield, New York, February 16, 1861, in Basler, *Collected Works of Abraham Lincoln*, 4:219.

32 *Philadelphia Inquirer*, February 20, 1861.

33 Harold G. and Oswald Garrison Villard, eds., *Lincoln on the Eve of '61: A Journalist's Story by Henry Villard* (New York: Alfred A. Knopf, 1941), 93.

34 Walt Whitman, *Specimen Days*, orig. pub, 1883, in *Memoranda During the War*, ed. Peter Coviello (New York: Oxford University Press, 2004), 39–40n. See also Daniel Mark Epstein, *Lincoln and Whitman: Parallel Lives in Civil War Washington* (New York: Ballantine Books, 2004), 66–68.

35 Remarks at City Hall, New York, February 20, 1861, in Basler, *Collected Works of Abraham Lincoln*, 4:233.

36 Quoted in Harold Holzer, ed., *State of the Union: New York & The Civil War* (New York: Fordham University Press, 2002), 8; for details on New York secession plan see Iver Bernstein, *The New York City Draft Riots and their Significance for American Society and Politics in the Age of the Civil War* (New York: Oxford University Press, 1990), 143.

37 See Paul M. Angle, "Fakery in the Name of Honest Abe," *Chicago History* 4 (1954–1955): 47–48, and Harold Holzer, "The Bearding of the President, 1860: The Portraitists Put on Hairs," *Lincoln Herald* 78 (Fall 1976): 99–101.

38 See Mark E. Neely and Harold Holzer, *The Union Image: Popular Prints of the Civil War North* (Chapel Hill: University of North Carolina Press, 2000), esp. "Flag Mania," 1–22.

39 See Harold Holzer, "The Image of Jefferson Davis as Commander in Chief," in *Jefferson Davis's Generals*, ed. Gabor S. Boritt (New York: Oxford University Press, 1999), 133.

40 Holzer, Boritt, and Neely, *The Lincoln Image*, 31; Mark E. Neely, Jr., Harold Holzer, and Gabor S. Boritt, *The Confederate Image: Prints of the Lost Cause* (Chapel Hill: University of North Carolina Press, 1987), 7.

41 The prints were *Chicago Platform and Candidates* (registered October 3), *Political Siamese Twins* (October 5), and *The Real Issue or What's The Matter* (October 6)—all anti-McClellan prints, as it happened. See Copyright Records, Southern District of New York, September 1864–December 1864, Rare Book Room, Library of Congress.

42 There are no issues of the *World*—reflecting the shutdown—between May 19 and May 22, 1864. For the paper's own account of the closure, see the issue of May 23, 1864. The best account of the shutdown is still Robert S. Harper, *Lincoln and the Press* (New York: McGraw-Hill, 1951), 289–93, 296–99.

43 *Bromley & Co's Publications*, Advertising Broadside, New York, 1864, Library of Congress. The firm listed no address—only a box number, perhaps to preserve anonymity—though an affiliated agent, J. F. Feeks, openly listed his location as 26 Ann Street.

44 In a related move, the newspaper also financed a hoax involving a book with the same title—mailing an advance copy to the White House in an effort to secure Lincoln's endorsement. Had Lincoln praised the *Miscegenation* tract, the *World* was poised to use his words to suggest that he did, indeed, secretly favor race mixing. But Lincoln was too smart for the New York publishers. He examined the letter and the booklet, and simply filed them away without responding. The miscegenation controversy is discussed in Neely and Holzer, *The Union Image*, 152–59. An excellent account of the hoax can be found in David E. Long, *The Jewel of Liberty: Abraham Lincoln's Re-election and the End of Slavery* (Mechanicsburg, PA: Stack-

pole Books, 1984), 153–66, 168–69, 172–77.

45 *Wilson's Business Directory of New York City*, 1860, advertisement opposite page 402; *Business Directory for 1863*, advertisement opposite page 378.

46 One of the surviving original copies of this print is in Lincoln Memorial University, Harrogate, Tennessee. See also Reilly, *American Political Prints*, 534.

47 See Carpenter, *Six Months at the White House with Abraham Lincoln*.

48 The accolade was used in a promotional appendix to a new Lincoln biography issued by the same publisher. See Henry C. Raymond, *The Life, Public Services and State Papers of Abraham Lincoln* (New York: Derby & Miller, 1865), endpapers.

49 *New York Independent*, February 2, 1871; J. C. Derby, *Fifty Years Among Authors, Books and Publishers...* (New York: Derby & Miller, 1884), 489.

50 *New York Evening Post*, quoted in *New York Times*, June 9, 1866.

51 *New York Herald*, April 26, 1865.

52 Original copies of both these titles are in the Print Collection of the New-York Historical Society.

53 Copyright Records, Southern District of New York, March 1–May 12, 1865. Currier & Ives registered its prints for federal copyright protection on April 26—the same day as Walt Whitman copyrighted his new collection of Civil War poetry, *Drum-Taps*.

54 *Ritchie's Historical Picture, Death of President Lincoln* [advertising brochure], (New York: A. H. Ritchie & Co., 1868), 8–9.

55 The original Marshall painting is in the New-York Historical Society; the print adaptation was issued by Ticknor & Fields in Boston. The Littlefield canvas was engraved by Henry Gugler and published by William Pate in New York. The Carpenter original, after its engraving by New Yorker Frederick Halpin, was later donated by the artist to the Union League Club of New York.

56 Holzer, Boritt, and Neely, *The Lincoln Image*, 211–12; Mary Lincoln to Francis B. Carpenter, December 25, 1866, in Justin G. Turner and Linda Levitt Turner, *Mary Todd Lincoln: Her Life and Letters* (New York: Alfred A. Knopf, 1973), 403–4.

57 The original painting is in the New-York Historical Society.

58 *New York Herald*, April 26, 1865.

CIVIL LIBERTIES
IN WARTIME NEW YORK

FRANK J. WILLIAMS

I N MARCH 1861, the United States stood on the threshold of civil war under the leadership of a newly inaugurated president who entered office vowing to unite the deeply divided nation. As political conflicts roiled the country, driving states to secede from the Union and join together in the newly formed Confederate States of America, President Abraham Lincoln's paramount initial goal was simply to restore and preserve the greater Union.

His decisions did not come easily, nor were they always well received. Even before Lincoln was inaugurated, he was challenged by Northerners who were sympathetic to the Confederacy. In January 1861, New York City's Democratic Mayor, Fernando Wood, made the unlikely proposal to the City Council that New York secede from the Union and declare itself a free city.

Wood told the Council, "While other portions of our State have, unfortunately, been imbued with the fanatical spirit which actuates a portion of the people of New England, the city of New York has unfalteringly preserved the integrity of its principles in adherence to the compromises of the constitution and the equal rights of the people of all the States."[1] Wood believed that the city could survive on its own, provided it maintained its profitable cotton trade with the Confederacy. Fortunately, Wood's proposal went no further. Rather, it drew bitter criticism from many in New York, including the *New York Tribune*'s Horace Greeley. In Greeley's words, "Fernando Wood evidently wants to be a traitor; it is lack of courage only that makes him content with being a blackguard."[2]

The president soon sought to impress upon Copperheads like Wood that during the coming struggle, he would do whatever was necessary to save the Union.[3] In February 1861, Lincoln ardently explained his position to the Mayor, who was

Studio of Mathew B. Brady (ca. 1823–96). *Abraham Lincoln*, Washington, DC, February 9, 1864. Albumen print on carte-de-visite mount. Library of Congress

Mathew B. Brady (ca. 1823–96).
Hon. Fernando Wood, N.Y.
(1812–81), ca. 1860–65. U.S.
National Archives and Records
Administration, ARC ID 529874,
LOCAL ID 111-B-5786

then in his second term in office. "There is nothing that can ever bring me willingly to consent to the destruction of this Union, under which not only the commercial city of New York, but the whole country has acquired its greatness," Lincoln wrote to the Democratic Mayor.[4] Lincoln's intent was to protect the civil liberties of those in the Union to the extent that they could be protected, but that the preservation of the Union came first. "So long, then, as it is possible that the prosperity and the liberties of the people can be preserved in the Union, it shall be my purpose at all times to preserve it."[5] Lincoln was attempting to impress his policy upon the Mayor who, despite his sympathies for the Confederacy, was later elected to two terms in the United States House of Representatives, serving from 1863 to 1865, then again from 1867 until his death.

In the earliest days of his presidency Lincoln kept his word, fearlessly exercising extraordinary powers to protect the failing nation—powers which many lamented were unconstitutional. Despite falling subject to tremendous criticism, especially in New York, President Lincoln remained proactive, convinced that extraordinary measures were necessary to save the nation from an unprecedented constitutional crisis.

As the war progressed, its battlegrounds never reached New York, but the nation's largest and wealthiest city became a political hotbed. As the home to the nation's most influential daily newspapers, the politically divided city would prove the perfect setting for criticism of the president's wartime decisions.

Protests erupted in New York and elsewhere—most, it should be remembered, unchecked by federal authorities. But two major incidents did provoke local and national attention, and generate enduring historical interest: a controversy involving arbitrary arrests in wartime, and another involving the right of newspapers to publish false reports about troop movements and enlistments. These cases aroused New Yorkers, and continue to arouse scholars in the ongoing, unending debates about executive power in wartime.

It began on September 24, 1862, when Lincoln issued a proclamation declaring martial law and authorizing the use of military tribunals to try civilians within the United States who were believed to be "guilty of disloyal practice" or who "afford[ed] aid and comfort to Rebels."[6] The proclamation also suspended the writ of habeas corpus "in respect to all persons arrested, or who are now, or hereafter during the rebellion shall be, imprisoned in any fort, camp, arsenal, military prison, or other place of confinement by any military authority or by the sentence of any Court Martial or Military Commission."[7]

By the time of Lincoln's proclamation, New York was already home to numerous prisoners of war who were held at one of the most feared Union war prisons, Fort Lafayette. The fort was referred to by Confederates as the American Bastille, reflective of its inaccessibility on a remote island a quarter mile from land in the

MASKS AND FACES.

King Abraham before and after issuing the EMANCIPATION PROCLAMATION.

Artist unknown. "Masks and Faces: King Abraham Before and After Issuing the Emancipation Proclamation." Wood engraving, published in *Southern Illustrated News*, November 8, 1862. Collection Western Reserve Historical Society

New York harbor.[8] Lincoln's suspension of the writ of habeas corpus prompted the arrest and detention of many more prisoners of war, causing the already crowded prison to reach three times its projected capacity during the war. The dilapidated fort was damp, poorly lit, and foul-smelling.[9] The cells were desperately overcrowded, precluding any exercise, and rations were of low quality and poorly prepared.[10] Not everyone saw the prison's conditions this way, however. The *New York Times* challenged the fort's nickname, stating that it was "not a Bastile at all, in fact the fort is more like a hotel than anything else."[11] Nevertheless, with the fort in full operation, New York's harbor held important Confederate leaders, blockade-runners, spies, and rebellious opponents of war.[12] Most of those imprisoned did not know the charges against them, leading one historian to recount that "Fort Lafayette was a symbol for New Yorkers of arbitrary arrests and denial of rights, but probably because of its elite character, it also was rated by some of its prisoners as the best military prison in the country."[13]

Anger over the administration's handling of civilian dissent was about to become worse in the Empire State. In March 1862, Major General Ambrose E.

William G. Jackman, engraver. *C[lement]. L[aird]. Vallandigham (1820–71)*, undated. Steel engraving, 4 ½ x 4 in (11.43 x 10.16 cm). PR 052

This is the way the North receives it.

THE PRESIDENT'S INAUGURAL.
And

This is the way the South receives it

Artist unknown. "The President's Inaugural." Wood engraving, published in *New-York Illustrated News*, March 23, 1861. E171.D38

Burnside assumed command of the Department of the Ohio.[14] Burnside made his headquarters at Cincinnati, where wholesale criticism of the war was as rampant as in New York. Agitated by anti-administration speeches, General Burnside responded on April 13, 1862, by issuing General Order No. 38, authorizing imposition of the death penalty for those who aided the Confederacy and who "declared sympathies for the enemy."

Among those who particularly irked Burnside was former Ohio Democratic Congressman Clement L. Vallandigham, the best-known anti-war Copperhead of the Civil War and perhaps Lincoln's sharpest critic.[15] Active in politics throughout most of his life, Vallandigham was elected to the House of Representatives from Ohio in 1856, 1858, and 1860. General Burnside knew him well from several speeches he had given while in Congress that had earned considerable publicity. Vallandigham charged Lincoln with the "wicked and hazardous experiment" of calling the people to arms without counsel and authority of Congress, with violating the Constitution by declaring a blockade of Southern ports, with "contemptuously" defying the Constitution by suspending the writ of habeas corpus,

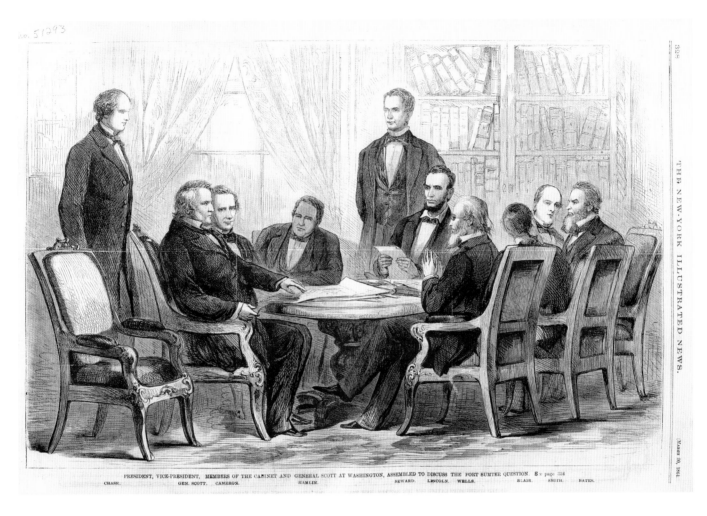

PRESIDENT, VICE-PRESIDENT, MEMBERS OF THE CABINET AND GENERAL SCOTT AT WASHINGTON, ASSEMBLED TO DISCUSS THE FORT SUMTER QUESTION. See page 324

CHASE.   GEN. SCOTT.   CAMERON.   HAMLIN.   SEWARD.   LINCOLN.   WELLS.   BLAIR.   SMITH.   BATES.

and with "cooly" coming before the Congress and pleading that he was only "pre-serving and protecting" the Constitution and demanding and expecting the thanks of Congress and the country for his "usurpations of power."[16]

Learning that Vallandigham was to speak again at a Democratic mass meeting in Mount Vernon, Ohio, Burnside dispatched two captains in civilian clothes to listen in on Vallandigham's speech. As anticipated, Vallandigham lambasted President Lincoln, referring to him as a political tyrant, and calling for his over-throw. The ex-Congressman proclaimed, among other things, that "the present war was a wicked, cruel, and unnecessary war, one not waged for the preservation of the Union, but for the purpose of crushing our liberty and to erect a despotism; a war for the freedom of the blacks and the enslavement of the whites."[17]

With General Order No. 38 as justification and at General Burnside's direction, 150 Union soldiers arrived at the Copperhead's home in Dayton at 2:40 a.m. on May 5, 1863.[18] When Vallandigham refused to let the soldiers in, they broke down his front door and forced their way inside.[19] They arrested him and escorted him to Kemper Barracks, a military prison in Cincinnati.[20] Although he was a United States citizen who would ordinarily be tried for criminal offenses in the civilian court system, Vallandigham was brought before a military tribunal a day after his

Artist unknown. "President, Vice-President, Members of the Cabinet and General Scott at Washington." Wood engraving, published in *New-York Illustrated News*, March 30, 1861. E171.D38

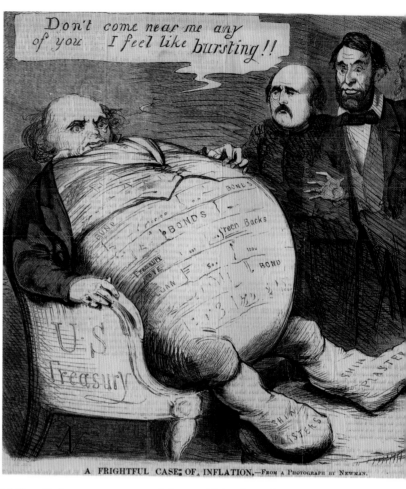

(above left) Artist unknown. "The Sowers." Wood engraving, published in *Fun*, October 17, 1863. Collection University of Minnesota Library

(above right) Artist unknown. "A Frightful Case of Inflation." Wood engraving after a photograph by Newman, published in *Frank Leslie's Budget of Fun*, April 1863. American Antiquarian Society.

arrest.[21] An attorney, Vallandigham represented himself before the military officers who presided over his case and protested that the commission had no authority to try him.[22] His protestations fell on deaf ears, however, as the case before the tribunal proceeded. The tribunal found Vallandigham guilty of violating General Order No. 38 and sentenced him to imprisonment for the duration of the war.[23]

Vallandigham's counsel then applied to the United States circuit court sitting at Cincinnati, for a writ of habeas corpus—a procedural method by which one who is detained can seek to have his imprisonment reviewed—but the writ was denied.[24] He later sought a writ of certiorari—an extraordinary writ used by an appellate court, at its discretion, to review a lower court record—from the United States Supreme Court, which was likewise denied, with the court ruling that it was without jurisdiction to review the military tribunal's proceedings.[25] The arrest, military trial, conviction, and sentence of Vallandigham aroused excitement throughout the country—but particularly in the Empire State. The "wiley agitator," [sic] as Lincoln later obliquely described the Ohioan, found many supporters in New York, particularly in the heavily Democratic state capitol of Albany.[26]

Sentiment in Albany was particularly strong, where Democrats held that Vallandigham's arrest was arbitrary and constituted an effort to exert military

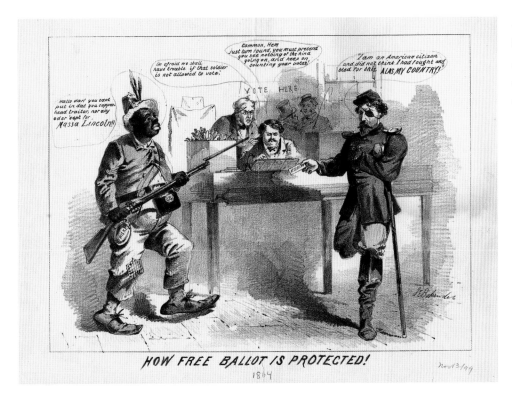

Artist unknown. Joseph E. Baker (ca. 1837–1914). *How Free Ballot is Protected!*, 1864. Lithograph, 9 3/8 x 12 9/16 in (23.81 x 31.91 cm). Gift of Daniel Parish Jr., PR 010

Artist unknown. *Heads of the Democracy*, 1864. Lithograph, 10 1/2 x 14 1/16 in (26.67 x 35.72 cm). Gift of Henry O. Havemeyer, PR 010

censorship of public discourse. One newspaper reported that the arrest was an experiment conducted by the Lincoln administration to test how much the public would tolerate.[27] Many New Yorkers feared that Vallandigham's arrest was a very real possibility for them too. The Albany *Atlas & Argus*, a Democratic newspaper, reported: "[T]he blow that falls upon a citizen of Ohio to-day, may be directed at a Democrat of New York to-morrow," the anti-administration paper wrote.

RUNNING THE "MACHINE".

John Cameron (b. ca. 1828).
Running the "Machine," 1864.
Lithograph, Currier & Ives,
publisher, 9 ¾ x 13 ¹¹⁄₁₆ in
(24.77 x 34.77 cm). PR 010

"The blow, therefore, is a threat at every Democrat."[28] Days later, the paper drove home this sentiment: "[T]he State of New York, and every citizen of the State, is equally threatened[.] We must make common cause with the citizens of other States, or we, too, are lost."[29]

Unlike the *Atlas & Argus,* the *New York Times* was supportive of the Lincoln administration. Immediately following Vallandigham's arrest, the *Times* offered its praise of the administration's action. "Of all Northern coadjutors of the rebellion, Vallandigham is the very one of whom an example ought to be made. His peculiar notoriety would make the example all the more signal in itself, and all the more effective as a warning," the paper's editors impressed upon its readers.[30] In the days following Vallandigham's trial, the *Times* reported its belief in evidence's truth and suggested that the best punishment for the ex-Congressman would be to exile him to the South. "Taking his life might seem too hard, imprisonment would quite likely make a martyr of him, but everyone will recognize the fitness of sending him to Dixie, to join that noble company of traitors whose praises he has sounded so loudly," the pro-administration paper opined.[31]

Democratic New Yorkers in Albany, incensed by Vallandigham's arrest,

Artist unknown. *Majr. Genl. Ambrose E. Burnside. At the Battle of Fredericksburg, Va., Dec. 13th 1862,* 1863. Hand-colored lithograph, Currier & Ives, publisher, 11 ¾ x 8 ¾ in (29.85 x 22.23 cm). PR 052

organized what the *Atlas & Argus* newspaper described as, "[o]ne of the largest and most respectable meetings ever held at the Capitol," to protest against the arrest and trial, which they believed was a "crime against the Constitution."[32] New Yorkers arrived at the Capitol in droves and by 8 p.m. the broad walk leading to the Capitol steps and the adjacent grounds were packed with citizens.[33]

Although unable to attend the public meeting, New York's Democratic

Mathew B. Brady (ca. 1823–96).
Erastus Corning (1794–1872),
ca. 1860. Albumen print,
carte-de-visite, E. Anthony,
publisher, 3 ⅜ x 2 ⅛ in
(8.57 x 5.40 cm). PR 011

Governor Horatio Seymour forwarded a letter that was read aloud to the spirited crowd of three thousand that filled the Capitol park.[34] Like many New Yorkers, Seymour was outraged at what he believed was a depredation of civil liberties. He wrote:

> The transaction involved a series of offences against our most sacred rights. It interfered with the freedom of speech; it violated our rights to be secure in our homes against unreasonable searches and seizures; it pronounced sentence without a trial, save one which was a mockery, which insulted as well as wronged. The perpetrators now seek to impose punishment, not for an offence against the law but for a disregard of an invalid order, put forth in an utter disregard of principles of civil liberty.[35]

At the rally, fiery speeches criticized General Burnside for his action against Vallandigham. Among those who spoke were Judge Amasa J. Parker, Congressman Francis Kernan and the Honorable John W. Murphy. Orator after orator expressed outrage against the allegedly arbitrary action of the Administration. Not everyone in attendance criticized the Lincoln Administration's actions. Several soldiers who had just returned from the battlefield displayed great dissatisfaction with the meeting's purpose, breaking chairs into pieces and hurling them into the crowd.[36] The *New York Times* reported that at one point during the disruption it appeared as though the soldiers might seize control of the meeting.[37] Their efforts were eventually thwarted, however, and the meeting returned to order.[38] Ultimately, the attendees adopted a series of resolutions and ordered that they be transmitted to the president "with the assurance of this meeting of their hearty and earnest desire to support the Government in every Constitutional and lawful measure to suppress the existing Rebellion."[39] The resolutions drove home the point that those who attended the meeting regarded Vallandigham's arrest and imprisonment as illegal and unconstitutional.[40] In the Albany Democrats' opinion,

> [the] assumption of power by a military tribunal, if successfully asserted, not only abrogates the right of the people to assemble and discuss the affairs of Government, the liberty of speech and of the press, the right of trial by jury, the law of evidence, and the privileges of *Habeas Corpus*, but it strikes a fatal blow at the supremacy of law, and the authority of the State and Federal Constitutions.[41]

On May 19, 1863, only days after this extraordinary public meeting, Albany's former Democratic Mayor, Erastus Corning, who had been elected as president of the assemblage upon Henry S. Crandall's nomination, addressed a copy of the resolutions to Republican President Lincoln. Corning also enclosed a brief note signed by himself, as president of the assemblage, and by its vice presidents and secretaries.

In the days and weeks that followed the Albany meeting, Democrats staged similar rallies that were held throughout the state of New York to protest what organizers insisted was the administration's infringement upon the "most sacred rights of American freemen."[42] One of the largest of these public meetings of indignation took place in New York City's Union Square, which the *New York Times* dismissed as a "ridiculous demonstration."[43] Describing themselves as arguably disgraced by the actions of fellow New Yorkers who attended the meeting, the editors at the *Times* wrote that "[t]here was hardly a sentiment uttered through the whole meeting that might not and would not, have been applauded in Richmond. The fellows were brimful of sympathy with the rebels, and gave themselves full swing."[44] Mass meetings also took place in Utica, Troy, and Waterloo, while in Brooklyn a sub-committee of the Democratic General Committee was appointed to "consider the subject of the recent arbitrary arrests by the Government, and draft resolutions expressive of the sense of the Union Democratic General Committee."[45]

Those loyal to the Union and the Republican administration, however, quickly challenged these meetings. In Albany, hundreds assembled on May 20, 1863, "to

Adalbert Johann Volck (1828–1912). *Writing the Emancipation Proclamation*, Baltimore, 1863. Etching, 4 13/16 x 6 1/2 in (12.22 x 16.51 cm). PR 010

Artist unknown. *Copperheads Worshipping their Idol*, 1864. Lithograph, 15 ½ x 12 ⅜ in (39.37 x 31.43 cm). PR 010

COPPERHEADS WORSHIPING THEIR IDOL.

The above is a design made by a prominent N.Y. Democrat for a monument, to be erected in honor of Mᶜ Clellan, the 1ˢᵗ Emperor of North America. The monument is to be erected after his election to the Presidency, when the independence of the South will be acknowledged, an Empire proclaimed in the North instead of our present form of Government, and Horace Greeley ! Wendell Phillips ! & five hundred more Abolitionists hung by the neck until they are dead.

give expression to their patriotic loyalty, and to vindicate the Capital of the State of New York from the imputation of indifference to the results of the war and to the integrity of the Nation."[46] Echoing the sentiments that filled the pages of the *New York Times*, the *Albany Evening Journal* described the assemblage of the Albany Democrats as "a meeting to justify a bad man, and to denounce those who sought to punish him."[47] The pro-administration paper continued: "The meeting was, and will be, recognized as a meeting to approve what a man, who is at heart a

THE COPPERHEAD PARTY.——IN FAVOR OF *A VIGOROUS PROSECUTION OF PEACE!*

traitor, has said and done, rather than what its responsible managers will wish it to be deemed, viz.: a meeting to maintain the supremacy of the civil law."[48]

It was not long before Lincoln himself replied to the Albany Democrats and he did so with an extremely long, closely reasoned document, constructed in lawyer-like fashion, and sprawling over twenty pages of handwritten sheets. Lincoln justified the action of the administration in the arrest, trial, imprisonment, and banishment of Vallandigham and elaborated on his view that certain proceedings are constitutional "when in cases of rebellion or invasion, the public Safety requires them, which would not be constitutional when, in [the] absence of rebellion or invasion, the public Safety does not require them."[49] More extraordinarily, Lincoln made sure copies of the letter went not only to Corning but also to friendly newspapers in New York City like Horace Greeley's *Tribune*.

In Lincoln's opinion, the framers of the Constitution had been wise to include a provision allowing for the suspension of the writ of habeas corpus "when in cases of Rebellion or Invasion, the public Safety may require it," as such a suspension

Artist unknown. "The Copperhead Party—In Favor of *a Vigorous Prosecution of Peace!*" Wood engraving, published in *Harper's Weekly*, February 28, 1863. Library of Congress, 2003663007

BROMLEY & CO'S PUBLICATIONS.

Yours till deth
Majer Jack Downing

LETTERS
—OF—
Major Jack Downing,
OF THE
DOWNINGVILLE MILITIA,
ON THE WAR.

In one Volume, 254 Pages, 12mo. Price in Paper, $1. $1.25 in Cloth. With Portrait of the Major and Seven Illustrations, of which the five on this sheet are specimens.

The Letters of Major Jack Downing, which has furnished such a rich fund of entertainment to the public for the past three years, are now ready. In these Letters the reader will find a thorough review of the war, and its causes, given in a homely, practical style, and enforced by quaint and original stories of the most side-splitting character, from both Mr. Lincoln and the Major. Underneath all is a vein of sound common sense which carries conviction with it, and renders the volume a capital campaign document. The Major's style is inimitable, and suited to the humorist and fun-loving, whether he be a philosopher, scholar, statesman, politician or preacher. The Major improves, like whisky, with age, and his wit sparkles like diamonds through the whole book.

POLITICAL CARICATURES,
No. 1.

(Price of each Caricature Twenty-five Cents per copy; five copies, $1, eleven copies, $2, post-paid. By Express, $16 per hundred.)

Major Jack Downing's Dream; or, The Grave of the Union.

This picture shows at a glance the entire object and design of the Abolition or Republican party. Ben. Butler, D. S. Dickinson, John Cochrane, Horace Greeley, Lincoln, Stanton, Chase, Seward, Sumner, Welles, Beecher, etc., figure in it. Greeley, in his old white hat and spectacles, rejoicing over the grave of the Union, and Beecher, with a negro baby in his arms, are irresistibly comic and amusing.

COPPERHEAD MINSTREL.

A choice selection of Democratic Poems and Songs for the use of Political Clubs and the Democratic Social Circle.

These Poems embrace all the best pieces, whether Patriotc, Sentimental, or Humorous, which have appeared during the progress of this most cruel and unnatural war. One object of the work is to preserve in book-form, the most thrilling, beautiful, and witty Songs which have been published in Democratic papers since the reign of Lincoln. It will be a "remembrancer" of these unhappy times.

Prices: Single copies, 25 cents, or five copies for $1, sent post-paid. Fifty copies, $8. One hundred, $15, per express, at expense of purchaser. For any number less than fifty, at the rate of five for a dollar, post-paid.

"I'm darned if the critter warnt bizzy tryin' to git on Linkin's trowses."—Page 80.

NO. 2.
Miscegenation; or, the Millennium of Abolitionism

This is a capital hit upon the new plank in the Republican platform. It represents society as it is to be in the era of "Equality and Fraternity." Lincoln, Sumner, Greeley, a female Lecturer, and a large number of "colored ladies and gentlemen," with white drivers and servants, show what society is to be in the millennium of Abolitionism. No description can do justice to the hits contained in this picture. Both Caricatures are excellent campaign documents.

"He sed he jest cum out to see and be seen, and didn't intend to blab enything about public affairs."—Page 111.

The Copperhead; or, Badge of Liberty.

This is a neat Pin, just the shape of the head and bust of the "Goddess of Liberty" on the old cent, made of pure copper, highly polished, and artistic and suitable either for ladies or gentlemen, who are fearless enough to declare their devotion to Free Speech, Free Press, and the Rights of White Men.

Price: Single Padges, 15 Cents; eight for $1, post-paid.

"So I told Seward an' Stanten to take hold, and the way we rolled the Kernel over was a caushin."—Page 128.

NO. 3.
The Abolition Catastrophe; or, The November Smash Up.

This picture represents the leading politicians of both political parties as engaged in a railway race for the Capitol at Washington. One train is engineered by Gen. McClellan—the other, by Mr. Lincoln. The latter train runs into the obstructions of "Emancipation, Confiscation, Public Debt, To Whom it may Concern," &c., &c., and is smashed into thousands of pieces; while the McClellan train with the Constitution for an engine, rides triumphantly into power. The leading men of both parties figure in the scene.

Any of the above sent promptly on the receipt of price. Write plainly your post-office address, County and State.

"Major, that is what I call goin' to the bottom of a subject."—Page 161.

BROMLEY & CO., Publishers,
Box 4,265 New York City.
J. F. FEEKS, General Agent, No. 26 Ann Street, New York.

was necessary to prevent "sudden and extensive uprisings against the government."[50] Lincoln explained to the Albany Democrats that Vallandigham's arrest was not premised on the ex-Congressman's criticism of the administration, nor was it in an effort to silence him, as Albany Democrats had charged,[51] The *Atlas & Argus* opined that "[t]he arrest is a threat against every public man who refuses to advocate the extreme measures of the Abolition Cabinet."[52] Lincoln sought to impart to those who harbored such mistaken beliefs that they were incorrect and to provide a global defense of his policies, not just aimed at the Albany Democrats, but at the United States as a whole. Indeed, he later distributed his letter to newspapers nationwide, just as he had earlier done with his Special Message to Congress in 1861. He explained that Vallandigham was arrested for his avowed hostility to the Union's war efforts, his laboring to prevent the raising of troops, and his encouragement of desertions from the army.[53]

In Lincoln's reasoning, Vallandigham's efforts, aimed at damaging the army and leaving the Union without an adequate military force to suppress the rebellion, were intolerable to the administration and antithetical to the Union's attempt to preserve the nation.[54] Lincoln argued that experience has shown that armies cannot be maintained unless those who desert are punished by death. He believed that Vallandigham's efforts to encourage soldiers to desert the army were equally detrimental to the nation and should likewise be punished by death. With this, came the most remembered passage of Lincoln's reply. The president wrote, "Must I shoot a simple-minded soldier boy who deserts, while I must not touch a hair of a wiley agitator who induces him to desert? ... I think that in such a case, to silence the agitator, and save the boy, is not only constitutional, but, withal, a great mercy."[55]

Political opposition notwithstanding, Lincoln did not back down from his belief that it was absolutely necessary to try insurrectionists, like Vallandigham, before military tribunals.[56] In Lincoln's opinion, the civilian court system was woefully inadequate to handle such matters.[57] He wrote to Corning that "a jury too frequently have at least one member, more ready to hang the panel than to hang the traitor."[58] Lincoln believed that the civilian court system was properly suited for trying individuals for crimes that were well defined in the law, but was ill suited for trying those charged with insurrection. Driving home the point, Lincoln wrote:

> he who dissuades one man from volunteering, or induces one soldier to desert, weakens the Union cause as much as he who kills a Union soldier in battle. Yet this dissuasion, or inducement, may be so conducted as to be no defined crime of which any civil court would take cognizance.[59]

On July 3, 1863, Corning replied to the president. Showing no signs of retreating himself, his committee charged Lincoln with "pretensions to more

(opposite page) Artist unknown. Advertisement for Bromley and Company's election campaign publications, 1864. Wood engraving, broadside. PS 991.A1.L4.1864

POLITICAL CARICATURE. N⁰.4.

Lith. Kimmel & Forster 250 & 256 Canal Street N.Y.

Entered according to act of Congress in the year 1864 by Bromley & Co New York in the Clerks Office of the Districts Court of the United States, for the Southern district of New York

THE MISCEGENATION BALL

at the Headquarters of the Lincoln Central Campaign Club, Corner of Broadway and Twenty Third Street New York Sept. 22ᵈ 1864 being a perfect fac simile of the room &c. &c. (From the New York World Sept. 23ᵈ 1864) No sooner were the formal proceedings and speeches hurried through with, than the room was cleared for a 'negro ball,' which then and there took place! Some members of the 'Central Lincoln Club' left the room before the mystical and circling rites of languishing glance and mazy dance commenced. But that MANY remained is also true. This fact WE CERTIFY, *that on the floor during the progress of the ball were many of the accredited leaders of the Black Republican party*, thus testifying their faith by their works in the hall and headquarters of their political gathering. There were Republican OFFICE-HOLDERS, and prominent men of various degrees, and at least one PRESIDENTIAL ELECTOR ON THE REPUBLICAN TICKET."

Single Copies sent pr. mail post paid.

Artist unknown. *Political Caricature No. 4. The Miscegenation Ball*, 1864. Hand-colored lithograph, Kimmel & Forster, lithographer, G.W. Bromley & Co., publisher, 18 ⁷/₁₆ x 22 ⁹/₁₆ in (46.83 x 57.31 cm). PR 010

than regal authority" and insisted that he had used "misty and cloudy forms of expression" in setting forth his pretensions. It also took issue with Lincoln's description of the group as Democrats, instead of as American citizens, despite the fact that the assemblage itself used this self-description in its own resolutions. To this, Lincoln, the "wily" politician and astute lawyer in the White House, did not respond.

Lincoln's actions in the summer of 1863 would not settle the civil liberties debate for New Yorkers and certainly would not be the last time that New Yorkers would challenge Lincoln over what they believed were deprivations of citizens' civil liberties. The next controversy arose not over freedom of speech, but over freedom of the press, and involved the city's opposition newspapers.

On May 17, 1864, the *New York World* and the *New York Journal of Commerce* apparently fell victim to a ruse by stock speculators trying to manipulate the markets, and both papers unknowingly published a false presidential proclamation.[60] The alleged decree set May 26 as a day of fasting and prayer and called for a military draft of an additional 400,000 men.[61] When the morning editions hit the stands on May 18, it appeared as though the *New York World* and the *New York Journal of Commerce* had scooped their competitors.[62] It was not long, however, before the Associated Press transmitted a denial of the proclamation to almost every Northern daily paper.[63] Meanwhile, many in Washington wondered whether the fraudulent report was a Confederate plot to expose the North as desperate and to incite more draft riots.[64] After all, the *New York World* was formerly operated by Mayor Wood; now, under the editorship of Manton Marble and directorship of August Belmont, chairman of the Democratic National Committee, it was an anti-administration paper that less than a year earlier had helped stir the city's violent outburst against conscription.[65] The *Journal of Commerce*, edited by William C. Prime, was likewise a Democratic paper that had for years defended the South and slavery.[66]

Advised by Secretary of State William Seward and Secretary of War Edwin M. Stanton, Lincoln ordered the arrest of the papers' editors and publishers, as well as the seizure of the premises.[67] Specifically, the president instructed General John Dix to "take possession by military force, of the printing establishments of the New York World and Journal of Commerce … and prohibit any further publication thereof … You are therefore commanded forthwith to arrest and imprison … the editors, proprietors and publishers of the aforementioned newspapers."[68] The order would have come as a surprise to those who knew of Lincoln's earlier stated commitment to a free press, but, much like Lincoln's earlier disdain for infringements on personal liberties, Lincoln had come to discover that things were different in wartime.

In 1861, while engaged in debate with James A. Seddon of Virginia at a peace convention in Washington, D.C., Lincoln had advocated eloquently for a free press. "Your press is incendiary," Seddon said of the Northern papers. "It advocates servile insurrection, and advises our slaves to cut their masters' throats. You do not suppress your newspapers. You encourage their violence."[69] To this, Lincoln replied,

> I intend no offence, but I will not suffer such a statement to pass unchallenged, because it is not true. No Northern newspaper, not the most ultra, has advocated a slave insurrection or advised the slaves to cut their masters' throats. A gentleman of your intelligence should not make such assertions. We do maintain the freedom

of the press—we deem it necessary to a free government. Are we peculiar in that respect? Is not the same doctrine held in the South?[70]

Now, only three years later, Lincoln felt justified in temporarily changing his position on free speech, again citing the first priority of his presidency—preservation of the Union at all costs.

In effect, the two New York newspapers remained out of business until Lincoln personally countermanded the order. During this time, the *World* and the *Journal of Commerce* prepared statements explaining the situation, which were published by other New York newspapers on their behalf. The *New York Tribune* supported the explanation, writing "[t]his we know, is a truthful statement of the facts." The *Tribune* also urged the administration to revoke the order "for certainly no journal should be punished for a mistake which might have very innocently been committed by the most loyal paper in the land."[71] By and large, other newspapers in New York were similarly outspoken on the matter and joined in condemning their competitors' suspension.[72] Nevertheless, a capital correspondent of the New York *Commerical Advertiser*, a pro-Republican journal, wired to his office: "We of the press are semiofficially cautioned not to criticize the recent newspaper seizure in New York. It is very easy to write about the liberty of the press, but one's personal liberty is more desirable these broiling days. Discretion is the better part of valor—mum's the word."[73]

Fortunately for the arrested editors, only two days passed before General Dix determined that the papers had, indeed, been tricked.[74] Armed with this new information, Lincoln immediately told Stanton that, although the editors were responsible for what they printed, he did not intend to be vindictive: the papers should be handed back to the editors.[75] Lincoln's reversal of the shutdown order reflected his earlier promise to Mayor Wood: the president would safeguard the civil liberties of individuals at all costs, except to the extent that the nation's preservation required otherwise.

Lincoln's countermand did not quell all fears in New York, however. Much as he had done with his earlier response to the Lincoln administration's trial of Vallandigham, Governor Seymour wrote a sharp-tongued letter to the District Attorney of the County of New York on May 23, 1864, charging the government with acts of violence without due legal process.[76] The letter, which was reprinted in the *New York Times*, argued that "[a]t this time of civil war and disorder, the majesty of the law must be upheld or society will sink into anarchy" and encouraged the District Attorney to investigate whether the government itself should be punished. Legal action was eventually taken against General Dix and members of his staff but it proved meritless as the case never proceeded past Judge A. D. Russell, who observed that the Habeas Corpus Act, if constitutional, "assimilates the

Artist unknown. *Political Caricature No. 3. The Abolition Catastrophe, or the November Smash-up*, 1864. Lithograph, G. W. Bromley & Co., publisher, 17 7/16 x 21 3/8 in (44.29 x 54.29 cm). PR 010

President of the United States during the existence of the present rebellion, to an absolute monarch, and makes him incapable of doing any wrong."[77]

Once reopened, the *New York World* bounced back to become one of Lincoln's most virulent critics in late 1863 and 1864. As Lincoln prepared for the election of 1864, the paper attacked him mercilessly, devising and executing against him what came to be known as the miscegenation campaign. In December 1863 reporters at the *New York World* concocted a pamphlet entitled, "Miscegenation:

The Theory of the Blending of the Races, Applied to the American White Man and Negro," a not-so-subtle attempt to advocate for mixing the races.[78] When the pamphlet made its debut, however, the authors were unknown and, from the pamphlet's context, appeared to be abolitionists.[79] The pamphlet urged Lincoln to add a miscegenation plank to the Republican Party platform.[80] It suggested that Lincoln proclaim that "the solution of the negro problem will not have been reached in this country until public opinion sanctions a union of the two races ... that in the millennial future, the most perfect and highest type of manhood will not be white or black but brown, or colored, and that whoever helps to unite the various races of man, helps to make the human family the sooner realize its great destiny."[81]

The Democratic Party took the ideas espoused in the pamphlet and ran with it, using it to depict Republicans as promoters of miscegenation.[82] Throughout the spring and summer of 1864, Democrats sought to appeal to the racism of white, working class Americans, hoping to convince them to vote against Lincoln in the election.[83] Although the controversy centered, yet again, in New York, unlike Lincoln's earlier response to the *New York World* and *Journal of Commerce*'s false reports, this time neither Lincoln nor his administration interfered with discussion about the pamphlet and chose to ignore it.[84] As it turned out, it was again the *New York World* who was at the center of the controversy, and two of its virulently anti-Abolitionist reporters were to blame for the pamphlet's content and dissemination.[85]

As the election drew near, the *World* continued to criticize the president, at one point writing the following in reference to the fitness of Abraham Lincoln and Andrew Johnson for the offices of president and vice president:

> In a crisis of the most appalling magnitude, requiring statesmanship of the highest order, the country is asked to consider the claims of two ignorant, boorish, third-rate, backwoods lawyers, for the highest stations in the government. Such nominations, in such a conjuncture, are an insult to the common sense of the people. God save the Republic!"[86]

Much to the *World*'s dismay, Lincoln won the November election, with the Republicans prevailing in New York, earning 50.46 percent of the vote in the Empire State, despite having lost heavily in New York City, where he received only 33.22 percent of the vote. Lincoln had fared no better in Kings, Albany, and Erie Counties. Lincoln's defeat in many New York cities and throughout significant portions of the state was attributed to the influx of Irish immigrants who supported the Democratic party, coupled with anti-Lincoln sentiment, especially on the issue of civil liberties. Fortunately, Lincoln had one last hope. For the first time in history, soldiers were allowed to cast absentee ballots and they did so in large number.[87] Of the total votes cast in the field, the nation's Commander-in-Chief received

121,152 to his opponent, George McClellan's 34,922.[88] The absentee ballots for New York ultimately led to Lincoln's victory in the state, as he prevailed by only 7,740 votes.[89]

In truth, the nation was fortunate that during the darkest days of civil war, it had held an election at all. Days after the vote, Lincoln spoke freely about the necessity of elections for the benefit of democracy. "We can not have free government without elections; and if the rebellion could force us to forego, or postpone a national election, it might fairly claim to have already conquered and ruined us," Lincoln stressed, perhaps demonstrating that he was a small "d" democrat at heart and that the reports of his stifling civil liberties may have been greatly exaggerated.[90]

Although New York served as one of the leading hosts of criticism of President Lincoln's wartime actions, the public debate spawned by such antagonism proved instrumental in helping the public comprehend Lincoln's wartime decisions. Lincoln understood the power of public opinion, remarking during his famous 1858 debates with Stephen A. Douglas that "public sentiment is everything."[91] Understandably, New Yorkers, like other Americans, disliked temporary curtailments of their civil liberties, but perhaps came to agree that, as historian Daniel Farber has recognized, "given the extremity of the country's situation, Lincoln's record on civil liberties was not at all bad."[92]

In the end, Lincoln's army won, leaving future generations with a singular, and not plural United States—and one that, as historian James McPherson has put it, "is" and not "are"—or were. As another scholar, Seventh Circuit Court of Appeals Judge Richard A. Posner, has aptly noted: "Lincoln's unconstitutional acts during the Civil War show that even legality must sometimes be sacrificed for other values. We are a nation under law, but first we are a nation."[93]

NOTES

Acknowledgment: The author is indebted to Nicole J. Dulude, Esquire, for her assistance on this article.

1   Edward McPherson, *The Political History of the United States During the Great Rebellion*, 2nd ed. (Washington, DC: Philp & Solomons, 1865), 43.

2   Edward Robb Ellis, *The Epic of New York City: A Narrative History* (New York: Basic Books 2004), 291.

3   Copperheads were Northern Democrats who sided with the South and opposed the Civil War. Republicans dubbed such war opponents Copperheads because of the copper liberty-head coins they wore as badges. David S. Heidler & Jeanne T. Heidler eds., *Encyclopedia of the American Civil War: A Political, Social, and Military History* (New York: W. W. Norton, 2000), 1:498-99. The term Copperhead was "borrowed from the poisonous snake of the same name that lies in hiding and strikes without warning. However, 'Copperheads' regarded themselves as lovers of liberty, and some of them wore a lapel pin with the head of the Goddess of Liberty cut out of the large copper penny minted by the Federal treasury."

Frank J. Williams, "Abraham Lincoln and Civil Liberties in Wartime," *Heritage Lectures* 5 (May 5, 2004): n.18, http://www.heritage.org/Research/NationalSecurity/hl834.cfm.

4   Roy P. Basler, ed., *The Collected Works of Abraham Lincoln* (New Brunswick: Rutgers University Press, 1953-1955), 4:233.

5   Ibid.

6   Ibid., 5:436-37.

7   Ibid.

8   Charles W. Sanders Jr., *While in the Hands of the Enemy: Military Prisons of the Civil War* (Baton Rouge: Louisiana State University Press, 2005), 56.

9   Ibid.

10 Ibid.

11 A Day at Fort Lafayette, *New York Times*, September 24, 1861.

12 Edward K. Spann, *Gotham at War: New York City, 1860-1865* (Lanham: SR Books 2002), 161.

13 Ibid.

14 General Order No. 37, in Benjamin Perley Poor, *The Life and Public Services of Ambrose E. Burnside, Solider-Citizen-Statesman* (Providence: J.A. & R.A. Reid Publishers, 1882), 204.

15 Ibid., 208-09.

16 Congressional Globe, 37th Cong., 1st sess., 1861, 57-59; see generally Frank L. Klement, *The Limits of Dissent* (New York: Fordham University Press,1998).

17 Ex parte Vallandigham, 68 U.S. 243, 244 (1864).

18 Michael Kent Curtis, *Lincoln, Vallandigham, and Anti-War Speech in the Civil War*, 7; Wm. And Mary Bill of Rts. J. 105, 107, 122 (1998) (hereinafter Curtis); *see also* Vallandigham Arrested, *Atlas & Argus*, May 6, 1863.

19 Curtis, *Lincoln, Vallandigham, and Anti-War Speech*, 107.

20 Poor, *Life and Public Services*, 208; William H. Rehnquist, *All the Laws But One* (New York: Vintage, 1998), 65-66.

21 Ex parte Vallandigham, 68 U.S. at 244; *see also* Curtis, 105, 121.

22 *Atlas & Argus*, May 13, 1863.

23 *The Trial of Hon. Clement L. Vallandigham by a Military Commission and the Proceedings under his Application for a Writ of Habeas Corpus in the Circuit Court of the United States for the Southern District of Ohio* (Cincinnati: Rickey & Carroll, 1863), 33.

24 Ibid., 37-39.

25 Vallandigham, 68 U.S. at 251.

26 Basler, *Collected Works of Abraham Lincoln*, 6:266.

27 Revival of Arbitrary Arrests, *Atlas & Argus*, May 12, 1863.

28 Ibid.

29 "The Vallandigham Outrage: Meeting at the Capitol in Behalf of Personal Freedom," *Atlas & Argus*, May 16, 1863.

30 "The Arrest of Vallandigham," *New York Times*, May 8, 1863.

31 "Where Shall Vallandigham Go?" *New York Times*, May 13, 1863.

32 "The Arrest of Vallandigham," *Atlas & Argus*, May 8, 1863, at 2.

33 "The Vallandigham Outrage: Immense Meeting at the Capitol," *Atlas & Argus*, May 18, 1863.

34 General News, *New York Times*, May 19, 1863.

35 "The Vallandigham Outrage: Immense Meeting at the Capitol," *Atlas & Argus*, May 18, 1863.

36 Ibid.

37 Ibid.

38 Ibid.

39 Ibid.

40 Ibid.

41 Ibid.

42 "The Vallandigham Outrage: The Voice of the People," *Atlas & Argus*, May 26, 1863.

43 "The Copperhead Indignation Meeting", *New York Times*, May 20, 1863.

44 Ibid.

45 "The Vallandigham Outrage: The Voice of the People," *Atlas & Argus*, May 26, 1863.

46 "The Union Must and Shall be Preserved," *Albany Evening Journal*, May 19, 1863; see also "The Great War Meeting," *Albany Evening Journal*, May 21, 1863.

47 "The Vallandigham Meeting," *Albany Evening Journal*, May 18, 1863.

48 Ibid.

49 Basler, *Collected Works of Abraham Lincoln*, 2:260, 267. The portions of Lincoln's letter to Erastus Corning are reprinted in the *Collected Works* as it appeared in the *New York Tribune* on July 15, 1863. This version incorporates revisions that Lincoln made in the copy prepared for the press as well as the final copy sent to Corning. The original letter has not been located.

50 Ibid., 265.

51 Ibid., 266.

52 "Revival of Arbitrary Arrests," *Atlas & Argus*, May 12, 1863.

53 Basler, *Collected Works of Abraham Lincoln*, 2:266.

54 Ibid.

55 Ibid., 266-67.

56 Ibid., 264.

57 Ibid.

58 Ibid.

59 Ibid.

60 Robert S. Harper, *Lincoln and the Press* (New York: McGraw-Hill, 1951), 289.

61 Ibid., 290-91.

62 Ibid., 291.

63 Ibid., 292.

64 Ibid., 293.

65 In 1863 draft riots broke out in New York City, brought about by conscription. Initially, the rioters, many of them Irish immigrants, targeted only military and governmental buildings but soon they came to attack blacks in the city and targeted those things that were symbolic of black political, economic and social power. Leslie M. Harris, *In the Shadow of Slavery: African Americans in New York City, 1626-1863* (Chicago: University of Chicago Press, 2003). The riots were finally quelled when General George Meade arrived from Gettysburg to restore order in the city.

66 Basler, *Collected Works of Abraham Lincoln*, 2:289, 293.

67 Ibid., 293.

68 Ibid., 7:347.

69 Charles Carleton Coffin, *Life of Lincoln* (New York: Harper and Brothers 1893), 235.

70 Ibid.

71 *New York Tribune*, May 19, 1864.

72 Harper, *Lincoln and the Press*, 299.

73 Ibid., 298.

74 Ibid., 297.

75 Ibid.

76 "The Seizure of the Press," *The New York Times*, May 25, 1864.

77 Harper, *Lincoln and the Press*, 302.

78 David E. Long, *The Jewel of Liberty* (Mechanicsburg: Stackpole Books,1994), 153-54.

79 Ibid., 154.

80 Ibid., 157.

81 Sidney Kaplan, *American Studies in Black and White: Selected Essays 1949-1989* (Amherst: University of Massachusetts Press, 1991), 53.

82 Long, *Jewel of Liberty*, 165.

83 Ibid., 156.

84 Jean H. Baker, *Affairs of Party: The Political Culture of Northern Democrats in the Mid-Nineteenth Century* (New York: Fordham University Press, 1998), 252.

85   Long, 154.

86 John C. Waugh, *Reelecting Lincoln: The Battle for the 1864 Presidency* (New York: Crown, 1998), 201.

87 Frank J. Williams, *Judging Lincoln* (Carbondale: Southern Illinois University Press, 2002), 115-17.

88 Ibid., 117.

89 Ibid.

90 Basler, *Collected Works of Abraham Lincoln*, 8:101.

91 Ibid., 3:27.

92 Daniel Farber, *Lincoln's Constitution* (Chicago: University of Chicago Press, 2003), 175.

93 Richard A. Posner, "The Truth About Our Liberties," in *Rights vs. Public Safety After 911: America in the Age of Terrorism*, ed. Amitai Etzioni and Jason H. Marsh (Lanham, MD: Rowman and Littlefield, 2003), 27.

MRS. LINCOLN IN WARTIME NEW YORK

CATHERINE CLINTON

R EADERS OF THE *New York Era* newspaper in July 1862 would have been intrigued by the following: "Minnie—What is Up? Why did you pass me in Broadway on Saturday with the air of an iceberg? Please answer my last letter and explain all, for this suspense is beyond endurance."[1] This sidewalk snub was recorded in July 1862, appearing alongside details about military operations, about slave emancipation in the District of Columbia, and side-by-side with marriage announcements and advertisements for theatrical performances. New York was awash with the business of the Civil War, but, as Minnie's friend demonstrated, New Yorkers being New Yorkers knew the show must go on.

The seat of national government had moved from the southernmost tip of Manhattan decades before young Abraham Lincoln daydreamed of escape from his Kentucky farmstead. His bride-to-be, the precocious Mary Todd, was a striving daughter of the bluegrass, whose youthful ambitions stoked her fascination with New York City.[2] Rhapsodic about fashion from an early age, she was perhaps even more eager to embrace the haute if not haughty standard by which Manhattan measured the rest of the world.[3] Once her husband was elected, Mary made almost a dozen excursions to Manhattan—including two visits between the time her husband was elected and the time he took office, eager to cash in on what she hoped would be the cachet to come.

New York City had been a tempting mirage for the young couple from their earliest days. After a difficult courtship, Mary Todd and Abraham Lincoln were married on November 4, 1842, in her older sister Elizabeth's Springfield, Illinois parlor, before moving into a boarding house, unable to afford their own home. Elizabeth Edwards was a member of the local aristocracy. Yet neither she, nor none

Lewis Emory Walker (1822–80). *Abraham Lincoln*, Washington, DC, ca. February 1865. Albumen silver print. Library of Congress

Artist unknown. *Elizabeth Todd Edwards.* Lincoln Presidential Library, Springfield, IL.

of her siblings or extended kin, were part of the fashionably mobile American set that seasonally moved from shore to springs, from country home to townhouse, free to move without financial concerns. Rather, Mary and her sisters were members of the hometown nobility who held sway over locals. This noblesse was something to which Mary had been born, but after her marriage to a poor man, something, she felt, had gone missing. She remained socially ambitious during her marriage, but it was only her status as First Lady that would elevate her to what she felt entitled.

Many in their hometown of Springfield grumbled about Mary Lincoln's snobbish demeanor long before Lincoln's prominence in politics, but most acknowledged that her grit and polish assisted her husband's ascent up the ladder. After Lincoln's election to serve in the Thirtieth Congress, Mrs. Lincoln insisted upon accompanying her husband to Washington, and it wasn't until 1849, when he was forty and his bride was not yet thirty-two, that the couple paid a first visit East together.[4]

Both were eager to return to the Atlantic seaboard, but it was nearly a decade before they visited Manhattan in 1857, when Lincoln decided to pay a call in person at the headquarters of the railway company that owed him a great deal of money. This jaunt to New York City turned into a family summer holiday, with a sightseeing detour to Niagara Falls, and stopovers in Chicago, to the delight of the Lincoln sons.

During Mary's first prolonged visit to Manhattan, she was definitely smitten and caught a terrible case of envy. She shared an anecdote that while surveying European-bound steamers in New York harbor, she sighed "that poverty was [her] portion." She laughingly reported that she told "Mr. L"—the way she most often identified her husband in letters—"that I am determined my next husband *shall be rich.*"[5] Her exposure to glittering allure in America's culture and fashion capital heightened her sense of wistfulness.

Fleeting Manhattan encounters left someone with Mary's tastes even more unsatisfied with modest prairie circumstances. Mrs. Lincoln continued to fret over her husband's fortunes, especially after 1858 when he was defeated in his race for the Senate for the second time in three years. But there was a different outcome two years later, when a rematch was mounted within the national arena in the race

for president. Beginning with a speech in New York at Cooper Union in February 1860, Lincoln upstaged Stephen Douglas, his dandified rival. Lincoln beat out three other candidates to become the country's first "western" president, and the first Republican to claim the Executive Mansion.[6]

When this "log cabin candidate" achieved the highest office in the land, his rise might have been admired by New York kingmaker Thurlow Weed and veteran journalist Horace Greeley.[7] Yet most New Yorkers joined the chorus of complaint that an unqualified bumpkin was invading the White House.

Mary's first trip to New York after her husband's election hinted at what lay ahead. While her husband grappled with unfolding events such as South Carolina's secession, forming a Cabinet, and other challenges, Mrs. Lincoln focused on the logistics of the family's move to Washington. Shortly after the New Year in 1861, she headed for New York to pick up a few things on her way to collect her son Robert, who was studying at Harvard. Robert could certainly make the journey home on his own, but Mary embraced the chance for a stopover in Manhattan following Lincoln's new status.[8] She basked in the celebrity, while becoming a target for the press.

Mrs. Lincoln left Springfield on January 8th, accompanied by her brother-in-law, local merchant Clark Smith. Even before she returned home, her conduct came under fire, as one Republican complained: "The idea of the President's wife kiting

(above left) Nicholas H. Shepherd. *Abraham Lincoln (1809–65)*, Springfield, IL, ca. 1846. Daguerreotype. Library of Congress, LC USZC4-2439, Dag no. 1224

(above right) Probably Nicholas H. Shepherd. *Mary Todd Lincoln (1818–82)*, Springfield, IL, ca. 1846. Daguerreotype. Library of Congress, LC USZC4-6189, Dag no. 1223

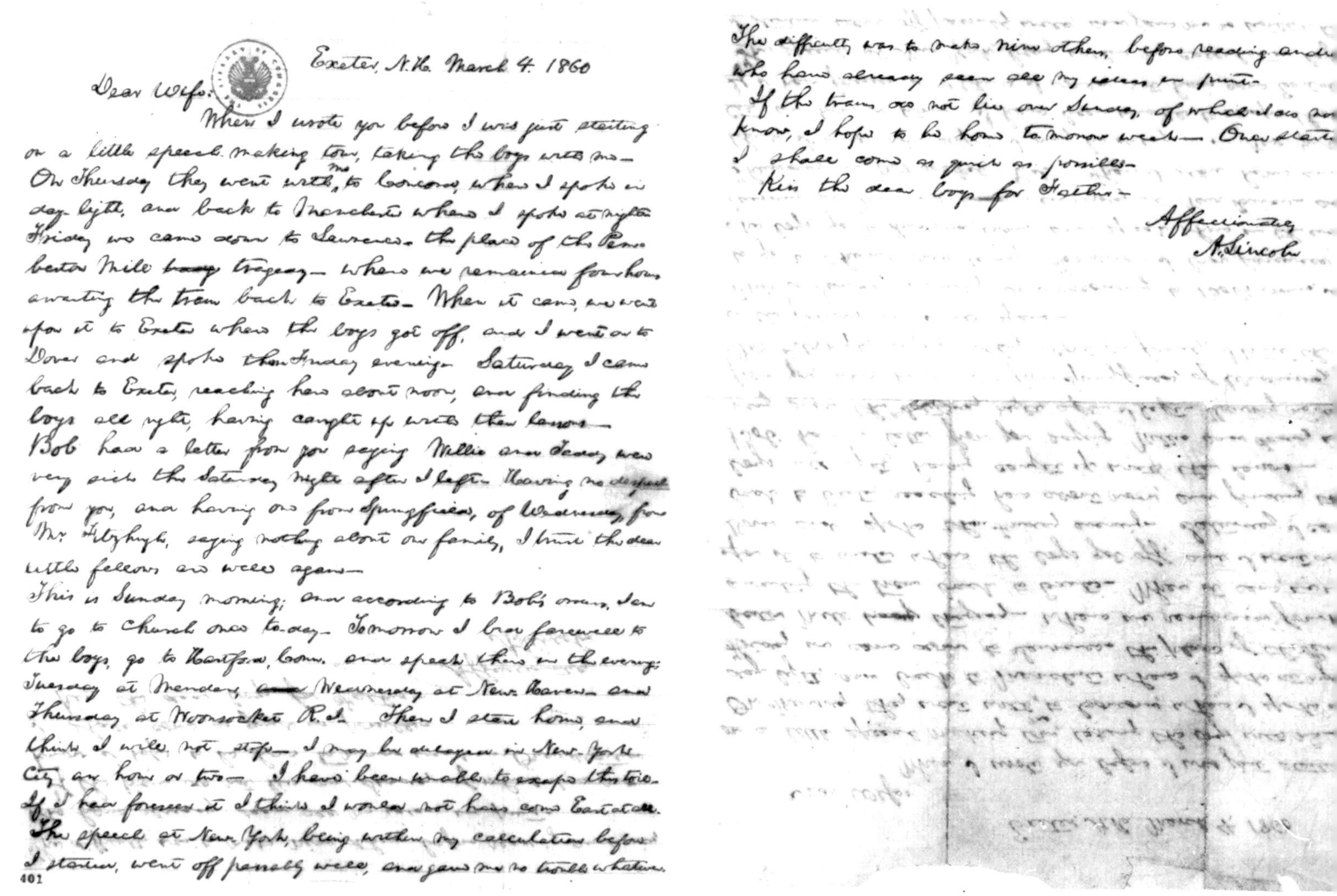

Exeter, N.H. March 4. 1860

Dear Wife:

When I wrote you before I was just starting on a little speech-making tour, taking the boys with me— On Thursday they went with me, to Concord, where I spoke in day-light, and back to Manchester where I spoke at night. Friday we came down to Lawrence— the place of the Pemberton Mill tragedy— where we remained four hours awaiting the train back to Exeter— When it came, we went upon it to Exeter where the boys got off, and I went on to Dover and spoke there Friday evening. Saturday I came back to Exeter, reaching here about noon, and finding the boys all right, having caught up with their lessons— Bob had a letter from you saying Willie and Taddy were very sick the Saturday night after I left— Having no dispatch from you, and having one from Springfield, of Wednesday, from Mr. Fitzhugh, saying nothing about our family, I trust the dear little fellows are well again—

This is Sunday morning; and according to Bob's orders, I am to go to Church once to-day— Tomorrow I bid farewell to the boys, go to Hartford, Conn. and speak there in the evening; Tuesday at Meriden, Wednesday at New-Haven— and Thursday at Woonsocket R.I. Then I start home, and think I will not stop— I may be delayed in New-York City an hour or two— I have been unable to escape this toil— If I had foreseen it I think I would not have come East at all. The speech at New-York, being within my calculation before I started, went off passably well, and gave me no trouble whatever.

401

The difficulty was to make nine others, before reading audie

who have already seen all my ideas in print—

If the train does not lie over Sunday, of which I do no

know, I hope to be home to-morrow week— Once start

I shall come as quick as possible—

Kiss the dear boys for Father—

Affectionately

A. Lincoln

Abraham Lincoln to Mary Todd Lincoln, March 4, 1860. Report from Exeter, New Hampshire, Letter. Abraham Lincoln Papers, Library of Congress.

Lincoln had been invited to speak in New England after his speech at Cooper Union in New York on February 27, 1860. While visiting his son Robert, a student at Phillips Exeter Academy in New Hampshire, Lincoln writes to Mary dramatically about his physical exhaustion, and modestly about his political success.

"*. . . I may be delayed in New-York City an hour or two-- I have been unable to escape this toil-- If I had foreseen it I think I would not have come East at all. The speech at New-York, being within my calculation before I started, went off passably well, and gave me no trouble whatever. The difficulty was to make nine others, before reading audiences, who have already seen all my ideas in print--.*"

ARRIVAL OF MR. LINCOLN, PRESIDENT ELECT AT THE ASTOR HOUSE, NEW YORK. See page 278.

Artist unknown. *Arrival of Mr. Lincoln, President Elect, at the Astor House,* 1861. Wood engraving, published in *New-York Illustrated News,* March 2, 1861. *E171.D38

MR. LINCOLN'S RECEPTION OF THE CITIZENS IN THE GOVERNOR'S ROOM, AT THE CITY HALL, NEW YORK. See page 279.

Artist unknown. *Mr. Lincoln's Reception of the Citizens in the Governor's Room,* 1861. Wood engraving, published in *New-York Illustrated News,* March 2, 1861. *E171.D38

about the country and holding levees at which she indulges in a multitude of silly speeches is looked upon as very shocking."[9] Her unconventional attachment to politics was condemned by many of Lincoln's supporters, as well as all of his detractors.[10]

Further, while in New York City, Mary was forced to confront the fact that electoral victory was the beginning, rather than the end of the struggle. The veil was most cruelly torn away from Mary's eyes.[11] While in the dining room of the

THE LINCOLN FAMILY IN 1861.

John Chester Buttre (1821–93) after Francis Bicknell Carpenter. *The Lincoln Family in 1861.* Handcolored engraving, J.C. Buttre Co., publisher, 17 ¹¹⁄₁₆ x 24 ³⁄₁₆ in (44.93 x 61.44 cm). PR 052

fashionable Metropolitan Hotel, she overheard gentlemen discussing her husband's shortcomings. One man loudly questioned: "Could he, with any honor, fill the Presidential Chair? Would his western gaucherie disgrace the Nation?"[12] These insults rattled Mary and foreshadowed what was to come.[13]

Yet when she next arrived in the city, surrounded by the cocoon of presidential trappings, her reception proved strikingly different, as a crowd estimated at 250,000 watched the parade of eleven carriages ferrying the president-elect's family and

GRAND RECEPTION NOTABILITIES NATION
AT THE WHITE HOUSE 1865

Dedicated to Mrs Abraham Lincoln

by the Publisher of Frank Leslie Chimney Corner

PRICE $3.00

Every Person who pays Ten Cents each for numbers 1 and 2 of
FRANK LESLIE'S
CHIMNEY CORNER,
The New Family Paper,
is entitled to a copy of this PLATE without extra charge. The Key to this Plate, giving the name of each individual portrait, will be published in No. 4 of the CHIMNEY CORNER.

entourage to the Astor House on February 19th.

By the time Mary settled into her new home in Washington, she found the condition of the White House to be more of a challenge than she had imagined. In 1860 an "auction" of over fifty items from the White House disposed of threadbare and unwanted goods, yet even her Springfield friends and relations found the Executive Mansion worn and shabby, with the air of a second-rate hotel.[14] Harriet Lane, who had served as her uncle James Buchanan's hostess, met with Mrs. Lincoln upon her arrival and reported, "Mrs. Lincoln is awfully *western*, loud & unrefined."[15] Clearly Mrs. Lincoln had her work cut out for her as society women up and down the East Coast were assessing her and finding her style considerably *de trop*. Mary determined that her new status would require several trips to Manhattan to put things right.

Lincoln did not discourage his wife's ambitions to make their new home a

Artist unknown. *Grand Reception of the Notabilities of the Nation,* 1865. Lithograph, Major & Knapp, printer, Frank Leslie, publisher, 14 ¾ x 20 ³⁄₁₆ in (37.47 x 51.28 cm). Gift of Henry O. Havemeyer, PR 052

GRAND BALL GIVEN BY THE CITIZENS OF NEW YORK AT THE ACADEMY OF MUSIC, IN HONOR OF THE PRINCE OF WALES—THE PRINCE OPENING THE BALL.—SEE PAGE 886.

"Grand Ball at the Academy of
Music to the Prince of Wales."
Wood engraving, published in
Frank Leslie's Illustrated Newspaper,
October 27, 1860. *E171.L63

showplace for the nation, even in the midst of unfolding rebellion.[16] Within weeks
of her arrival on the scene, Mrs. Lincoln's fondness for shopping had become part
of her image—with reporters hounding her every move. One journalist observed:
"If she but drives down Pennsylvania Avenue, the electric wire trills the news to
every hamlet in the Union."[17]

Shopkeepers in the nation's capital lured Mary Lincoln into their stores, but
she was drawn most to New York's emporiums. As one nineteenth-century chronicler
confessed: "extravagance is the besetting sin of New York society."[18] Merchants
vied to flatter and dress the First Lady, but none was more eager than the patriotic
and flamboyant A.T. Stewart.

In 1823, Irish-born Stewart opened his "linen and lace" shop in downtown
Manhattan. By 1848, the Belfast native transformed his shop into a five-story dry
goods emporium, stretching the entire block from Chambers to Reade streets along
Broadway, north of City Hall Park. His impressive expansions stimulated great
fortune, and Stewart became the first New Yorker to be dubbed a "merchant
prince."[19] In 1862, Stewart built an even more breathtaking marble palace near

Photographer unknown. *Beginning of Department Stores*, ca. 1853. 8 7/16 x 6 ½ in (21.43 x 16.51 cm). Subject files, N-YHS Department of Prints, Photographs, and Architectural Collections. Gift of Mrs. Elihu Spicer, PR 020

Tenth Street and Astor Place, with the world's largest cast iron building front. By 1865, Stewart's total sales were nearly fifty million dollars. His personal wealth a decade later made him the seventh richest person in the country.

In downtown Manhattan, Stewart's store, Lord & Taylor's, and what would become Macy's department store flourished during the American Civil War. George Huntington Hartford launched his Great American Tea Company, which would expand into the A&P retail food chain. In 1860, Madame Demorest opened her own shop and began to sell tissue-papered dress patterns,

Tiffany & Co. Ewer presented to Abraham Lincoln on his first inauguration from his Washington friends, March 4, 1861. Sterling with gold wash. Marked *Tiffany & Co/550 Broadway/English Sterling 925–1000*, with mark for J. C. Moore and Son. Courtesy Cowan's Auctions

netting as much as three million dollars a year by 1876.

Although Paris boasted its "grand magasins de nouveautés" and London supported several "universal providers," American retailers were urban pioneers, creating a new and swelling flock of devoted consumers.[20] Branding became a part of the American retail experience, beginning with Charles Lewis Tiffany, who parlayed his experience working as a clerk in his father's dry goods store into owning a thriving glass, porcelain, silver, and jewelry business. His 1845 catalogue promoted his store as a cultural destination. In 1854, Tiffany's settled into 550 Broadway, a location near the St. Nicholas Hotel, which was especially popular with visitors from the West who came to New York to gawk and shop.[21]

Often, the local gentry were not amused. New York's social establishment, with its Dutch and British origins, had a clear set of rules and regulations, betraying its culturally royalist roots, despite claims of republican or even "Republican" egalitarianism. Manhattan society on the brink of the Civil War focused its frenzied energies on the Academy of Music ball given for the Prince of Wales in 1860.[22] Balls and weddings were the moments when would-be doyennes looking to move up the ladder hoped that taste and wealth might be played to their best advantage: where jewels and gowns, and gestures and deportment were all closely scrutinized and decoded for deeper meanings. These were public spectacles where reputations could be made as well as ruined.[23]

The Manhattan society dance was a grand occasion. During the opening march and mid-point quadrille, followed by a lavish supper, elaborate rituals unfolded. Especially important were the New York assembly balls given in January, where young women from the best families made their debuts. The fondness for costume balls swept in during the 1840s, but faded with the sobering realities of war. Prior to the Civil War, gentlemen's clubs were popular—the Union Club and the Century Association, for example—but one commentator observed, "the ladies are among the bitterest opponents of the system."[24] War brought other sea changes.

MRS. LINCOLN IN WARTIME NEW YORK 205

The established aristocracy feared the "degeneracy" introduced by wartime lapses, as two society women lamented "married ladies supping at Delmonico's without their husbands and the rompishness of the younger ladies."[25] Nevertheless, all this rompishness and hijinks were what attracted outsiders to New York, along with the fine European imports and the exquisite range of goods offered and on such lavish display. After Mrs. Lincoln was given her $20,000 for the White House's refurbishment, she naturally headed for what awaited her in the crowded aisles of America's trendsetting isle of Manhattan.

During her shopping excursion in May 1861, Mary might even be commended for selecting a fine Haviland dinner service with solferino and gilt detail for state occasions, decorated with the seal of the United States on each piece. Jean Baker suggests that the entwining of a gold border with two lines is "signifying the Union of North and South."[26] However, what is remembered is neither Mrs. Lincoln's taste nor her patriotism, but that she ordered a second set, at a cost of $1,100, and had her own initials emblazoned on this tableware.[27]

John William Orr (1815–87). Tiffany & Co., 1850. Wood engraving, 8 ¾ x 6 in (22.23 x 15.24 cm). Gift of Daniel Parish Jr., PR 020

While a New York reporter accompanied her wardrobe shopping, she told him that she could not afford the cost of some luxury goods in cashmere and lace with which merchants tempted her, and she was "determined to be very economical." But when luxury items ended up in her personal trunks, and she appeared in a parade of new fashions, an avalanche of bad press followed. One New York reporter fumed that Mrs. Lincoln's china would match "the mulberry colored livery of her footmen."[28] This kind of shrill attack persisted throughout her husband's presidency.

A few blocks away from where Mrs. Lincoln was conducting her shopping campaigns in May 1861, a group of New York women were launching their own

BALL, BLACK & CO., MANUFACTURERS & IMPORTERS OF SILVER & PLATED WARE, DIAMONDS, WATCHES &c
Sign of theGolden Eagle, **247 BROADWAY**, South Corner of Murray Street, opposite the City Hall, **NEW YORK.**

Artist unknown. "Ball, Black & Co., Manufacturers & Importers of Silver & Plated Ware, Diamonds, Watches &c.," 1857. Wood engraving, 6 ³⁄₁₆ x 8 ¹³⁄₁₆ in (15.72 x 22.38 cm). PR 020

new enterprise. Many of them, brought up in affluent surroundings, now found the maintenance of elegant décor and social obligation passé. The bracing atmosphere of flag waving and patriotic sacrifice appealed to many women of means in New York City. The president's appeal for military volunteers energized these females to mobilize and offer themselves to the Union effort as well.

First and foremost, the audacious campaign launched by women and for women to channel their energies into soldiers' aid was intended to supplant the frippery of fashion. There would always be obsession with hats, ribbons, and hemlines, but Lincoln's call to arms catapulted women's possibilities into a different orbit. New York women hoped to rise to the occasion.

Pioneering medical reformers Elizabeth and Emily Blackwell called a meeting of women in New York City to coordinate efforts for soldiers on the homefront. On April 29, 1861, between 2,000 and 3,000 women responded to the Blackwells' call. The gathered assemblage decided to train nurses for work in the field and to establish a network of soldiers' aid societies: the Women's Central Relief Association [WCRA]. Unitarian minister Henry Bellows was elected president of the group,

MRS. LINCOLN'S WARDROBE ON EXHIBITION IN NEW YORK.—SKETCHED BY STANLEY FOX.—[SEE PAGE 686.]

with a board of twelve (six men and six women) delegated to oversee the organization's goals. While in Washington to coordinate with government efforts, Bellows caved in to the many restrictive demands of Secretary of War Simon Cameron, much to the disappointment of the Blackwells.[29]

Despite misgivings about female nurses in Washington, the WCRA women trained nearly one hundred nurses over the course of the war. Volunteers such as Georgeanna Woolsey gave themselves wholeheartedly to this cause, although these nurses might find themselves ill equipped and stranded on hospital ships with a boatload of wounded and dying men, with no supplies.

Less than six months after it had been founded as an independent woman's organization, wartime exigency demoted the group to an affiliate of the United States Sanitary Commission, with Bellows at the helm. Nevertheless, this auxiliary became one of the most dynamic of voluntary organizations engineered by women. Leadership featured charismatic reformers such as Louisa Lee Schuyler, the unmarried daughter of an aristocratic New York family. By the fall of 1861, Schuyler's group had collected roughly 30,000 items of clothing, over 15,000 pieces of bedding, over 6,000 havelocks, and nearly 2,000 packages

Stanley Fox. "Mrs. Lincoln's Wardrobe on Exhibition in New York." Wood engraving, published in *Harper's Weekly*, October 26, 1867. G71.H29 oversize

Mathew B. Brady (ca. 1823–96).
Mary Todd Lincoln (1818–82),
1861. Published in Meserve
Historical Portraits. Albumen
silver print from albumen print,
3 ¼ x 2 ⅛ in (8.26 x 5.40 cm).
PR 231

of preserves.[30] Through Schuyler's prodigious efforts, the group ballooned to nearly 1,500 affiliated societies, concentrated in New York, New Jersey, Connecticut, and Massachusetts. New York women were up against difficult economic trends, struggling to assist simultaneously soldiers in the field and families on the home front.

Schuyler discovered the problems average women encountered with finding basic goods such as sugar, eggs, and bread, as wartime inflation doubled prices between 1861 and 1863. And poor women in the needle trades—who along with domestic servants were at the bottom rungs of the economic ladder—found themselves in desperate straits by 1863, when one New York newspaper reported that

Eastman Johnson (1824–1906). *Knitting for the Soldiers*, 1861. Oil on millboard, 9 ⅜ x 11 ¾ in (23.81 x 29.85 cm). The Robert L. Stuart Collection (S-26)

women's wages had decreased from 25 to 50 percent since 1860, while the cost of living had increased more than 50 percent.[31]

But once again, activist women stepped into the breach with a crop of New York charities. Reformer Mary Anne Hawkins described the "walks of usefulness" made by "female city missionaries" during wartime.[32] Hawkins chronicled activities in her organization's publication, *The Seabird*, which "awakened in the minds of many who their secluded homes in the interior, were almost wholly unacquainted with the want and woes of seamen and their families."[33] The society workhouse with six new sewing machines, as well as the society store, followed an antebellum practice of offering charity for the selected worthy poor.

At the same time, the war forced reform organizations to expand their portfolios, like the New York Ladies Educational Union, established in May 1862:

> The object of this society shall be to establish an Educational Industrial Institution and Asylum, where the homeless or destitute children of our deceased or disabled soldiers may be furnished with food, clothing, mental and moral instruction, combined with such training in the arts or daily life as will be designed to fit its beneficiaries for usefulness and respectable self-support.[34]

Like most groups during the war, they complained about an inability to keep up with demand: they could only house fifty orphans, when hundreds continued to apply.[35]

(next page) Winslow Homer (1836–1910). *Making Havelocks for the Volunteers.* Wood engraving, published in *Harper's Weekly*, June 29, 1861. 10 ⅞ x 9 ¼ in (27.62 x 23.50 cm). PR 049

HARPER'S WEEKLY.

A JOURNAL OF CIVILIZATION.

VOL. V.—No. 235.]   NEW YORK, SATURDAY, JUNE 29, 1861.   [SINGLE COPIES SIX CENTS.
[$2 50 PER YEAR IN ADVANCE.

Entered according to Act of Congress, in the Year 1861, by Harper & Brothers, in the Clerk's Office of the District Court for the Southern District of New York.

THE WAR—MAKING HAVELOCKS FOR THE VOLUNTEERS.

Photographer unknown. *WCRA (Women's Central Relief Association) in Cooper Union, New York City,* ca. 1864. Albumen print, 12 x 13 ⅞ in (30.48 x 35.24 cm). PR 164

Networks of women volunteers constituted a patriotic "sisterhood."[36] An ethic of patriotic sacrifice—giving up curtains so hospital patients might have bedding—demonstrated the contagion of Union esprit. Louisa Schuyler's group of volunteers "began life in a little room which contained two tables, one desk, half a dozen chairs, and a map on the wall." From these humble beginnings, a mighty tide of female activism spread across the North.

The twenty-four-year-old Schuyler became known as "Lou" among her fellow workers, and relied heavily on her own sister, Georgina (with whom she would live for over fifty years).[37] Ellen Collins, nearly ten years Schuyler's senior, became head of the women's supplies committee, and Angelina Post co-chaired the correspondence committee with Schuyler.[38] Schuyler credited this experience as one of the most significant for her generation: "The work of the Sanitary Commission was a great educator to women of the day."[39]

Josephine Shaw, who later married into a wealthy New York family, recorded her commitments in a diary: "December 16th: today is my birthday, —18 years. Sent today 42 pairs of mittens to Rob."[40] She lost her beloved brother, war hero Colonel Robert Gould Shaw, during the Second Battle of Fort Wagner in July 1863 when he led his African American troops into combat. Effie Shaw and her circle struggled to introduce discipline and efficiency into their reform activities, as during wartime, acts of charity became even more a matter of life and death.

Effie was actually sewing for her own husband, Charles Russell Lowell, and eight months pregnant when news came of his death on October 24, 1864.[41] But her husband had urged her during their few months of marriage to "live like a plain Republican, mindful of the beauty and duty of simplicity. … I hope you have outgrown all foolish ambitions and are now content to become a 'useful citizen.'"[42] So even as she donned her widows' weeds, Josephine Shaw Lowell invested herself in women's warwork until Confederate surrender, and devoted herself to reform. But this turn toward simplicity was not always adopted.

Indeed, a "smart set" of women commingled their interests in high society and charity. In Chicago, the first Sanitary Fair (a bazaar run by the U. S. Sanitary Commission to raise money for soldiers' aid) ran for two weeks in October 1863, and generated nearly $80,000 in profits. Thus the craze for the social extravaganzas was set in motion.[43]

Schuyler and other WCRA leaders were extremely ambivalent about this development. As they suspected, many New York City society women, tired of social abstinence, might eagerly abandon their mundane clothing and food drives in favor of a grandiose society event. The money raised by fairs could be diverted to buy supplies for dwindling warehouses, but depleting supplies worried the reformers. Once Chicago raised such a spectacular sum, the women of New York coveted the chance to best their Midwestern sisters. First, the women from the great city of

(opposite page) Winslow Homer (1836–1910). *Post-Office of the Brooklyn Fair in Aid of the Sanitary Commission.* Wood engraving, published in *Harper's Weekly,* March 5, 1864. 13 ⅝ x 9 in (34.61 x 22.86 cm). PR 049

J. Gurney & Son. *Art Gallery, New York Metropolitan Fair*, 1864. Stereograph (detail), 3 x 5 ⁵⁄₁₆ in (7.62 x 13.49 cm). Gift of Charles W. Kirby, 1936, PR 065-0500-0052

Entry tickets for Metropolitan Fair, 1864. Metropolitan Fair Papers

Brooklyn took up the challenge and generated nearly half a million dollars in cash donations for widows and orphans at their grand fair in February 1864.

But two months later, Manhattan women built themselves a fairground at the corner of Sixth Avenue and Fourteenth Street, where they sold donated goods from around the country. Organizers combined female persuasiveness with male business acumen to raise over a million dollars for their Metropolitan Fair, which opened on April 4, 1864, attracting an opening parade of nearly 10,000. This extravaganza's entrance fee limited attendance to none but the fashionable elite.[44] But the fashionable kept lining up to attend, and bought over 30,000 tickets during the fair's three weeks. Visitors viewed Frederick Church's *Heart of the Andes* and Emanuel Leutze's *Washington Crossing the Delaware* in an art gallery. These women also created a children's department, a music hall, and a "Knickerbocker Kitchen" at facilities nearby.

One-of-a-kind entertainments were staged by Manhattan society women, including Jessie Benton Fremont, one of a smattering of illustrious wartime refugees

E. & H. T. Anthony & Co.
[Ticket Office, Metropolitan Fair,
New York], 1864. Stereograph
(detail), 3 x 6 in (7.62 x 15.24 cm).
PR 065-0500-0010

J. Gurney & Son. *Department of Photographs & Engravings, N.Y. Metropolitan Fair.*, 1864. Stereograph (detail), 3 x 5 ⅝ in (7.62 x 14.29 cm). PR 065-0500-0041

who settled in Manhattan. With her husband General John Fremont's fall from favor, the couple retreated to New York in 1863. Both Fremonts saw the city as an ideal spot to relaunch his political career.[45] In the midst of other activities, Jessie organized over two hundred offspring of the local elite into a spectacular children's pageant for the Metropolitan Fair. And so the passion for spectacle and fundraising went into high gear in 1864.

New York society women loved a good benefit. They initiated one of the most successful charity nights during wartime on November 25, 1864. This time the money raised did not go to soldiers' aid. Rather, a Booth-studded cast performed *Julius Caesar* and raised almost four thousand dollars to erect a statue of Shakespeare (a bronze by sculptor John Quincy Adams Ward) in Central Park.[46] It was a particularly festive event, reuniting the three Booth brothers, the actors Edwin, John Wilkes, and Junius Brutus Booth, Jr., for one night only; John Wilkes and Edwin had been estranged over sectional politics (which would become permanent with John Wilkes Booth's assassination of Lincoln—and subsequent death). This charity performance was interrupted by alarm when Confederate arsonists allegedly tried to burn

Bierstadt Brothers. *Exhibition Room, Metropolitan Fair, N. Y.*, 1864. Stereograph (detail), 3 x 5 ¹³⁄₁₆ in (7.62 x 14.76 cm). PR 065-0500-0037

E. & H. T. Anthony & Co. *Entrance to the Grand Moving Diorama and Miniature Battle Field, Metropolitan Fair, New York*, 1864. Stereograph (detail), 2 ¾ x 6 ¹⁄₁₆ in (6.99 x 15.40 cm). Gift of Charles W. Kirby, 1936, PR 065-0500-0036

Photographer unknown. *John Wilkes Booth, Edwin Booth, and Junius Brutus Booth* [from left to right] *in* Shakespeare's Julius Caesar, 1864. Photograph. Brown University Library

down the Winter Garden Theater—but following Edwin's reassurances that there was no fire (a small blaze was doused), the play continued. The interruption did not dampen what was proclaimed by all to be a resounding success, and led to Edwin's resuming his theatrical career and performing *Hamlet* for a record-breaking one hundred nights.[47]

While Mrs. Charles Eames ruled Washington society from her eclectic Sunday salon at her Fourteenth and H Street home, her sister Marion Campbell Gouverneur proved an equally formidable force within New York's most socially exclusive circles.[48] While Mrs. Eames ruled unchallenged, Marion's social network was but one of several intersecting circles of Knickerbocker Dutch and Astor wealth, among other cliques. But all these groups had one thing in common: they spared no criticism for the First Lady, and gossip about her flowed freely. New York matron Mary Daly, a staunch Unionist, confessed to her diary, "Mrs. Lincoln behaves in the most undignified manner possible ... she seems to be easily flattered. She is not a young woman by any means, but dresses like one ... ."[49]

When her son Willie died in February 1862, Mrs. Lincoln went into a period of deep and profound mourning. Her visit to Manhattan that summer was in stark contrast to her trip the year before: she was swathed from head to toe in black, accompanied by her sons, and the only public outing that attracted press attention was a visit to the Broadway clinic run by the New England Relief Association. Following this stop, she headed for the Park Hospital, where the First Lady was escorted through the wards and greeted wounded soldiers, where they "fully appreciated her kindness and womanly sympathy."[50]

Yet following her year of mourning, after she resumed her social schedule, press attacks continued. Despite her detractors, the First Lady continued to

THE ASSASSINATION OF PRESIDENT LINCOLN,
AT FORD'S THEATRE WASHINGTON, D.C. APRIL 14TH 1865.

Artist unknown. The Assassination of President Lincoln, at Ford's Theatre Washington, D.C. April 14th 1865, 1865. Lithograph, Currier & Ives, publisher, 7 ³/₁₆ x 12 ⅛ in (18.26 x 30.80 cm). PR 052

influence trends, and New York fashion plates revealed a craze for flowers in the hair—copying her style. Mary Daly complained about women "bare to the waist and dressed for show."[51] She confessed in the winter of 1863 that "the supper and dinner parties are far more numerous than they have been for several winters. … Gold is at one hundred sixty-eight; it will soon be two hundred, I suppose. How will all this end? What is to become of the poor?"[52] New York society matrons, even from the enviable perch of fashionable salons, were finding it difficult to ignore the poverty in their streets. It was perhaps no surprise to Daly that riots broke out in the streets of Manhattan when the draft was instituted in July 1863, in what one eyewitness called "the bloody week." To many it seemed a kind of class war had broken out—with the looting of Brooks Brothers, among other stores, signalling rage against "bastions of wealth" while so many endured wartime hardship. Mob violence led to murder and mayhem, which was only quelled when Union troops marched in to restore order.[53]

And once order was restored, the women of New York resumed business as usual, gossiping about the First Lady. In April 1864 when Mrs. Lincoln again visited, the *New York Herald* took sharp aim: "Mrs. Lincoln ransacked the treasures of the Broadway dry good stores."[54] Social arbiter Mary Clemmer Ames complained, "While her sister women scraped lint . . . the wife of the president of the United States spent her time rolling to and fro between Washington and New York, intent on extravagant purchases for herself and the White House."[55] By war's end, Mrs. Lincoln was once again fair game for scandalmongers and critics, the easy target for the press that she remained for the rest of her life.

New York women spared little charity for Mrs. Lincoln even after the long nightmare of war, when she and her husband might have found the long awaited port in storm, and her husband was assassinated. Lincoln's murder plunged his wife into a permanent period of grief and mourning. She joined the rest of the nation, wondering what lay ahead. Lincoln's final visit to New York was on the funeral train, which carried his body back to Springfield, retracing his trip from Illinois to the White House. More than half a million people lined the streets of New York City, along the route from the station to City Hall, where his body lay in state for three days.[56]

While the whole nation suffered post-traumatic shock at war's end and Lincoln's death, Mary Lincoln lay in a darkened room at the White House, unable to rouse herself from her grief until long after her husband was brought home to Springfield. She would never take up residence in a town so associated with traumatizing memories, and would never visit Washington again—except for a brief stay, when she came to town only long enough to attend her son Robert's wedding before heading off to Europe. But for the rest of her life, Mary Lincoln made periodic visits to New York—seeking help from her husband's business associates, seeking a reversal of fortune following the loss of her son Tad in 1871, and seeking medical advice after European exile. Seeking, always seeking, Mrs. Lincoln spent the rest of her life roaming. Yet Manhattan kept drawing her back, as it rhythmically spun along, drawing thousands—and by century's end—millions into its unique orbit. Although it would be granite men and bronze horses memorialized in decades following the war, the lifeblood of women kept New York City humming. Even the mysterious and aloof Minnie was part of the Manhattan throng defining the era, as she sailed down Broadway and faded into the pages of Civil War history.

NOTES

1   *New York Era*, July 12, 1862.

2   On the character of Mary Todd, and her relationship with Abraham Lincoln, please consult Catherine Clinton, *Mrs. Lincoln: A Life* (New York: Harper Collins, 2009), chapters 1-3.

3   New Yorkers remain extremely parochial about their role within the United States of America—in much the way Parisians divide the world into "Paris" and "Deep France" in conversational terms.

4   A tour back to Illinois through New England, about which, sadly, little is known about their itinerary.

5   Justin G. Turner and Linda Levitt Turner, eds., *Mary Todd Lincoln: Her Life and Letters* (New York: Knopf, 1972), 50.

6   Lincoln was born outside the original thirteen colonies, and much of his political career was staked on his identity as a candidate from the plains.

7   Lincoln was considered an "unqualified bumpkin," even though the Eastern press sympathetic to Lincoln's bid during the campaign had reported on the "gentility" of his home—

(opposite page) Probably Henry Ulke (1821-1910). *Mary Lincoln*, ca. 1866. Photographic print, 9 ½ x 5 ⅝ in (24.13 x 14.29 cm). Collection of Harold Holzer

albeit often with a tone of surprise. See, for example: *New York Herald*, August 13, 1860 and *New York Daily Tribune*, August 23, 1860.

8   She was much pleased by being given a "Sewing Machine, mounted in a solid rosewood full case, and altogether a bijou of an affair, destined as a present to the wife of the president elect, and to find a location in one of the apartments of the White House. It is richly silver plated and ornamented with inlaid pearl and enamel. It is worthy the possession of a duchess, and indeed the very companions of this superb sewing machine have actually been finished and sent to the English Duchess of Sutherland, and the Russian Duchess of Constantine." *Chicago Tribune*, January 24, 1861. Mary swaddled herself with the faux trappings of royalty, cushions she learned to enjoy, came to expect—and, at times, demanded. Both the Lincolns were showered with attention and gifts, with the President-elect often attracting hats.

9   Ruth Painter Randall, *Mary Lincoln: Biography of a Marriage* (Boston: Little Brown, 1953), 193.

10   It might have been with some relief to Lincoln's closest advisors that his wife went away, however briefly, during those few weeks between her husband's election and his inauguration. Clearly Mrs. Lincoln had strong ideas about whom her husband should appoint, and voiced her opinion in ways that were not condoned by many contemporaries, nor by later generations of critics. Her absence from Illinois, however, did not prevent Mary from making her wishes known. On January 17th she wrote a strongly worded letter [marking it CONFIDENTIAL] to David Davis, one of Lincoln's closest advisors, reporting that she had overheard some gossip about Norman Judd, a Republican party leader from Illinois. She did not want Judd in her husband's cabinet and joined forces with David Davis to block his appointment. In her letter she suggested that Judd's rise to the cabinet might harm her husband's sterling reputation "when honesty in high places is so important." She further flattered Davis to use his influence to prevent such an appointment, and concluded with the obligatory apology that she would not intrude, but "for the good of the country." In reality, Judd was Mrs. Lincoln's enemy from the days of Lincoln's failed Senate bid in 1855. Although Lincoln forgave Judd, who became a strong Republican ally in the years to follow, Mary Lincoln did not. In her letter to Davis, she supplied him with ammunition for their mutual goal of knocking Judd out of the running.

11   It was perhaps appropriate that Mrs. Lincoln would discover on this trip that New York was also the home to a strong "copperhead" community—the Democrats hidden away in Northern towns and cities. And New York would become a copperhead stronghold as well by 1863. See Jennifer L. Weber, *Copperheads: The Rise and Fall of Lincoln's Opponents in the North* (New York: Oxford University Press, 2006).

12   Elizabeth Todd Grimsley, "Six Months in the White House," *Journal of the Illinois State Historical Society* 19, no. 3: 43.

13   Threats would become dire even before the Lincolns left Springfield, as according to Henry Villard, a few weeks after the election "a scandalous painting on canvas was received by Mrs. Lincoln, expressed from South Carolina. It represented Mr. Lincoln with a rope around his neck, his feet chained and his body adorned with tar and feathers." Harold G. & Oswald Garrison Villard, eds., *Henry Villard, Lincoln on the Eve of '61; a Journalist's Story* (New York: Knopf, 1941), 52–53. In another case, an actual "noose" was reported to have been delivered to the president-elect. Mary, along with others, became increasingly concerned about the safety of her husband, as press attacks seemed the least of her worries with the outbreak of war.

14   In the Buchanan administration, new furnishings for the mansion (which included a circular divan which remained in the White House into the twentieth century) and new chandeliers for the state dining room cost approximately $23,000. William Seale, *The President's House* (Washington, DC: White House Historical Association, 1986), 1:342. See also, Jerrold Packard, *The Lincolns in the White House: Four Years that Shattered a Family* (New York: St. Martin's, 2005), 10–11.

15   Seale, *The President's House*, 1:363.

16   Nevertheless, Lincoln clearly and famously would not stand for any overspending; Benjamin French reported the president complaining, "it would stink in the land to have it said that an appropriation of $20,000 for furnishing the house had been overrun by the President when the poor freezing soldiers could not have blankets, & [he] swore he would never approve the bills for flub dubs for that damned old house!" See Donald B. Cole and John J. McDonough, eds., *Witness to the Young Republic: A Yankees's Journal—the Diary of Benjamin Brown French, 1828–1870* (Hanover, NH: University Press of New England, 1989), 382.

17   William Howard Russell, *My Diary, North and South*, ed. Fletcher Pratt (New York: Harper, 1954), 27. See Clinton, *Mrs. Lincoln*, chap. 7, "Hope All That Will Yet Be Well" and chap. 9, "Dashed Hopes."

18   James McCabe, *Lights and Shadows of New York Life* (Philadelphia: National Publishing, 1872), 141.

19   He built a two million-dollar mansion at the corner of Fifth Avenue and Thirty-fourth Street in 1873, which became the talk of the town.

20   William Leach, *Land of Desire: Merchants, Power, and the Rise of a New American Culture* (New York: Pantheon Books, 1993).

21   See Joseph Devorkin, *Great Merchants of Early New York* (New York: Society for the Architecture of the City, 1987) and McCabe, *Lights and Shadows*, 306.

22   See Susan Bindig, "New York Welcomes the Prince of Wales, 1860," *Dance Chronicle* 12, no. 2 (1989): 221–43.

23   Mrs. Lincoln was put on display at her inaugural ball in March 1861. The next day, the *New York Herald* weighed in: "She is more self-possessed than Lincoln and has accommodated more readily than her taller half to the exalted station to which she has been so strangely advanced from the simple social life of the little inland capital of Illinois." See Jean Baker, *Mary Todd Lincoln* (New York: Norton, 1987), 179.

24   McCabe, *Lights and Shadows*, 396.

25   Jerry E. Patterson, *The First Four Hundred: Mrs. Astor's New York in the Gilded Age* (New York: Rizzoli, 2000), 18

26   Baker, *Mary Todd Lincoln*, 52.

27   See Clinton, *Mrs. Lincoln*, 135–37 and 153–55. For a contrasting interpretation, see Michael Burlingame, "The Lincolns' Marriage: A Fountain of Misery of a Quality Absolutely Infernal," in *The Inner World of Abraham Lincoln* (Urbana: University of Illinois Press, 1994).

28   Turner and Turner, *Mary Todd Lincoln*, 88. Such a suggestion—that Mrs. Lincoln bought china to match servants' livery—proves less likely when contemporary descriptions of the Lincoln White House reveal quite the opposite. A diplomat's wife described: "There were before the White House no sentinels, not even a porter… no crowd of gorgeous liveried footmen was to be seen …" See Princess Felix Salm-Salm, *Ten Years of My Life* (Detroit: Bedford Brothers, 1878), 45. This observation was echoed by William Russell who noted at the State dinner on March 28th there was "no parade or display, no announcement—no gilded staircase, with its liveried heralds" and again, the dinner "was not remarkable for ostentation. No liveried servants…" Russell, *My Diary*, 23–24. Prince Napoleon was taken aback when he arrived at the White House on an official visit and there was no one to greet him. His diary recorded "one goes right in [the White House] as if entering a café." John Whitcomb and Claire Whitcomb, *Real Life at the White House* (New York: Routledge, 2000), 136. So the idea that Mary Lincoln would pick out china to match liveried footmen was not just fanciful, but purposely misleading. These libels were published and circulated even before she arrived back in Washington from her trip in May. See Turner and Turner, *Mary Todd Lincoln*, 87.

29   Elizabeth Blackwell was passed over for a role on the national board of the United States Sanitary Commission, established in June 1861. Dorothea Dix was given an official position as Superintendent of Female Nurses, rather her better-qualified rival, Elizabeth Blackwell.

Blackwell conceded that the male physicians effectively blocked their path: "They refused to have anything to do with the nurse education plan if the Miss Blackwells were going to engineer the matter." See Jeanie Attie, *Patriotic Toil: Northern Women and the American Civil War* (Ithaca, NY: Cornell University Press, 1998), 82.

30 Ibid., 83.

31 Mary Elizabeth Massey, *Bonnet Brigades: American Women and the Civil War* (New York: Knopf, 1966), 145.

32 Mary Anne Hawkins, *Record of Benevolent Efforts in Behalf of Seamen's Destitute Families in the City of New York* (New York: Mariner's Family Industrial Society, 1865), 62.

33 Ibid., 69.

34 *Patriot Orphan Home—Under the Care of the New York Ladies Education Union* (New York: Sanford, Harroun & Co., 1864), 3.

35 Ibid., 7.

36 See Judith Ann Giesberg, *Civil War Sisterhood: The U.S. Sanitary Commission and Women's Politics in Transition* (Boston: Northeastern University Press, 2000).

37 Ibid., 63.

38 Giesberg, *Civil War Sisterhood*, 39.

39 Ibid., 60.

40 Joan Waugh, *Unsentimental Reformer: The Life of Josephine Shaw Lowell* (Cambridge: Harvard University Press, 1997), 53.

41 His bride of less than a year was unable to attend his funeral at Harvard College Chapel and his burial at Mt. Auburn cemetery. She also bore the brunt of his family's disappointment when she gave birth to a daughter instead of a son, a few weeks later. Ibid., 84–85.

42 Ibid., 85.

43 Women in the Chicago-based Northwest Sanitary Commission decided to hold fairs—with entrance tickets offered at 75 cents and donated goods for sale. They set a goal of $25,000, and President Abraham Lincoln contributed an original draft of the Emancipation Proclamation, which was auctioned off at $3,000.

44 See William Y. Thompson "Sanitary Fairs of the Civil War," *Civil War History* 4, no. 1 (March 1958): 51–57.

45 See Carol K. Bleser and Lesley J. Gordon, eds., *Intimate Strategies of the Civil War: Military Commanders and Their Wives* (New York: Oxford University Press, 2001) and Tom Chaffin, *John Charles Frémont and the Course of American Empire* (New York: Hill and Wang, 2002).

46 See Robert Berkelman, "Lincoln's Interest in Shakespeare," *Shakespeare Quarterly* 2, no. 4 (October 1951): 303–12.

47 Michael W. Kauffman, *American Brutus: John Wilkes Booth and the Lincoln Conspiracies* (New York: Random House, 2004), 149–50.

48 See Marion Campbell Gouverneur, *As I Remember: Recollections of American Society During the Nineteenth Century* (New York: Appleton, 1911).

49 Mary Lydig Daly, *Diary of a Union Lady, 1861–1865*, ed. Harold Earl Hammond (New York: Funk and Wagnalls, 1962), 62 and 86.

50 *New York Herald*, July 17, 1862.

51 Daly, *Diary*, 331–32.

52 Ibid., 219 and 222.

53 See Iver Bernstein, *The New York City Draft Riots: Their Significance for American Society and Politics in the Age of the Civil War* (New York: Oxford University Press, 1990) and Ellen Leonard, *Three Days Reign of Terror, or the July Riots of 1863* (New York: s.n., 1867). One eyewitness revealed: "Prominent among those who made the first attack, and who also urged on their relatives and acquaintances in order to carry on the work of demolition, were quite a large number of women." See *The Bloody Week!: Riot, Murder & Arson, Containing A Full Account Of This Wholesale Outrage On Life And Property* (New York: Coutant & Baker, 1863).

54 *New York Herald*, May 2, 1864.

55 Mary Clemmer Ames, *Ten Years In Washington. Life And Scenes In The National Capital, As A Woman Sees Them* (Hartford, CT: A.D. Worthington & Co., 1875), 237. Even more bitter eruptions broke out later in the election year, as one New York society matron raged over White House chicanery: "It is humiliating to all American women who have to economize and struggle and part with their husbands, sons and brothers in these sad times, to see this creature sitting in the highest place as a specimen of American womanhood, and "Uncle Ape," as he should be called, the specimen of man." See Daly, *Diary*, 305.

56 And like the tabloid town New York was, a photographer took a photo of the president's body—the only post-mortem photo of Lincoln to surface. See page 251.

MOURNING FOR A LOST CAPTAIN: NEW YORK CITY COMES TO TERMS WITH A NATIONAL TRAGEDY

MICHAEL KAMMEN

ALTHOUGH THE City of New York did have a viable Republican presence by the early 1860s, it remained largely unsympathetic to Abraham Lincoln throughout his presidency, and for no single reason although certain crucial ones stand out. The sizeable Irish population was overtly hostile to African Americans because of competition for employment and overt racism. Hence their disdain for the Emancipation Proclamation of 1863, and followed by the dangerous draft riots that year in which blacks were targeted and killed. The Mayor of New York, C. Godfrey Gunther, was a Copperhead quite sympathetic to the South. The Common Council and Board of Aldermen were both dominated by Democrats who remained consistently critical of Lincoln, and they strongly supported General George B. McClellan, his presidential rival in 1864. Because Lincoln had received such a frosty reception in 1861, and knowing full well that most of the Manhattan newspapers largely opposed his policies— *The World* ran racist cartoons aimed at Lincoln—he rarely visited the city between his inauguration and his assassination on Good Friday in 1865.[1]

George Bancroft, the nation's most distinguished historian and a very prominent Democrat, had been unimpressed when he first met Lincoln in 1860; yet he gave the principal oration at a massive funeral ceremony held at Union Square late on April 25. The fact that his remarks were altogether laudatory, and sincerely so, is emblematic of a remarkable turnaround in city sentiment that began fairly promptly as news of Booth's successful assassination attempt spread throughout New York on Saturday, April 15. A yearning for vengeance was expressed publicly and often, especially during the first week following the president's death. The local press covered both the quest for Lincoln's killer and rumors of a possibly

Alexander Gardner (1821–82). *Abraham Lincoln*, Washington, DC, February 5, 1865. The Collection of Keya Morgan, Lincolnimages.com.

larger conspiracy, almost as thoroughly as it reported stories of mourning through-out the nation, especially in Washington.

Nasty "threats and prophecies" that had occurred intermittently during Lincoln's presidential administration now felt like ominous warnings and fore-shadowings that should have been taken more seriously. A superstitious populace found strange solace in the bizarre timing of this catastrophe. Because it coincided with the day that traditionally marked Christ's death, the accent upon Lincoln's *martyrdom* became not merely instantaneous, but ubiquitous. Some sermons even stressed that God had perhaps allowed this tragedy to occur on Good Friday to provide potent moral lessons for sermons on Easter Sunday![2]

James Gordon Bennett's independent newspaper, the *New York Herald*, the only city paper with a Sunday edition, editorialized on the 16th that the president's death

> has created a keener sorrow, a deeper, broader and more universal sense of the public loss, than, we dare say, has been experienced in any age, in any country, or by any people, over the death of one man ... Steadily following the drift of events and the developments of public opinion through all the progressive changes of this gigantic war of ideas, President Lincoln, we can all now com-prehend, pursued the paths of safety, wisdom and success. In this masterly pol-icy that plain, unpretending man exhibited a breadth of sagacity which though perplexing to politicians of one idea, has given us the practical results of the highest statesmanship to both our domestic and foreign affairs.

Most other papers, such as Horace Greeley's *New-York Tribune*, sympathetic to Lincoln, printed similar sentiments. But the *Tribune* also included a particular observation that catches our notice because it uncannily anticipates what so many observers wrote right after Franklin Roosevelt died: "When we last saw Mr. Lincoln, he looked so weary and haggard that he seemed unlikely to live out his term."[3]

The response of the press to Lincoln's death is fascinating and significant for multiple reasons. Within just a few days of his demise most papers felt compelled to offer an estimate of "his place in history," which became rather awkward for those that had been his harshest critics. The *New York World*, for example, acknowledged:

> It is probable that the judgment of history will differ in many respects from that of Mr. Lincoln's contemporaries; and in no respect, perhaps, more than in reversing the current tenor of the public thinking on what has been con-sidered the vacillation of his character. It must never be overlooked that Mr. Lincoln was elevated to the presidency without previous training; that he was a novice in the discharge of high executive functions.[4]

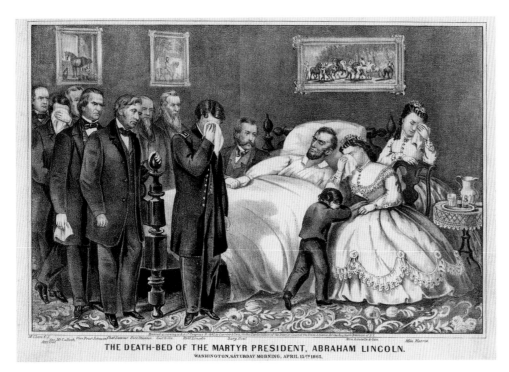

THE DEATH-BED OF THE MARTYR PRESIDENT, ABRAHAM LINCOLN.
WASHINGTON, SATURDAY MORNING, APRIL 15TH 1865.

Artist unknown. *The Death-Bed of the Martyr President, Abraham Lincoln. Washington, Saturday Morning, April 15th 1865,* 1865. Lithograph, Currier & Ives, publisher, 12 ⅞ x 8 ½ in (32.70 x 21.60 cm). PR 052

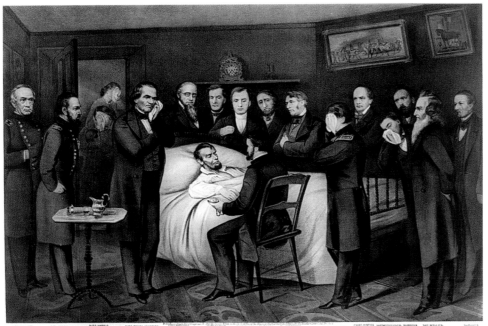

THE DEATH BED OF THE MARTYR PRESIDENT ABRAHAM LINCOLN.
WASHINGTON, SATURDAY MORNING, APRIL 15TH 1865, AT 22 MINUTES PAST 7 O'CLOCK

Artist unknown. *The Death Bed of the Martyr President, Abraham Lincoln Washington, Sunday Morning April 15th 1865 at 22 Minutes Past 7 o'clock,* 1865. Lithograph, Currier & Ives, publisher. Library of Congress, 91792453

The *World* then added, with more than a touch of casuistry, that if the country had only foreseen a Civil War, it would not have chosen such an inexperienced and "peculiar type of character." The editors remarked that "what was wanting in the flexibility of our political system was made up in the character of Mr. Lincoln. Whatever may be thought of the absolute merits of the late President's administration—on which it would not be decorous to express our views on this occasion—it cannot well be denied that it has been throughout, a tolerably faithful reflex of the predominant public opinion of the country." While apparently

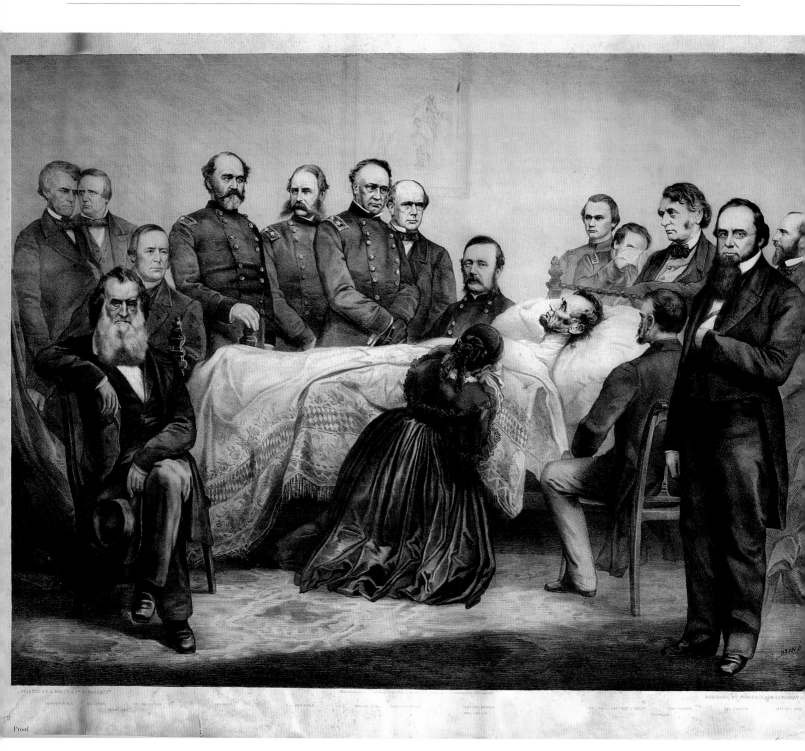

Peter Kramer (1823–1907).
[Lincoln's Deathbed], 1865.
Lithograph, A. Brett & Co.,
printer, Jones & Clark, publisher,
18 5/8 x 24 7/8 in (47.31 x 63.18 cm).
PR 052

accusing Lincoln of being guided by (or else blindly following) public opinion, this paper seemed to concede that its own coverage might have been somewhat out of touch with public views elsewhere in the North. At least it acknowledged that the president's death was indeed a "calamity," and that among the sources of his influence was the "quaint and peculiar character of his written and spoken eloquence."[5]

Although we do not ordinarily associate Abraham Lincoln with quaintness, the word seems to have had a certain resonance at that time. The *New York Herald's* assessment of his place in history used it as well, though much less grudgingly in an editorial that remains one of the most memorable.

> All men of undisturbed observation must have recognized in Mr. Lincoln a quaintness, originality, courage, honesty, magnanimity and popular force of character such as have never heretofore, in the annals of the human family, had the advantage of so eminent a stage for their display. He was essentially a mixed product of the agricultural, forensic and frontier life of this continent—as indigenous to our soil as the cranberry crop, and as American in his fibre as the granite foundations of the Apalachian [sic] range.[6]

From there the *Herald* added a crucial insight that we find echoed in papers of diverse political persuasions: namely, that American institutions do not depend upon the life of any single individual for their maintenance or progress. As even the hypercritical *World* remarked on the very day Lincoln expired: "Its effect upon the political future of the nation will, at least, not be such as when a dynasty is overthrown. Our laws provide for the succession to such remote degrees that even assassination cannot leave the nation without a visible leader and head."[7] That sentiment appeared across party lines despite the dramatic decline in leadership ability represented by the transition from Abraham Lincoln to Andrew Johnson. Even though we have long known that the course of Reconstruction might have been very different if Lincoln had lived, his contemporaries clearly agreed that they lived under a constitutional government of law, not of men, and one that carefully provided for a quick and clear line of succession.

The *New York Times*'s coverage seemed to damn with faint praise by noting that Lincoln prevailed in the governing process "by the passionless simplicity of his integrity and unselfish patriotism over the larger experience and more brilliant gifts, and more vigorous purpose of his constitutional advisers." The novice politician was fortunate to have such a splendid cabinet! The *New York Evening Post*, William Cullen Bryant's newspaper, ran laudatory columns from the outset despite the fact that Bryant, the nation's most distinguished poet, had expressed occasional reservations about Lincoln's policies. The intensely political editor wanted immediate and universal emancipation in 1862 and lamented the president's tolerance of mediocre generals and poor performance by the army. But Bryant did make the astute observation that "No one who reads our papers will for a moment doubt that their political discussions are too virulent and personal."[8]

On April 18 the *Tribune* attacked the *World* because of its grudging words of faint praise for Lincoln. For example, it observed that the president had been saved by the "unaffected kindliness of his disposition and the flow of his homely and somewhat grotesque mother-wit—the most popular of all the minor mental endowments." That is what shielded him from the "inflammable

(above left) Mourning Ribbon, April 1865. Inscribed, "In Memory of A. Lincoln, Assassinated April 14, 1865, May His Soul Rest in Peace," silk albumen photograph, metal. 4 ½ x 1 ⅛ in (11.40 x 2.75 cm). INV 5478

(above right) Mourning Ribbon, April 1865. Inscribed, "A Nation Mourns! Abraham Lincoln, E Pluribus Unum. 'The Union must and shall be preserved.' Born Feb. 12th, 1809. Died April 15th, 1865." Ink on silk, 1 x 9 x 10 in (2.54 x 22.86 x 25.40 cm). INV 2885

natures around him," thereby referring to what the *Times* considered his brilliant cabinet. *The World* responded two days later by attacking the *Herald* for using a fabricated story about Lincoln back in 1861. The *Tribune*, however, expressed astonishment that the *Daily News*, a Copperhead paper, could conceivably run a seemingly suitable statement lamenting the assassination.[9]

On the following day *The World* proclaimed that the *New York Times* did itself and American journalism "great discredit by lending itself to a senseless and scandalous attack on the theatrical profession in general as being some way 'involved' in Booth's atrocious crime." Edwin Booth, the most popular Shakespearean actor in the United States and the brother of John Wilkes Booth, suffered deeply and became depressed because of his brother's crime. Booth's highly successful American career might have effectively ended at that point. He swore that he would never act again; but he did, returning to his most famous role as Hamlet. In 1864 he had voted in his first presidential election—for Abraham Lincoln.[10]

On Monday, April 17 all the papers gave comprehensive and detailed coverage of a city that seemed spontaneously and instantaneously to clad itself in mourning—mostly meaning endless festoons of black crepe (always spelled *crape* in the press at that time), American flags, presidential photographs with black surrounds, and the wearing of badges commercially produced on very short notice: with silver eagles, miniature portraits of Lincoln, red, white, and blue ribbons, and black crepe bands worn on the left arm. Girls tended to wear black and white ribbons. George Templeton Strong described the scene he witnessed going to Trinity Church on Easter morning.

Nearly every building in Broadway and in all the side streets, as far as one could see, festooned lavishly with black and white muslin. Columns swathed in the same material. Rosettes pinned to window curtains. Flags at half-mast and tied up with crape. I hear that even in second and third class quarters, people who could afford to do no more have generally displayed at least a little twenty-five cent flag with a little scrap of crape annexed. Never was a public mourning more spontaneous and general.[11]

Every church was filled to overflowing and their sermons were reported in remarkable detail. Because Henry Ward Beecher was visiting Fort Sumter in South Carolina for a memorial service, a replacement provided his huge Plymouth [Congregational] Church in Brooklyn with a suitable eulogy. At the largest Roman Catholic Church the priest spoke of the late president in reverential terms and deplored his death as "not only a national but a world-wide calamity." According to the *Tribune* "There were representatives of many foreign nations in this congregation. The Irishman, the German, the Frenchman, the Swiss, the Italian was there; but upon no face did we discover the trace of anything but profound regret at the terrible national tragedy at Washington." The *Tribune* made the arresting observation that "If ever man made war in a Christian spirit, Mr. Lincoln was that man."[12]

At the Broadway Synagogue on Saturday, where Passover was being observed, Rabbi Isaacs offered an impressive prayer that God might bless the United States and be with the people in their hour of trial. The congregation was moved to tears. The *Herald* noted that Passover marked the anniversary of the time when Jews escaped the land of Egypt and were "freed from the chains of slavery. The recent [Union] victories, occurring as they did just on the eve of this feast [Lee had surrendered on April 10], were in a certain manner commemorative of their delivery. And as the forefathers of the Jews passed over the Red Sea at the time of which this festival is the anniversary, so also the American people seemed to have passed over and beyond the red sea of blood which has been spilt so freely during the last four years."[13]

Despite this pervasive display of genuine shock and grief, dissidents did not entirely disappear, at least not directly, and the press reported the fate of many. Near the Custom House a man was heard to say, "It served Old Abe right." He was immediately set upon by a mob, crying "Lynch him. Lynch him." He escaped into a building where police protected him. A man who favored the Confederacy was caught by a crowd bent upon vengeance and severely beaten. When the treasurer of the Winter Garden Theatre, Thomas J. Jackson, declared he was glad that Booth had shot Lincoln ("I would have done it myself"), he was arrested for disloyalty. The same thing happened to a "disloyal" policeman, while three men were arrested for rejoicing over the president's death. When a passenger aboard a Brooklyn ferryboat expressed "obnoxious opinions," bystanders heaved him overboard; a small passing craft rescued him. An anti-Lincoln socialite woman observed that a nearby house, "having not been put in mourning, was tarred and for two days men have been at work at it."[14]

In the privacy of her extensive diary, Maria Lydig Daly, a New Yorker well

Mourning Ribbon, April 1865. Inscribed, "A Nation's Loss. Died April 15, 1865." Black ink on silk, 1 x 9 x 10 in (2.54 x 22.86 x 25.40 cm). INV 2885

WE MOURN Our Country's Loss.

We Mourn Our Country's Loss,
[1865]. Woodcut banner,
12 ⅞ x 37 in (32.70 x 95.25 cm).
PR 052

connected with Copperhead leaders, could preserve such opinions for posterity. As she recorded on April 19, the assassination

> will make a martyr of Abraham Lincoln, whose death will make all the short-comings of his life and Presidential career forgotten in, as Shakespeare says, "the deep damnation of his taking off." People had been arrested in the streets only for saying, "Pity it had not been done before," and the Loyal Leaguers are in a furious state of patriotism. The houses are all draped in mourning, each house striving to outdo the other. … Nor can we blame [Lincoln] that when elected by a legal majority, he accepted the Presidency. Every American feels competent for any place. It is a wise man indeed who feels that he knows but little, and as President of the United States, his government as that of right and law was the one to be sustained by all lovers of their country.[15]

Many events that had been scheduled for the coming week were postponed, and in a few instances, with some reservations or regrets. The Democratic Tammany Society, which dominated the City Council, met at the Old Wigwam where William Marcy Tweed spoke, and a resolution was passed acknowledging that Lincoln acted from patriotic motives and therefore deserved praise for his forbearance and leadership. A group called the McClellan Sociable postponed their annual ball until April 28. The "colored people," on the other hand, quite willingly postponed a jubilee scheduled for April 18.[16] Most important, however, because of Lee's surrender and a series of major victories in the deep South by General Sherman, Governor Fenton had declared Wednesday, April 19 a day of thanksgiving and celebration. Instead, it became a day of mourning and prayer that spilled over to the next day with most offices and stores remaining closed.[17]

For a solid week beginning on April 17, every imaginable organization met by day and by night to express grief, console one another, discuss the political situation, convey condolences to the Lincoln family, and pass resolutions expressing concern and support for the government. Students at Columbia College and what

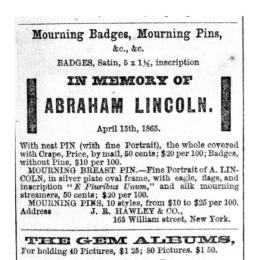

Advertisements from *Frank Leslie's Illustrated Newspaper* for Lincoln merchandise, May 1865.
*E171.L63

became New York University met on the 17th, as did citizens of the Fifth Ward, and eventually most other wards. On the 18th, bank officers met at the American Exchange Bank and resolved that next to George Washington, Lincoln was the greatest American. So did the faculty of the Free Academy, the Commissioners of Emigration, and members of the theatrical profession who met at the Metropolitan Hotel and decided to wear badges of mourning for thirty days. With no touch of irony intended, they acknowledged that Lincoln had liked theater and that as professionals they had lost a patron and true friend. The Knights of St. Patrick met and decided that a committee should represent the association at the "funeral obsequies" scheduled for April 24th and 25th, when Lincoln's funeral procession would march through lower Manhattan.[18]

When Alexis de Tocqueville wrote *Democracy in America*, published in 1835–40, he placed great emphasis upon the active and vital role played by voluntary associations in American civic life.[19] Much as he dreaded the prospect of sectional conflict in the United States, which he did not live to see, Tocqueville might have felt reassured about the future of the Union if he could witness all of these dozens if not hundreds of gatherings that took place during the week following April 17, culminating in a memorial meeting held at the New-York Historical Society on the evening of the 25th.[20] Frederick De Peyster chaired the session, Mr. Brodhead

Author unknown. Pages from a diary, New York City, April 15, 1865. McLellan Lincoln Collection, John Hay Library, Brown University. Following news of Lincoln's assassination, an anonymous New Yorker traveled the city, sketching in a diary the makeshift shrines erected in countless windows and storefronts.

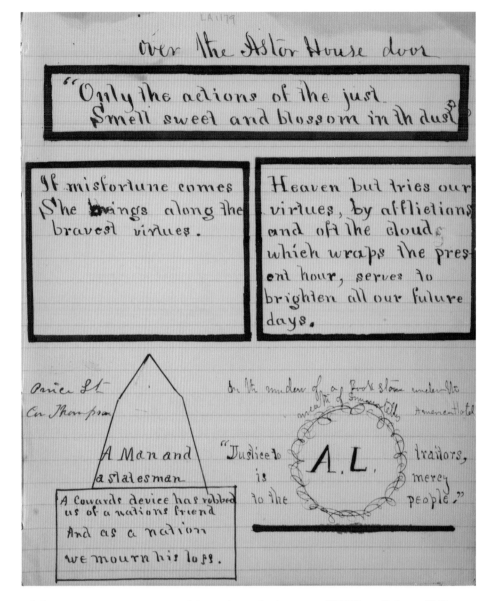

read the now customary preamble and resolutions, and William Maxwell Evarts, a lawyer and rising Republican activist who soon became Attorney General of the United States and later Secretary of State, gave the major address.[21]

Tocqueville also devoted a famous chapter to "Relationships Between Civil and Political Associations" in which he expressed grave reservations about the evils that might arise from "unlimited political freedom of association."[22] The Tammany Hall General Committee, presided over by Tweed, met promptly and passed three gracious resolutions praising Lincoln, pledging support to the Federal government, and draping its rooms with mourning muslin, yet sharp conflicts arose when the Tammany committee of the Twenty-first Ward spurned "with contempt the unseemly and meaningless action" taken several days earlier by the Democratic General Committee of Tammany Hall. This ward-level group did not want to be viewed as an "exponent" of the Democratic masses and merely the "degenerate machine" of a few unprincipled and corrupt office-holders, office-seekers, and

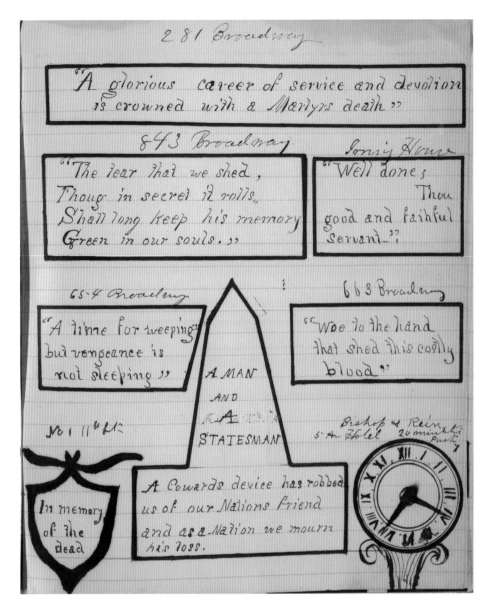

demagogues. Instead, they committed themselves to supporting Lincoln's successor, Andrew Johnson.[23] These fractious differences resulted from a struggle between competing blocs to control the City Democrats, and it is apparent that there were tensions and recriminations among members as to the most appropriate course of action to be followed at a time of political tumult and uncertainty.

Part of the problem may very well have involved race, because Tammany Hall had insisted that blacks *not* be permitted to march in the grand procession to be held on April 25, the principal day devoted to Lincoln's New York funeral. William Cullen Bryant's *Evening Post* declared that excluding blacks would be mortifying and humiliating. When the Common Council predictably supported Tammany's position, the Union League raised a furor and went directly to Secretary of War Stanton, who overruled Tammany at the last minute (the 24th) and allowed blacks to march the next day, albeit at the very end in Phase Eight of the procession, following the delegation from Brooklyn, then a separate city engaged in considerable rivalry with New York. Stanton's telegram insisted "that no discrimination respecting color should be exercised in admitting persons to the funeral procession."[24]

The *Tribune* sounded rather sanctimonious in accepting the racist rejection (approved by the Joint Municipal Committee in Charge of Obsequies) in an editorial while slamming their Democratic opponents: "as the Blacks of our City do not need any display of banners, mottoes, regalia, &c., to convince any body that *they* grieve for the loss of our good President, we suggest that they do not need to take to heart their exclusion from the parade of tomorrow." As it turned out, Thomas C. Acton, President of the Board of Police, supported Stanton's directive, overruled the Common Council, and about two to three hundred Blacks did march, most notably a platoon of the First Loyal League (colored) of Brooklyn, who carried a large banner. On the front it read: "Abraham Lincoln: Our Emancipator," and on the back, "to Millions of Bondmen He Liberty Gave." The banner was actually made on the 24th by women from Beecher's Plymouth Church in Brooklyn and was carried by four freedmen recently arrived from the South who were "perfectly astonished to know that there were so many more 'Yankees' than blacks!"[25]

Two entire platoons of police walked before and after the African Americans to ensure that their rights would be respected, and the blacks were greeted with cheers and waving handkerchiefs.[26] They were the *only* group in the entire procession to receive an ovation from the sorrowing crowd; and as members of the Union League marched past the blacks, who were patiently awaiting their turn to step off, they raised their hats in homage to the Emancipator and the blacks, and were saluted in return. On Easter Sunday, Reverend Cheever preached at the Plymouth Church, proclaiming that "if our nation does not now do justice to the loyal blacks, the present rebellion will soon be followed by another conflict which will enter into all the intricacies of social life. ..." How prophetic he proved to be.[27]

On April 18 the *Tribune* and other papers received a proposal that a monument to the president should be erected in New York as soon as possible. Horace Greeley responded that the matter should be left to Lincoln's home state of Illinois to be placed above the president's remains, though a bust or some other memento might be placed in Madison Square or Central Park. He then added that one of these days the Freedmen of the United States will most likely erect from their own offerings "a monument to their emancipator on the site of one of the principal slave-pens of Richmond, Charleston, or New Orleans. But there is no hurry." Was Greeley being facetious about the possible site, or simply unrealistic? It's unclear; but unsurprisingly, no memorial to Lincoln has ever appeared at any of these sites.[28]

If Greeley's reluctant response seems surprising, it should be kept in mind that mounting memorials and statues to American heroes did not become the norm

(opposite page) Artist unknown. *Our Fallen Heroes: Abraham Lincoln National Monument*, 1865. Hand-colored wood engraving, Haasis & Lubrecht, publisher, 33 ⅝ x 28 ⅜ in (85.41 x 72.07 cm). PR 052

until the latter third of the nineteenth century. Partially that was because of Congress's costiveness in appropriating money, and partially because raising the necessary funds by public subscription proved very difficult. As early as 1783 the Continental Congress had wanted to erect an equestrian statue to George Washington in Roman garb; and in 1791 Pierre L'Enfant's plan for the new capital city also called for an equestrian statue of the Founder where the two central axes running from the White House and Capitol building would intersect on what became the Mall. The notion was too much at odds with the anti-monarchical republicanism of the time, and neither proposal would be realized. More than half a century later, money for a great obelisk began to be raised by public subscription, which totally stalled in 1855. An embarrassed Congress eventually provided funds to finish the monument in 1885![29]

Wednesday, April 19, the day of Lincoln's funeral in Washington, would be called a "mid-week sabbath" in New York because places of worship were filled to capacity, with all stores, courts, and offices closed. As Helen Grinnell summarily remarked in her diary: "We *all* went to church." Bryant's *Evening Post* even chose not to publish at all on that most solemn day. According to the *Tribune* it was a moment of "the greatest solemnity that ever dawned upon this continent. The city began to assume its widow's weeds at an early hour on Saturday morning, day by day becoming blacker and more profound." But on the 19th all buildings now wore "habiliments of woe," and manifestations of sorrow were universal. Guns were fired from the forts in the harbor and other locations throughout the city. Every flag flew at half-staff bound with black. No word was heard more often in church services than "martyr." At the Jewish temple on East Twelfth Street, following an eloquent discourse on the life and character of Lincoln, the mourner's kaddish was also recited, "which is never used except on the death of the nearest relatives of a family." At another congregation on East Ninth Street, the rabbi contrasted the congregation's joy on the first day of Passover with their sorrow on the closing day.[30]

Bryant's *Evening Post* had declared a day earlier that the political opposition, "malignant as they sometimes have been, have now joined hands with the professed supporters of the administration, and the nation which was to have been destroyed, or at least crippled by this foul blow, is more united and stronger than ever." The paper rejected a proposal that Lincoln be buried with Washington at Mount Vernon, suggesting instead that he should repose in a "noble porphyry sarcophagus to be placed in the centre of the Rotunda of the Capitol," where future millions would see it. Meanwhile an array of banners bearing slogans emerged ubiquitously: "May he rest in peace" appeared in many windows. "Our Martyr President" could be seen throughout the city along with "God moves in a mysterious way his wonders to perform." Below City Hall Park, which very soon became the focal site

(opposite page) Artist unknown. *Washington and Lincoln. The Father and the Saviour of Our Country*, 1865. Hand-colored lithograph, Currier & Ives, publisher, 15 1/16 x 11 1/8 in (38.26 x 28.26 cm). PR 052

for New York's viewing of the body, all banks, hotels, newspaper offices, stores, insurance and telegraph offices were heavily draped with mourning cloths and appropriate signs of grief. The *Post* did, however, challenge the propriety and bad taste of decorating Indians and bare-legged Scotchmen standing in front of cigar stores with mourning scarves.[31]

A problem arose over which the *Evening Post* seemed to agonize more than any other paper. The mayor and aldermen, who had never shown any enthusiasm for Lincoln, wanted Thursday the 20th to be a day of Thanksgiving, with all homes illuminated, to mark the important Union victories still very much in progress in the deep South, from Georgia to Mobile and Biloxi. Although victory was won, the war had not quite ended. Yet there was also very widespread sentiment to hold still another day of fasting and prayer. The *Post* felt that "the transactions of the city cannot suffer a sudden suspension of two consecutive days in the middle of the week." Life must go on and commerce could not remain in abeyance indefinitely.[32]

As it turned out, public sentiment won, Thursday became a legal holiday, and most churches remained open for public worship. An immense congregation gathered at the Plymouth Church in Brooklyn. The Third Avenue Presbyterian Church was packed, and so was the Bloomingdale Baptist Church at Forty-second Street near Seventh Avenue. The Portuguese Synagogue on Nineteenth Street held a solemn funeral service on the evening of the April 20.[33]

By the weekend, however, commerce had inevitably resumed, most notably with the sale of Lincoln memorabilia, such as copies of the Emancipation Proclamation engraved on the best paper and suitable for framing, deemed "an appropriate ornament for the parlor or office." Well, perhaps it would be for Republicans, though less likely for Democrats—Copperheads as well as others. Ads proliferated for engraved portraits and biographies of Lincoln, accounts of the assassination, and *The History of Julius Caesar* ($2.50 in fancy binding, $1 in paper covers). When Edwin Booth eventually announced that he would resume his stage career on January 3, 1866, the *New York Herald* asked sardonically: "Is the Assassination of Julius Caesar to be Performed?"[34]

Even so, the *Evening Post* wondered when public amusements would fully reopen, noting the significant "pecuniary loss" incurred by so many days set aside for mourning. With Lincoln's body arriving and more solemnities scheduled for the city on Monday and Tuesday, it looked as though business as usual would once again be suspended. It seemed a pleasing prospect that theaters would surely re-open on the 26th, once the Lincoln train had left for Albany; and on Saturday (the 22nd) the *Post* ran ads for an array of amusements that would soon be available once again: the Academy of Music, the Broadway Theatre, Niblo's Garden, Barnum's American Museum, St. Alban's Bazaar and Promenade, and the Philharmonic Society of New York.[35]

(opposite page) Programme of the Funeral Obsequies of the Lamented Late President, Abraham Lincoln!, 1865. Broadside, The Republican Print, Sing Sing, NY, publisher. SY 1865 no. 17

PROGRAMME

OF THE

FUNERAL OBSEQUIES

Of the lamented late President,

ABRAHAM LINCOLN!

ON TUESDAY, APRIL 25th, 1865.

The citizens of the Town of Ossining and vicinity will meet at TALLCOT'S HALL, in the village of Sing Sing, on TUESDAY AFTERNOON, at 4 o'clock, and will be formed in procession and march through Main Street to the Rail Road Depot, where it will be formed in line under the direction of the Marshal. The procession will be formed and march in the following order:

GRAND MARSHAL,
Aids,
Leggett's Brass Band,
Committee of Arrangements and Finance Committee,
Clergymen,
Cadets of Mr. Churchill's School,
Cadets of Maj. Benjamin's School,
Cadets of Mr. Tracy's School,

Fire Department of the Village,
Supervisor and other officers of the Town,
President and Trustees, and other Village Officers,
Officers of the Sing Sing Prison,
Union League,
Democratic Union Club,
Citizens of neighboring Towns,
Citizens of the Town of Ossining.

Minute Guns will be fired and the Church Bells tolled during the ceremonies.

The citizens of the village are requested to close their places of business between the hours of 4 and 6 o'clock on that day.

The undersigned would particularly request that all citizens form in the line of procession as designated in the foregoing programme, and not march promiscuously upon the side-walks as is often the case.

COMMITTEE OF ARRANGEMENTS:

C. C. CHILDS, JR.,
N. O'BRIEN, JR.,
JAMES M. BARD,
OSCAR RESSEGIUE,
A. B. REYNOLDS,
ABRAM HYATT,

G. T. E. SHELDON,
J. A. AITCHISON,
J. H. PLATT,
H. HERRINGSHAW,
THOMAS McLEAN,
DAVID REED,

POWLES J. PALMER

FINANCE COMMITTEE:

W. J. WIXSON,
D. D. MANGAM,
WILLIAM C. HOWE,
THOMAS McLEAN,

F. C. BURRHUS,
C. F. MAURICE,
E. G. BLAKSLEE,
A. G. ROSE,

JAMES T. COLLYER.

W. W. BENJAMIN,
Grand Marshal.

Ossining, April 24th, 1865.

"THE REPUBLICAN" PRINT, SING SING.

THE NATION MOURNS.

Photographer unknown. Lincoln's Funeral, City Hall, New York City, 1865. Stereograph (detail), 3 ½ x 7 in (8.89 x 17.78 cm). Gift of Mrs. Elihu Spicer, PR 065

Anticipating the culminating days of bidding farewell to Lincoln, New York welcomed home its most popular preacher, Henry Ward Beecher, on the 23rd. (Lincoln had actually attended Beecher's church the day before his Cooper Union speech in 1860.) His sermon that Sunday at the Plymouth Church compared Lincoln extensively with Moses, emphasizing the late president's "spirit of leniency and indifference toward leading rebels."[36] Beecher may or may not have been out of touch, or simply hopeful when he insisted that "the popular grief at the assassination of President Lincoln has already obliterated all party lines at the North and united the country in a sentiment of loyal sorrow and patriotic indignation."[37] That was a half-truth at best because the next day, when Lincoln's nine-car funeral train arrived, there would be open mud-slinging between Republicans and Democrats.[38]

Common Council spent the weekend making plans for New York's funeral, which required much deliberation. A major discussion centered on what kinds of vehicles should be included in the procession. When one alderman proposed that

several states should be represented by carriages, another argued that that seemed very unwise because this was to be a demonstration of mourning rather than celebrating the return of peace. Ultimately the Council decided upon very few vehicles, except for specified purposes, other than the enormous one on which the casket would ride.[39]

It was determined that religious exercises should be conducted by the most eminent clergy, and all organizations, including private clubs (Tocqueville's singularly American participants in civic life), should be invited to take part in the ceremonies. Citizens engaged in the pursuit of commerce, letters, and the arts, along with all "industrial professions" were especially encouraged to assemble at Union Square late on Tuesday afternoon for a massive gathering to hear the

Photographer unknown.
Lincoln's Funeral Procession,
Seventh Regiment in advance of
the catafalque, New York City,
1865. Stereograph (detail),
William Evans James, publisher,
3 ¼ x 6 ½ in (8.26 x 16.51 cm).
Gift of Mrs. Elihu Spicer, PR 065

Broadside with crape from Lincoln's coffin attached, 1865. N.C.S.N.Y., publisher. Gallatin Papers, Box 76

Head-quarters 1st Division N. G. S. N. Y.

New-York, April 20, 1865.

Special Orders,
No. 8.

This Division will unite with their fellow-citizens in rendering appropriate honors to the Remains of that Illustrious Patriot, whose loss, in the hour of victory, the nation now deplores.

Upon the arrival of the Funeral Cortege in this City on Monday next, it will be received at the landing by the Seventh Regiment, which will escort it to the City Hall, and will mount guard there until the Funeral Parade on Tuesday Morning.

The Division will parade on Tuesday next, the 25th instant, with the usual badges of mourning, as the Funeral Escort to the Remains of the late President Lincoln.

The Division Line will be formed on Broadway, with the right on Warren Street, at twelve o'clock, M., precisely.

The Field and Staff of the Infantry Regiments will parade dismounted.

Brigadier-General YATES will direct minute guns to be fired in Union Square, from one o'clock, P. M. until the close of the procession.

The Division Staff will assemble at the quarters of the Major-General, at eleven o'clock, A.M., and Captain Otto will report at the same hour.

The Commissary-General will furnish ammunition upon the requisition of the proper officer.

Major-General Duryea, Commanding the Second Division, National Guards, will unite with this Division in the Funeral Parade on Tuesday next. His Division or such part thereof as can conveniently parade on that day will form line in Broadway on the left of the First Division.

The Fourth Artillery will parade with full batteries.

By order of

Major-General CHAS. W. SANDFORD.

ALEXANDER HAMILTON, *Division Inspector.*

CHAS. H. TOMES, *Major and Vol. Aid-de-Camp.*

Head-quarters Second Brigade N. G. S. N. Y.

GENERAL ORDER,
No. 8

The above orders are hereby promulgated. The Brigade Line will be formed in Broadway, with the right on Worth Street, at 11½ o'clock, A. M.

Colonel Teller, commanding the Fourth Regiment, will detail a detachment from his Regiment to fire the minute guns as above stated, and will make requisition for the necessary ammunition.

By order of

Brigadier-General CHARLES YATES.

B. S. CHURCH, *Brigade-Major and Inspector.*

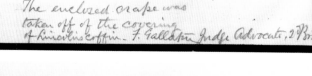

The enclosed crape was taken off of the covering of Lincoln's coffin. F. Gallatin Judge Advocate, 2 B'd'

NEW YORK'S HONORS TO PRESIDENT LINCOLN'S REMAINS.

This reproduction of a wood engraving printed in an illustrated paper of 1865 shows the funeral cortege passing up Broadway in April, 1865. It was one of the most notable events in the history of the city. The funeral car was drawn by twelve coal-black horses, and was accompanied by a military guard of 15,000 men.

principal oration given by historian George Bancroft. German musical societies and glee clubs would attend the procession in a body numbering about nine hundred singers and perform in front of City Hall, where Lincoln would lie in state for twenty-four hours from noon on Monday until nearly noon the next day.[40]

William Cullen Bryant's *Evening Post*, perhaps the most art and history-oriented among the newspapers, printed an interesting letter to the editor on the 24th. It noted: "Our city has been of late a curious and rich museum of funereal art, and it is desirable that some adequate record of the most characteristic specimens should be preserved. We call attention to two specimens that are in admirable taste, and worthy of being remembered." First the writer singled out the impressive drapery in front of Trinity Church bearing the inscription "The memory of the just shall live" in antique letters. Cited second was a rich altarpiece in the Church of the Messiah: a marble monument, cruciform, standing on a well-suited pedestal.[41]

Differences of opinion also arose over the optimal location at City Hall for Lincoln's coffin to be situated. The Aldermen wanted it placed in the Governor's Room on the second floor, to which a double staircase led from the rotunda. It seemed logical to have mourners ascend one staircase and descend on the other. The *Herald*, however, made a case that the coffin could optimally be situated on

Artist unknown. "New York's Honors to President Lincoln's Remains." Published in *Frank Leslie's Illustrated Newspaper*, May 1865. Columbia University Libraries

Framed leaves from Abraham Lincoln's bier, 1865. Albumen photograph, plant material, ink, silk ribbon, wood, and gilding; inscribed in ink: *This laurel lay on President Lincoln's heart/while lying in state for three days in/City Hall in New York, April 25th/1865.* 8 ¾ x 7 ¼ x 1 in (22.23 x 18.42 x 2.54 cm). Gift of Mrs. Georgine Wood Charlton, Z.2603

the fine esplanade in front of the Hall, arguing that doing so would improve the traffic flow and enable more people to view the president, avoid a crush in the rotunda and human traffic problems on the narrow staircases. Using the esplanade would also mean that many citizens with no desire to go inside and see Lincoln's face "up close" could be content with a view of the magnificent catafalque and coffin upon it.[42] That proposal did not prevail.

Monday April 24 dawned with clear skies, balmy air, and gentle breezes, "one of the most perfect days of spring," according to the press. Lincoln's funeral train crossed the Hudson at Jersey City and arrived at the Manhattan ferry slip on DesBrosses Street precisely on schedule at 10:50. The coffin, placed on a hearse drawn by six horses, was escorted by two companies of the spit-spot, socially elite Seventh Regiment, New York State National Guard, and passed very large crowds through Hudson Street to Broadway and then to City Hall. According to one account, "as the solemn procession swept past the Alhambra palace, a saloon of pleasure on Canal Street, the windows were crowded with the sad faces of negroes and mulattoes, most of whom were ladies, and all of whom were bathed in tears."[43]

The magnificent coffin, reputed to have cost about $2,000, was then carried up the circular staircase under the rotunda and placed on a black velvet bier resting on a dais as eight hundred choristers sang the "Pilgrims' Chorus" from Wagner's *Tannhäuser*. The German Liederkranz Band then played a solemn dirge and several German singing clubs of the Liederkranz Society sang additional dirges. Meanwhile, a woman placed a floral tribute in the form of a cross on the coffin followed by Mrs. N. C. Bishop and her eight-year-old son (George Washington Irving Wellington Bishop) carrying the letters A.L. "made entirely of rare and most beautiful flowers," which he placed upon Lincoln's chest. After generals and other dignitaries had an opportunity to witness the scene set up in the Governor's Room, Gurney & Son took photographs of the opened coffin and artists sent by illustrated newspapers made sketches of the deceased. Finally, soon after one o'-

clock, the general public was admitted.[44]

The *Tribune* contrasted the overwhelming response that day with the cool reception Lincoln had received from the city in 1860 and 1861: "the public reception was feeble and cold, marked chiefly by features of curiosity. How all this is changed! Now a million people join in expressing horror of the 'deep damnation' of his taking off," a curious expression used twice in the same article. While Greeley's paper emphasized the unanimity of classes and nationalities in mourning the nation's loss, the rival *New York World* struck a very different and far more partisan tone.[45]

Democrats disciplined by four years of injustice bravely borne, should calmly now bear with all that is not flagrantly aggressive and indecent in the conduct

Photographer unknown. [Abraham Lincoln's catafalque], 1865. Stereograph (detail), 3 5/16 x 6 15/16 in (8.41 x 17.62 cm). Gift of Mrs. Elihu Spicer, PR 065

Jeremiah T. Gurney (1812–86).
Entrance to Catafalque at City
Hall, 1865. Stereograph (detail),
3 ⅛ x 5 ⅝ in (7.94 x 14.29 cm).
Purchase, PR 065

of Republicans. It is Republicans who most need now to remember that
Democrats may sometimes have right and reason on their side, and to admit
that, since the future of the nation absolutely depends on the establishment of
right and reason, a Democratic victory in policy may possibly be the salvation
of their own fortunes and happiness.

Although the *World* acknowledged that "the determination, the heroism of the
crowd of mourners was marvelous," it made no mention of slavery ending or of
blacks being in New York, present or future.[46]

During the next twenty-three hours crowds streamed through City Hall to
view the body, their numbers expedited during the night as decisions were made
to ease the long lines of people waiting by increasing the numbers admitted each

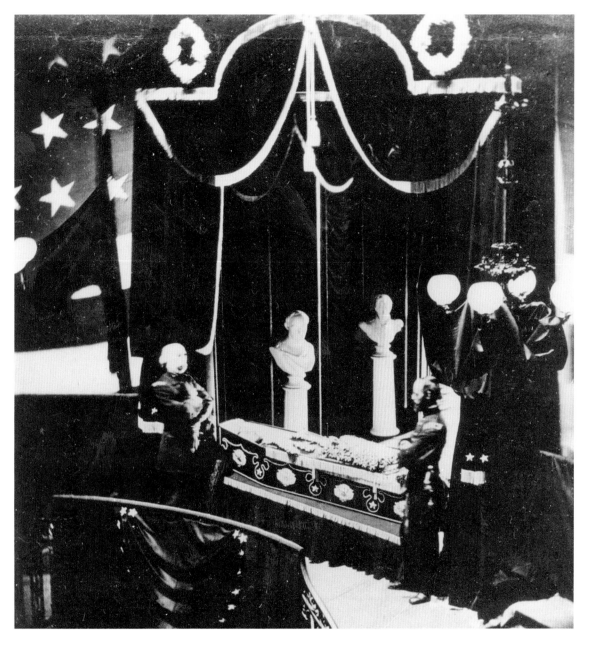

hour. The German Club, Quartette Club, the Concordia, and the Harmonia remained all night, chanting appropriate stanzas at regular intervals. Initially the column passing through the west entrance averaged forty-five people per minute and from the east entrance about fifty per minute. The following day police admitted people at a still more rapid rate, and it was estimated that between 120,000 and 150,000 viewed the body before the coffin was closed at noon on the 26th. Some guessed that as many as half a million had hoped to.[47]

Some resentment occurred because "private passes" were issued to aldermen, councilmen, supervisors, and possibly members of the famous Seventh New York Regiment which had the honor of accompanying the coffin on the 25th. Each member was entitled to issue twelve cards to family and friends, but the *Post* complained that twelve seemed to mean 1,200. "Certainly the privilege was as

Jeremiah Gurney (1812–86). [Lincoln Lying in State in New York City Hall], 1865. Abraham Lincoln Presidential Library and Museum.

inclusive as it was professed to be exclusive, and the crowds with passes embraced all classes of citizens, from well-to-do merchants to small newsboys."[48]

Then there were men simply trying to sneak in without waiting their turn by posing as journalists, or by accompanying one. When women attempted to lean over the coffin to kiss Lincoln's face, they were jerked back by guards.[49] All things considered, however, no reports of rowdiness or fighting appeared, and there were no arrests except for pickpockets seeking wallets, watches, and other valuables. In fact, the Board of Police announced that during the previous week there were fewer arrests for drunkenness or disorder than in any week since the time New York City's population exceeded 100,000.[50] Those who waited in line for hours hoping to glimpse the president seemed to accept that in a democracy, some people are more equal than others. And most important, perhaps, a great many of those who waited patiently to pay their last respects were men who had not even voted for Lincoln in 1860 or 1864.

The public fully expected an open coffin, of course, but Lincoln had now been dead for ten days, and the art of modern embalming was still in its infancy. Although the president's face had been touched up cosmetically in Washington, Baltimore, Harrisburg, and Philadelphia, by the time it reached Manhattan, the visage had become discolored and sunken. The *New York Times* grimly reported a "face dark to blackness, features sharp to a miracle, an expression almost horrible in its un-nature, a stiff, starched countenance resembling none they knew of and expressive of nothing familiar." Nevertheless, glimpsing that face even momentarily seemed meaningful. Writing inclusively in her diary once again, and with no qualms about viewing a gruesome visage, Helen Grinnell declared that we *all* went down to see "the dead face of our good President." As the *Evening Post* put it, most likely written by Bryant himself, people were witnessing "but a sad reflection of the real person" and not the "genial, kindly face of Abraham Lincoln but a ghastly shadow." If the man had seemed sallow and gaunt in life, he appeared even more so in death.[51]

Prior to closing the coffin at noon, Captain Parker Snow, commander of the Arctic and Antarctic exploring expeditions, presented to General John A. Dix, commander of the New York military district, for placement with Lincoln some relics of Sir John Franklin's ill-fated expedition, most notably, a tattered leaf of a prayer book on which the first word legible was "Martyr."[52]

Lincoln's casket was then carried out of City Hall and loaded onto the so-called funeral car that would carry it during the over two-hour-long procession that would culminate in a four o'clock departure on the train up the Hudson to Albany. Several papers carried a full description of the funeral car, the likes of which had never before been seen. What follows is one of the most complete accounts, containing an odd mixture of tenses, as though the author had seen the car nearly finished but not entirely.

> The main platform will be fourteen feet long, eight feet wide, and fifteen feet one inch in height. On this platform, which is five feet from the ground, is a dais six inches in height, on which the coffin rests.
>
> Above the dais is an elegant canopy, supported by four columns curving upward at the centre, and surmounted by a miniature temple of liberty. The platform is covered with black cloth, which falls at the sides nearly to the ground, and is edged with silver bullion fringe; festoons of black cloth will also hang from the sides, festooned with silver stars, and also edged with silver bullion.
>
> The canopy will be trimmed in like manner with black cloth, festooned and spangled with silver bullion, the corners surmounted by a rich plume of black and white feathers. At the base of each column will be three American flags, slightly inclined, festooned and covered with crape.
>
> The temple of liberty is represented as deserted, having no emblems of any kind in or around it, except a small flag on the top, at half-mast. The inside of the car is lined with white satin, fluted. From the centre of the roof is suspended a large eagle, with outspread wings, having in its talons a laurel wreath. The platform around the coffin was strewn with flowers. The car was drawn by sixteen gray horses, covered with black cloth trimmings, each led by a groom.[53]

Estimates of those who walked in the funeral procession ranged from sixty-five to seventy-five thousand, including eleven thousand from the military, though all agreed that it was democratically diverse. As one headline put it: "All Nationalities, All Religions, All Trades, All Classes, All Politics, All Colors Are Represented." And there may well have been as many as 750,000 spectators watching who remained for several hours after the funeral car had been loaded on the train. The procession (referred to in some accounts as a cortège) must have been an awesome sight. As it moved north past Union Square it "seemed to have no model in history. It was prodigious in magnitude and perplexing to ordinary conception." James Gordon Bennett's *Herald* singled out the Irish groups, the Masons, and the Odd Fellows for praise because of their bright regalia and banners containing patriotic legends.[54]

One of the Celtic societies carried a beautiful miniature monument inscribed with the name LINCOLN on the pedestal. Within the shaft there was a clock whose hands were stopped at twenty minutes past seven, the moment of the president's death on the 15th. "This tribute had more than ordinary signification," the paper remarked. "It is a Celtic and Castilian custom of the present day to stop a clock the moment a relative or friend departs in the house, as a token that time for the deceased had closed forever and that eternity had been opened for his view."[55]

Lincoln's Funeral Procession, Union Square, New York, 1865. Stereograph (detail), 3 7/16 x 6 15/16 in (8.73 x 17.62 cm). Gift of Mrs. Elihu Spicer, PR 065

There seems to have been concern expressed because Tammany Hall marched as a singular unit proclaiming its identity, in violation of a rule against "political inscriptions" intended to apply to politically partisan organizations; but with all of the ethnic groups and civic societies marching as units, no action was taken. The *New York World* found cynical irony in the ovations received by the groups of black soldiers, especially in the more affluent neighborhoods. "A queer city is New York," it noted. "Less than two years since, for one entire week [the notorious Draft Riots of 1863] it was as much as a negro's life was worth to be seen in the streets, while now they are on the very topmost wave of fashionable favor! What next, we wonder?" (Although estimates of the number of African Americans actually marching ranged from two hundred to two thousand, the smaller figure reported by the *Times* seems much more likely.)[56]

The press waxed hyperbolic about the grandiosity of it all, regardless of where particular papers stood politically. The *Tribune* called it "the most sublime and solemn funeral in history." (They had not witnessed the elaborately planned funeral procession of Habsburg Emperor Charles V in 1558, which the monarch viewed in a full dress rehearsal the year before he died.) But unlike the Holy Roman Emperor's procession, Lincoln's was egalitarian. "Never did all classes stand more nearly on the same level. Whether the humble had been exalted or the high had been depressed, it is not for us now to inquire." Not to be outdone, the *World* acknowledged that the funerals of Napoleon, Wellington, and Prince Albert had surely been impressive, but "all of them must pale their ineffectual fires before the obsequies of Abraham Lincoln."[57]

Despite such apparent equanimity, the *World* persisted in sniping at its rivals, noting that the *New York Times* is "preaching moderation" in the language used by journals that had opposed Lincoln. We stand in no need of such lessons, quipped the *World*, "and repudiate the *Times* as a teacher of them. For four years the *Times* has used violent epithets with utter and shameless recklessness. ... Let the *Times* mend its own manners, which are bad, and its morals, which are worse."[58]

The procession made its way up Broadway to Fourteenth Street, turned west in front of Union Square, then over to Fifth Avenue, up Fifth to Thirty-fourth Street and across to Ninth Avenue, and then down a few blocks to the Hudson River Railroad Depot at Thirtieth Street and Tenth Avenue.[59] At 3:30 the approach of the hearse became known by the solemn refrains of bands. Regiments soon presented arms, officers saluted with their swords, and colors draped in mourning were lowered to acknowledge the president's arrival. Brisk but stately preparations were made for departure on a train headed by the *Union*, which in turn was guided by a pilot locomotive called the *Constitution*, which would lead the cortège up the Hudson. At 4:15 the station bell clanged a final warning, the conductor boarded, and the Lincoln Special headed for Peekskill and beyond.[60]

The *Tribune* heaped praise upon A.T. Stewart's "uptown" department store for the elegant elaborateness of its decorations, found the windows of Lord & Taylor among the most attractive, and singled out Mathew Brady's Gallery at the corner of Broadway and Tenth Street because it displayed a fine portrait of Lincoln draped in black with a silver-lined wreath. Beneath it was the very same inscription that Greeley had placed on the *Tribune* building: "With malice toward none, with charity for all." Above the portrait was an American shield with flags gracefully festooned around it. Elegant homes along Fifth Avenue were lauded for their decorations, as were the New-York Club House and the Fifth Avenue Hotel.[61]

Amidst all the compliments given to commercial establishments for closing and making Broadway look so solemn—"the sable weeds of woe were found alike

O Captain! my Captain!

O Captain! my Captain! our fearful trip is done,
The ship has weather'd every rack, the prize we sought
        is won,
The port is near, the bells I hear, the people all exulting,
While follow eyes the steady keel, the vessel grim and daring,
        But O heart! heart! heart!
            O the bleeding drops of red,
                Where on the deck my Captain lies,
                    Fallen cold and dead.

O Captain! my Captain! rise up and hear the bells;
Rise up—for you the flag is flung—for you the bugle trills,
For you bouquets and ribbon'd wreaths—for you the shores
        a-crowding,
For you they call, the swaying mass, their eager faces turning,
        Here, Captain! dear father!
            This arm beneath your head;
                It is some dream that on the deck
                    You've fallen cold and dead.

My Captain does not answer, his lips are pale and still,
My father does not feel my arm, he has no pulse nor will,
The ship is anchor'd safe and sound, its voyage closed
        and done,
From fearful trip the victor ship comes in with object won;
        Exult, O shores, and ring, O bells!
            But I with mournful tread
                Walk the deck my Captain lies,
                    Fallen cold and dead.

Walt Whitman
March 9 1887

in all streets"—the impact of the president's death on business and the economy did not go unnoticed, especially with so many days having been set aside for official holidays and prayer. Although commerce became largely paralyzed for more than a week, the market remained notably steady. After reviewing that steadiness in detail, Horace Greeley offered this comforting comment. "We are the greatest people on the globe. The assassination of the head of an European government [*sic*] would have convulsed their society," he explained, and

> collapsed their credit, struck down capital seeking investment, and precipitated a drastic fall in values. But look what happened when this nation, now in the fifth year of a civil conflict unparalleled for costliness and bloodiness. ... The people have rallied as one man to support the administration; increasing their faith in the power to govern; and intensifying their purpose to purify the Republic and establish it forever, cost what it may. We are seeing the footprints of history in the incidents that mark the progress of this crisis.[62]

Arrangements had predictably been made to conduct a formal outdoor program at Union Square immediately following the train's departure so that community leaders could offer their final professions of spiritual reverence and secular respect. George Bancroft spoke for an hour in a manner that combined historical perception with a climactic peroration. He acknowledged that the mourners present, along with the nation, lacked the judicious perspective that only time and wisdom would provide:

> Those who come after us will decide how much of the wonderful results of his public career is due to his own good common sense, his shrewd sagacity, readiness of wit, quick interpretation of the public mind, his rare combination of fixedness and pliancy, his steady tendency of purpose; how much to the American people, who, as he walked with them side by side, inspired him with their own wisdom and energy; and how much to the overruling laws of the moral world by which the selfishness of evil is made to defeat itself.[63]

The Reverend Joseph P. Thompson then read Lincoln's Second Inaugural Address; Reverend E. P. Rogers invoked Psalm 94 (written by King David against enemies of Israel) followed by musical selections; Rabbi Samuel M. Isaacs read passages from the Old Testament; Reverend Samuel Osgood read a hymn; and Reverend Roswell D. Hitchcock closed the occasion by reading an ode composed that morning by William Cullen Bryant. The second and third stanzas are most notable:

> In sorrow by thy bier we stand,
> Amid the awe that hushes all,

(opposite page) Walt Whitman (1819–92). Manuscript copy of 'O Captain! My Captain!' Poem, March 9, 1887. Brown University, John Hay Library

> And speak the anguish of a land
> That shook with horror at thy fall.
>
> Thy task is done; the bond are free;
> We bear thee to an honored grave,
> Whose noblest monument shall be
> The broken fetters of the slave.[64]

Between 1865 and 1900, an extraordinary number of works—poetry and prose, but especially biographies—lauded Lincoln.[65] Some verged upon canonization. They highlighted his capacity to rise from humble origins, overcome poverty and the lack of formal education, and ultimately guide the nation through a tragic war and free the slaves. But as Barry Schwartz and others have observed, "once the emotional climate attending his death dissipated, however, divisions of opinion about him reverted toward (without actually reaching) their original state. Conflicts of interest and opinion were not as severe as they had been during the war, but they could not be easily healed." By the mid-1880s, however, that mending process began to be evident, at times achieving mystic chords of memory.[66]

On April 15, 1887, the twenty-second anniversary of Lincoln's death, an aged, white-maned Walt Whitman appeared at New York's Madison Theatre and recalled the catastrophe and events leading up to it. His distinguished audience included James Russell Lowell, the beloved naturalist John Burroughs (Whitman's friend and biographer), John Hay (once Lincoln's secretary and now his biographer), the great sculptor Augustus St. Gaudens, Richard Watson Gilder, editor of the *Century Magazine*, President Daniel Coit Gilman of Johns Hopkins University, Andrew Carnegie, and many other notables.[67] Whitman concluded by reading "O Captain! My Captain." Recall the last of his three memorable stanzas:

> My captain does not answer, his lips are pale and still,
> My father does not feel my arm, he has no pulse nor will,
> The ship is anchor'd safe and sound, its voyage closed and done,
> From fearful trip the victor ship comes in with object won;
> Exult O shores, and ring O bells!
> But I with mournful tread,
> Walk the deck my Captain lies,
> Fallen cold and dead.[68]

During his talk, Whitman mentioned that on the day of Lincoln's murder, the lilacs seemed to be blooming in profusion, and he had never since then seen them in their season without promptly remembering the late president. When Whitman finished reading "O Captain!" a "little bit of a maiden in a white Normandy cap and a little suit of Quaker gray" walked on the stage with a beautiful basket of lilac blossoms, and without saying a word presented them to the soulful poet. He took them and conveyed his tearful appreciation by kissing her, not once but twice.[69]

NOTES

1   Ernest A McKay, *The Civil War and New York City* (Syracuse: Syracuse University Press, 1990), esp. chaps. 15–16. Although it is conventional wisdom that New York City held Lincoln in low regard, the brilliant speech he gave at Cooper Union on February 27, 1860, which introduced the unknown westerner to New York, was exceedingly well received by local Republicans. It was interrupted by "frequent applause" and four New York newspapers printed the entire text the next day. According to the *New-York Tribune*, "The vast assemblage frequently rang cheers and shouts of applause, which were prolonged and intensified at the close." It was then printed in pamphlet form by the Young Men's Central Republican Union and by the *Tribune*. Quotations from William Lee Miller, *Lincoln's Virtues: An Ethical Biography* (New York: Alfred A. Knopf, 2002), 383–84. See especially Harold Holzer, *Lincoln at Cooper Union: The Speech That Made Abraham Lincoln President* (New York: Simon & Schuster, 2004).

2   David Herbert Donald and Harold Holzer, eds., *Lincoln in the Times: The Life of Abraham Lincoln as Originally Reported in The New York Times* (New York: St. Martin's Press, 2005), 273.

3   *New York Herald*, April 16, 1865; *New-York Tribune*, April 17, 1865. Greeley especially blamed the "incessant persecutions of office-seekers."

4   *New York World*, April 17, 1865.

5   Ibid.

6   *New York Herald*, April 17, 1865.

7   *New York World*, April 15, 1865.

8   Donald and Holzer, *Lincoln in the Times*, 276; *New York Evening Post*, April 21, 1865. For Bryant's occasional frustration with Lincoln, see Parke Godwin, *A Biography of William Cullen Bryant* (New York: D. Appleton & Co., 1883), 2:162, 170–76; Curtiss S. Johnson, *Politics and a Belly-full: The Journalistic Career of William Cullen Bryant* (New York: Vantage Press, 1962), 115–16.

9   *New-York Tribune*, April 18, 1865; *New York World*, April 20, 1865.

10 *New York World*, April 22; Eleanor Ruggles, *Prince of Players: Edwin Booth* (New York: W.W. Norton, 1953), 195–201; Richard Lockridge, *Darling of Misfortune. Edwin Booth: 1833–1893* (New York: The Century Co., 1932), 139, 152–63.

11 *New York World*, April 20, 1865; Allan Nevins and Milton Halsey Thomas, eds., *The Diary of George Templeton Strong* (New York: Macmillan, 1952), 3:585. By Sunday the 16th, merchants had totally run out of black muslin and dealers in dry goods began taking orders for prompt delivery.

12 *New-York Tribune*, April 17, 1865.

13 Ibid.; *New York Herald*, April 16, 1865.

14 *New York Herald*, April 16 and April 17, 1865; Harold Earl Hammond, ed., *Diary of a Union Lady, 1861–1865* (New York: Funk & Wagnalls, 1962), 357.

15 Hammond, *Diary of a Union Lady*, 354–55.

16 Donald and Holzer, *Lincoln in the* Times, 280; *New York Herald*, April 17, 1865.

17 *New York Herald*, April 16 and April 18, 1865.

18 *New-York Tribune*, April 18, April 19, and April 22, 1865.

19 Alexis de Tocqueville, *Democracy in America*, ed. Isaac Kramnick (New York: Penguin, 2003), 595–600; Johann N. Neem, "Squaring the Circle: The Multiple Purposes of Civil Society in Tocqueville's *Democracy in America*," *The Tocqueville Review* 27, no. 1 (2006): 99–121.

20 See Aurelian Craiutu and Jeremy Jennings, "The Third *Democracy*: Tocqueville's Views of America after 1840," *American Political Science Review* 98 (August 2004): 391–404.

21 *New York Evening Post*, April 26, 1865.

22 See Michael Kammen, *Alexis de Tocqueville and Democracy in America* (Washington, DC: Library of Congress, 1998), 41–42.

23 *New-York Tribune*, April 21, 1865.

24 Victor Searcher, *The Farewell to Lincoln* (New York: Abingdon Press, 1965), 139; Donald and Holzer, *Lincoln in the Times*, 312.

25 *New-York Tribune*, April 24, April 25, and April 26, 1865. Most contemporary sources say that around two hundred blacks marched. The figure three hundred is insisted upon by Dorothy Meserve Kunhardt and Philip B. Kunhardt Jr, *Twenty Days: A Narrative in Text and Pictures of the Assassination of Abraham Lincoln and the Twenty Days and Nights that Followed . . .* (New York: Harper & Row, 1965), 154, 169.

26 Maria Lydig Daly snidely observed that the "few colored soldiers" required a police guard. Hammond, *Diary of a Union Lady*, 358.

27 *New-York Tribune*, April 26, 1865; Cheever reported in the *New York Times* and quoted in Donald and Holzer, *Lincoln in the Times*, 274. For the ongoing plight of African Americans, see Martha Banta, *Barbaric Intercourse: Caricature and the Culture of Conduct, 1841–1936* (Chicago: University of Chicago Press, 2003), 268–82.

28 *New-York Tribune*, April 20, 1865. See Kirk Savage, *Standing Soldiers, Kneeling Slaves: Race, War, and Monument in Nineteenth-Century America* (Princeton: Princeton University Press, 1997), 90–94, and 63 for the memorial by sculptor Edmonia Lewis.

29 See Kirk Savage, "The Self-Made Monument: George Washington and the Fight to Erect a National Memorial," in *Critical Issues in Public Art: Content, Context, and Controversy*, ed. Harriet F. Senie and Sally Webster (Washington, DC: Smithsonian Institution Press, 1992), 8.

30 Diary of Helen (Lansing) Grinnell, April 19, 1865, New York Public Library; *New-York Tribune*, April 20, 1865.

31 *New York Evening Post*, April 18, 1865.

32 Ibid., 2; McKay, *Civil War and New York City*, 302–3.

33 *New-York Tribune*, April 21, 1865.

34 Ibid., April 24, 1865; Ruggles, *Prince of Players: Edwin Booth*, 205. He made his return as Hamlet.

35 *New York Post*, April 21, 2; ibid., April 22, 4.

36 See "Abraham Lincoln," in Henry Ward Beecher, *Patriotic Addresses in America and England, from 1850 to 1885, on Slavery, the Civil War, and the Development of Civil Liberty in the United States*, ed. John R. Howard (New York: Fords, Howard, & Hulbert, 1889), 701–12. Miller, *Lincoln's Virtues*, 376.

37 Like those who had long opposed Lincoln, the empathetic Beecher was also capable of enigmatic sophistries. At one point in his sermon on the 23rd he exclaimed: "I bless God that there is some argument of consolation in the matter and manner of his going, as there was in the matter and manner of his staying." Beecher, *Patriotic Addresses*, 707.

38 *New York World*, April 24, 1865; *New York Herald*, April 24, 1865.

39 *New-York Tribune*, April 22, 1865.

40 Ibid.

41 *New York Evening Post*, April 25, 1865. To the best of my knowledge, neither one has survived, though both would be most welcome at the Museum of the City of New York or the New-York Historical Society.

42 *New York Herald*, April 23, 1865.

43 *New-York Tribune*, April 25, 1865.

44 Scott D. Trostel, *The Lincoln Funeral Train: The Final Journey and National Funeral for Abraham Lincoln* (Fletcher, OH: CAM-TECH Publishing, 2002), 83–86; Kunhardt and Kunhardt, *Twenty Days*, 162, 166; *New-York Tribune*, April 25, 1865. In the *Tribune's* account the public was not admitted until two o'clock, but most sources say one.

45 *New-York Tribune*, April 25, 1865.

46 "An Era of Good Feelings," *New York World*, April 25, 1865.

47 *New-York Tribune*, April 25, 1865; *New York Evening Post*, April 25, 1865. The *New York Herald* declared that more than 150,000 had passed the coffin during the twenty-three hour span. April 26, 1865.

48 *New York Evening Post*, April 25, 1865.

49 Kunhardt and Kunhardt, *Twenty Days*, 166.

50 *New York Herald*, April 25, 1865; *New York Evening Post*, April 26, 1865.

51 Donald and Holzer, *Lincoln in the Times* [April 25], 331; Diary of Helen (Lansing) Grinnell, April 24, 1865; Searcher, *Farewell to Lincoln*, 130–33. Grinnell acknowledged that "the face was worn and shrunken, but we felt satisfied to have seen it."

52 *New York Herald*, April 26, 1865.

53 *New York Evening Post*, April 25, 1865. See also Trostel, *The Lincoln Funeral Train*, 87.

54 *New York Herald*, April 26, 1865.

55 Ibid.

56 *New York World*, April 26, 1865; Donald and Holzer, *Lincoln and the Times*, 339 (regarding Tammany), 340 (for the estimate of 200).

57 *New-York Tribune*, April 26, 1865; *New York World*, April 26, 1865.

58 *New York World*, April 26, 1865.

59 A photograph of the procession passing Union Square shows two small boys watching from a second-story window. One of them is six-year-old Theodore Roosevelt, and the other his four-year-old brother Elliott. See David McCullough, *Mornings on Horseback* (New York: Simon & Schuster, 1981), 64 and the picture facing 128.

60 Trostel, *Lincoln Funeral Train*, 87.

61 *New-York Tribune*, April 26, 1865.

62 Quoted in Searcher, *The Farewell to Lincoln*, 149–50. Vendors, by the way, had a very big day on the 25th selling memorial buttons and badges.

63 *New-York Tribune*, April 26, 1865. Printed in full by the *New York Times* on April 26, 1865, it is accessible as "How Shall the Nation Show its Sorrow?" in *Building the Myth: Selected Speeches Memorializing Abraham Lincoln* ed. Waldo W. Braden (Urbana: University of Illinois Press, 1990), 62–71.

64 *New-York Tribune*. April 26, 1865.

65 On the day of Lincoln's departure from New York, a friend pleaded with Bryant to write Lincoln's biography: "you have it in your power to make the impression it has left on the mind of the people very lasting by preparing a memoir of Mr. Lincoln which would be worthy of him & of the feelings that now fill the heart of the Nation. … The lives of Mr. Lincoln we have, are [unreadable] biographies which do not inspire the confidence and meet the feelings of the people. They are written from a low point of view & are unilluminated by the splendor which his Setting Sun reflects upon his whole career." Henry W. Bellows to William Cullen Bryant, April 25, 1865, Bryant-Godwin Papers, New York Public Library.

66 Barry Schwartz, *Abraham Lincoln and the Forge of National Memory* (Chicago: University of Chicago Press, 2000), 70–74; Merrill Peterson, *Lincoln in American Memory* (New York: Oxford University Press, 1994), chaps. 2 and 3.

67 Donald and Holzer, *Lincoln in the Times*, 397–401.

68 Malcolm Cowley, ed., *The Complete Poetry and Prose of Walt Whitman* (New York: Pellegrini & Cudahy, 1948), 305–6.

69 Donald and Holzer, *Lincoln in the Times*, 401–2. Reported in the *New York Times* on April 16, 1887. For Whitman's great poem, "When Lilacs Last in the Dooryard Bloom'd," see Cowley, *Complete Poetry*, 298–305.

SELECT BIBLIOGRAPHY

LINCOLN, SLAVERY, NINETEENTH-CENTURY ICONOGRAPHY,
AND THE CIVIL WAR

Barton, William E. *Abraham Lincoln and Walt Whitman.* Indianapolis: Bobbs Merrill, 1928.

Basler, Roy P. *The Lincoln Legend: A Study in Changing Perceptions.* New York: Bonanza Books, 1969.

Basler, Roy P, ed. *The Collected Works of Abraham Lincoln*, 8 vols. New Brunswick, NJ: Rutgers University Press, 1953–55, plus supplements.

Berlin, Ira, and Leslie A. Harris, eds., *Slavery in New York.* New York: New-York Historical Society, 2005.

Bernard, Kenneth A. *Lincoln and the Music of the Civil War.* Caldwell, ID: Caxton Printers, 1966.

Bernstein, Iver. *The New York City Draft Riots and their Significance for American Society and Politics in the Age of the Civil War.* New York: Oxford University Press, 1990.

Blight, David W. *Race and Reunion: The Civil War in American Memory.* Cambridge, MA: Harvard University Press, 2001.

———. *Frederick Douglass' Civil War.* Baton Rouge: Louisiana State University Press, 1989.

Boritt, G[abor] S. *Lincoln and the Economics of the American Dream.* Memphis: Memphis State University Press, 1978.

Bunker, Gary L. *From Rail-Splitter to Icon: Lincoln's Image in Illustrated Periodicals, 1860–1865.* Kent, OH: Kent State University Press, 2001.

Cox, LaWanda. *Lincoln and Black Freedom.* Columbia: University of South Carolina Press, 1981.

Cunningham, Noble E., Jr. *Popular Images of the Presidency: From Washington to Lincoln.* Columbia: University of Missouri Press, 1991.

Epstein, Daniel Mark. *Lincoln and Whitman: Parallel Lives in Civil War Washington.* New York: Ballantine Books, 2004.

Donald, David Herbert. *Lincoln.* New York: Simon & Schuster, 1995.

Donald, David Herbert and Harold Holzer. *Lincoln in the Times: The Life of Abraham Lincoln as Originally Reported in the New York Times.* New York: St. Martin's Press, 2005.

Foner, Eric. *Forever Free: The Story of Emancipation and Reconstruction.* New York: Alfred A. Knopf, 2005.

Foner, Philips S. and Yuval Taylor, *Frederick Douglass: Selected Speeches and Writings.* Chicago: Lawrence Hill Books, 1999.

Freeman, Andrew. *Abraham Lincoln in New York.* New York: Coward-McCann, 1960.

Gale Research Co., *Currier & Ives: A Catalogue Raisonné*, 2 vols. Detroit: Gale Research, 1984.

Guelzo, Allen C. *Lincoln's Emancipation Proclamation*. New York: Simon & Schuster, 2005.

Hamilton, Charles and Lloyd Ostendorf. *Lincoln in Photographs: An Album of Every Known Pose*, rev. ed. Dayton, OH: Morningside Press, 1985.

Harper, Robert S. *Lincoln and the Press*. New York: McGraw-Hill, 1951.

Holzer, Harold. *Lincoln at Cooper Union: The Speech that Made Abraham Lincoln President*. New York: Simon & Schuster, 2005.

————. *Washington and Lincoln Portrayed: National Icons in Popular Prints*. Jefferson, NC: McFarland, 1993.

Holzer, Harold, Mark E. Neely, Jr., and Gabor S. Boritt. *The Lincoln Image: Abraham Lincoln and the Popular Print*. New York: Scribner's, 1984.

Holzer, Harold, Gabor S. Boritt, and Mark E. Neely, Jr. "Francis Bicknell Carpenter (1930–1900): Painter of Abraham Lincoln and His Circle," *American Art Journal*, 16 (spring 1984): 66–89.

Horan, James D. *Mathew Brady: Historian with a Camera*. New York: Crown Publishers, 1952.

Horton, James Oliver and Lois E. Horton. *Slavery and the Making of America*. New York: Oxford University Press, 2005.

McPherson, James M. *Battle Cry of Freedom: The Civil War Era*. New York: Oxford University Press, 1988.

————, ed. *The Most Fearful Ordeal: Original Coverage of the Civil War by Writers and Reporters of the New York Times*. New York: St. Martin's Press, 2004.

Mahin, Dean B. *One War at a Time: The International Dimensions of the American Civil War*. Washington, DC: Brassey's, 1999.

Mayhaffer, Harry J. *War of Words: Abraham Lincoln and the Civil War Press*. Washington, DC: Brassey's, 2001.

Miers, Earl Schenck, ed. *Lincoln Day by Day: A Chronology, 1809–1865*. Washington, DC: Lincoln Sesquicentennial Commission, 1960.

Mitgang, Herbert. *Lincoln as they Saw Him*. New York: Rinehart & Co., 1956.

Neely, Mark E., Jr. *The Fate of Liberty: Abraham Lincoln and Civil Liberties*. New York: Oxford University Press, 1991.

————. *The Boundaries of American Political Culture in the Civil War Era*. Chapel Hill: University of North Carolina Press, 2005.

Neely, Mark E., Jr. and Harold Holzer. *The Union Image: Popular Prints of the Civil War North*. Chapel Hill: University of North Carolina Press, 2000.

Oakes, James. *The Radical and the Republican: Frederick Douglass, Abraham Lincoln, and the Triumph of Antislavery Politics*. New York: W. W. Norton, 2007.

Panzer, Mary. *Mathew Brady and the Image of History*. Washington, DC: Smithsonian Institution Press, 1997.

Peters, Harry Twyford. *America on Stone: The Other Printmakers to the American People*. New York: Doubleday, 1931.

Peterson, Merrill. *Lincoln in American Memory*. New York: Oxford University Press, 1994.

Reilly, Bernard. *American Political Prints, 1766–1876: A Catalog of the Collections of the Library of Congress*. Boston: G. K. Hall & Co., 1991.

Schwartz, Barry. *Abraham Lincoln and the Forge of National Memory*. Chicago: University of Chicago Press, 2000.

Searcher, Victor. *The Farewell to Lincoln*. New York: Abingdon Press, 1965.

Sullivan, Edmund B., and Roger A. Fischer. *American Political Ribbons and Ribbon Badges, 1825–1981*. Lincoln, MA: Quarterman Publishing, 1985.

Waugh, John C. *Reelecting Lincoln: The Battle for the Presidency*. New York: Crown, 1997.

Williams, Frank J. *Judging Lincoln*. Carbondale: Southern Illinois University Press, 2001.

Wilson, Rufus Rockwell. *Lincoln in Caricature*. New York: Horizon Press, 1953.

NEW YORK

Foner, Philip S. *Business and Slavery: The New York Merchants and the Irrepressible Conflict.* Chapel Hill: University of North Carolina Press, 1941.

Henderson, Mary C. *The City and the Theatre: New York Playhouses from, Bowling Green to Times Square.* Clifton, NJ: James T. White & Co., 1973.

Holzer, Harold, ed., *State of the Union: New York and the Civil War.* New York: Fordham University Press, 2002.

———, ed. *The Union Preserved: A Guide to Civil War Records in the New York State Archives.* New York: Fordham University Press, 1999.

Homberger, Eric. *Scenes from the Life of a City: Corruption and Conscience in Old New York.* New Haven, CT: Yale University Press, 1994.

Spann, Edward K. *Gotham at War: New York City, 1860–1865.* Wilmington, DE: SR Books, 2002.

SELECTED PRIMARY SOURCES

New-York Historical Society Library Manuscripts and Collections:

Account Book, Moses Taylor & Company, 1855–78

Documents of the United States Sanitary Commission, 1862–63

Minturn, Robert Bowne. *Memoirs of Robert Bowne Minturn. Printed for Private Circulation.* New York: A. D. F. Randolph & Co., 1871.

Publications Relating to the Union League Club (includes charters, registers, publications, periodicals, membership registers)

Seventh Regiment Records, New York Infantry Regiment, 7th Militia, 1767–1983 (include collection of printed material pertaining to Seventh Regiment, New York National Guard)

Seward, William H. *Autobiography of William H. Seward.* New York: D. Appleton and Co., 1877.

———. *The Works of William H. Seward.* New York: Redfield, 1853–84.

Records of the National War Committee of the Citizens of New York, 1862–63 (includes correspondence related to Peter Cooper, General Michael Corcoran)

Records of Union Defense Committee of the City of New York, 1861–85 (includes correspondence with Moses Grinnell, George Opdyke, John Austin Stephens)

United States Army, Department of the East, District of Southern New York, Collection of General and Special Orders Issued in New York City, 1863–65

Private Collections:

Gilder-Lehrman Collection:

Roger Hertog Collection

Harold Holzer Collection

Frank and Virginia Williams Collection

John Monsky Collection

Morris Offit Collection

Other Sources:

August Belmont Papers, Columbia University Library

Peter Cooper Papers, Cooper Union

Lincoln Papers, Library of Congress

Moses Taylor Papers, New York Public Library

Bound Volumes:

Carpenter, Francis B. *Six Months at the White House: The Story of a Picture.* New York: Hurd & Houghton, 1866.

Greeley, Horace. *Recollections of a Busy Life.* New York: J. B. Ford, 1868.

Maverick, Augustus. *Henry J. Raymond and the New York Press for Thirty Years.* Hartford, CT: A. S. Hale & Co., 1870.

CONTRIBUTORS

HAROLD HOLZER, editor, is Senior Vice President for External Affairs at the Metropolitan Museum of Art, serves also as co-chairman of the U. S. Abraham Lincoln Bicentennial Commission, and is the author, co-author, or editor of thirty-four books on Lincoln and the Civil War era. Among his award-winning works are *The Lincoln Image* (1984), *The Lincoln-Douglas Debates* (1993), *Lincoln as I Knew Him* (1999), *Dear Mr. Lincoln: Letters to the President* (1993), *Mine Eyes Have Seen the Glory: The Civil War in Art* (1993), *The Lincoln Family Album* (1990), and with Governor Mario Cuomo, *Lincoln on Democracy* (1990), which has been published in four languages. His latest book is the acclaimed *Lincoln President-Elect: Abraham Lincoln and the Great Secession Winter 1860–1861*, which has won the 2009 Barondess Award and the Award of Achievement of the Lincoln Group of New York. His two books for the Lincoln bicentennial year are *The Lincoln Anthology: Great Writers on His Life and Legacy*; and *In Lincoln's Hand: His Original Manuscripts with Commentary by Distinguished Americans*.

JEAN H. BAKER is the Bennett-Harwood Professor of History at Goucher College in Baltimore, Maryland where she has taught American history for over thirty years. She is the author of numerous books and articles including *Affairs of Party: The Political Culture of Northern Democrats in the Mid-Nineteenth Century* (1993), *Mary Todd Lincoln: A Biography* (2008), *James Buchanan* (2004), and *Sisters: The Lives of America's Suffragists* (2005). She is currently writing a biography of Margaret Sanger.

CATHERINE CLINTON is the author or editor of over two dozen books, including *Mrs. Lincoln: A Life* (2009) and *Harriet Tubman: The Road to Freedom* (2004), named as one of the best nonfiction books of 2004 by the Christian Science Monitor and the Chicago Tribune. She has published numerous articles, including "Lincoln: The Family Who Made Him, The Family He Made." Educated at Harvard, Sussex, and Princeton, she is a member of the advisory committee to the Abraham Lincoln Bicentennial Commission, a member of the Screen Writers Guild, and holds a chair in U. S. history at Queen's University Belfast in Northern Ireland.

JAMES OLIVER HORTON is the Benjamin Banneker Professor of American Studies and History at the George Washington University and Historian Emeritus, National Museum of American History, Smithsonian Institution. He is a member of the U. S. Abraham Lincoln Bicentennial Commission and has served as Senior Advisor on Historical Interpretation and Public Education for the Director of the National Park Service, chair of the National Park System Advisory Board, and President of the Organization of American Historians. His books include *The Man and the Martyr: Abraham Lincoln in African American History and Memory* (2006), *Free People of Color* (1993), *The Landmarks of African American History* (2004), *In Hope of Liberty* (1997), and *Slavery and the Making of America* (2005).

MICHAEL KAMMEN is the Newton C. Farr Professor of American History and Culture (emeritus) at Cornell University, where he taught from 1965 until 2008. In 1980-81 he held a newly created visiting professorship in American history at the École des Hautes Études in Paris. He is an elected member of the American Academy of Arts and Sciences and served in 1995–96 as President of the Organization of American Historians. His books include *People of Paradox: An Inquiry Concerning the Origins of American Civilization* (1972), awarded the Pulitzer Prize for History in 1973; *A Machine That Would Go of Itself: The Constitution in American Culture* (1986), awarded the Francis Parkman Prize and the Henry Adams Prize; *Mystic Chords of Memory: The Transformation of Tradition in American Culture* (1991); and *Visual Shock: A History of Art Controversies in American Culture* (2006).

BARNET SCHECTER is the author of *The Devil's Own Work: The Civil War Draft Riots and the Fight to Reconstruct America* (2005) and *The Battle for New York: The City at the Heart of the American Revolution* (2002). A contributing editor of the three-volume *Encyclopedia of the American Revolution* (2006) and *Landmarks of the American Revolution* (2006), he is also a contributor to the *Encyclopedia of New York City* (2009). He is a fellow of the New York Academy of History.

CRAIG L. SYMONDS is Professor of History Emeritus at the United States Naval Academy and the author of thirteen books on the Civil War and naval history, including biographies of Patrick Cleburne and Joseph E. Johnston. His most recent book is *Lincoln and His Admirals: Abraham Lincoln, the U.S. Navy, and the Civil War* (2008), which won the 2009 Lincoln Prize, the most prestigious award in the field. He and his wife Marylou live in Annapolis, Maryland.

FRANK J. WILLIAMS retired in 2009 as Chief Justice of the Supreme Court of Rhode Island. The founding chairman of the Lincoln Forum, he has written and edited several books, including *Judging Lincoln* (2002). In 2003, President Bush, through the Secretary of Defense, invited Chief Justice Williams to be a member of the Military Commissions Review Panel for military trials to be held in Guantanamo Bay, Cuba with the rank of Major General. In 2006, Congress reconstituted that panel as the United States Court of Military Commission Review, on which Williams serves as Chief Judge. He is a member of the U. S. Abraham Lincoln Bicentennial Commission.

INDEX